D0773424

OMNIVM   LVX   CIVIVM

BOSTON
PUBLIC
LIBRARY

William Trevor

Twayne's English Authors Series

Kinley Roby, Editor
Northeastern University

TEAS 501

William Trevor
Photograph courtesy Mark Gerson

William Trevor

Kristin Morrison

Boston College

Twayne Publishers ■ New York

Maxwell Macmillan Canada ■ Toronto

Maxwell Macmillan International ■ New York Oxford Singapore Sydney

William Trevor
Kristin Morrison

Twayne Publishers
Macmillan Publishing Company
866 Third Avenue
New York, New York 10022

Maxwell Macmillan Canada, Inc.
1200 Eglinton Avenue East
Suite 200
Don Mills, Ontario M3C 3N1

Library of Congress Cataloging-in-Publication Data

Morrison, Kristin
  William Trevor / Kristin Morrison.
    p. cm. – (Twayne's English authors series; TEAS 501)
    Includes bibliographical references and index.
    ISBN 0-8057-7032-1 (alk. paper)
    1. Trevor, William, 1928- – Criticism and interpretation. 2. Ireland and literature. 3. Irish in literature. I. Title. II. Series.
PR6070.R4Z78 1993
823'.914 – dc20   93-12080
                                                              CIP

10 9 8 7 6 5 4 3 2 1

Printed in the United States of America.

Contents

Acknowledgments

The writing of this book on William Trevor's fiction formally began in 1985 during a summer spent in Dublin, followed by a semester's academic leave as a fellow in the Department of English at Edinburgh University. My paper "William Trevor's 'System of Correspondences,'" presented at the annual meeting of the American Conference for Irish Studies held at Boston College in the spring of 1986, was published in the *Massachusetts Review*, in an issue on contemporary Ireland (1987). Since then discussions with various colleagues in Irish studies and with students in my courses on twentieth-century Irish fiction have contributed to my understanding of Trevor's work. I am particularly grateful to Adele Dalsimer for her initial suggestion to work on Trevor, for her interest, and for her unfailing enthusiasm not only with regard to this project but throughout our 24 years of collegiality and friendship. Special thanks to my husband, Robin Popplestone, who for our mutual pleasure has read aloud these and many other novels and stories, in a dazzling variety of appropriate voices and accents. Finally, my thanks to William Trevor, for his kindness in answering questions about his life and work.

Chronology

1928   William Trevor Cox born 24 May in Mitchelstown, County Cork, of middle-class Irish Protestant parents, James William Cox and Gertrude (Davison) Cox. During his boyhood the family moves frequently throughout the south of Ireland.

1941-1950   Attends Sandford Park School, Dublin; St. Columba's College, Dublin; and Trinity College, Dublin.

1950   Receives B.A. in history from Trinity College, Dublin.

1951-1955   Teaches school (history, art) in Northern Ireland and in England.

1952   Marries Jane Ryan.

1955-1965   Enjoys successful career as sculptor. Begins writing. He and his wife move to Devon (where they continue to live). They have two sons, Patrick and Dominic.

1958   *A Standard of Behaviour* (first novel).

1964   Trevor awarded the *Transatlantic Review* Prize for fiction. *The Old Boys* (novel).

1965   Trevor awarded the Hawthornden Prize for fiction. *The Boarding-House* (novel).

1966   *The Love Department* (novel).

1967   *The Day We Got Drunk on Cake and Other Stories*.

1968   *The Girl* (one-act play).

1969   *Mrs. Eckdorf in O'Neill's Hotel* (novel).

1971   *Miss Gomez and the Brethren* (novel). *The Old Boys* (play adapted from the novel; staged at the Mermaid Theatre, London, in 1970).

1972   *The Ballroom of Romance and Other Stories. Going Home* and *A Night with Mrs. da Tanka* (one-act plays). Trevor awarded Society of Authors traveling fellowship.

1973   *Elizabeth Alone* (novel).

1974   *Marriages* (one-act play).

1975   *Angels at the Ritz and Other Stories*; wins the Royal Society of Literature Award.

1976   *The Children of Dynmouth* (novel); wins the Whitbread Award. *Old School Ties* (stories and memoirs). Trevor receives the Allied Irish Banks Prize for fiction and the Heineman Award for fiction.

1977   Trevor awarded the CBE (Commander of the Order of the British Empire) in recognition of his valuable services to literature.

1978   *Lovers of Their Time and Other Stories.*

1979   *The Distant Past* (Trevor's selection of his "Irish stories" for a series devoted to the Irish short story). Trevor awarded the Irish Community Prize.

1980   *Other People's Worlds* (novel). Trevor receives Giles Cooper Award for "Beyond the Pale" (radio play).

1981   *Beyond the Pale and Other Stories. Scenes from an Album* (full-length play; staged at the Abbey Theatre, Dublin, in August).

1982   Trevor receives Giles Cooper Award for "Autumn Sunshine" (radio play).

1983   *Fools of Fortune* (novel); wins the Whitbread Award. *The Stories of William Trevor* (collected stories).

1984   *A Writer's Ireland: Landscape in Literature* (photo essay). Trevor awarded Hon. D.Lit., Exeter University.

1986   *The News from Ireland and Other Stories.* Trevor awarded Hon. D.Lit., Trinity College, Dublin.

1987   *Nights at the Alexandra* (short novel).

1988   *The Silence in the Garden* (novel); wins one of the Irish *Sunday Independent* Arts awards and is named *Yorkshire Post* Book of the Year.

1989   Trevor edits *The Oxford Book of Irish Short Stories*; awarded Hon. D.Lit., Queen's University, Belfast.

1990   *Family Sins and Other Stories.* Trevor awarded Hon.D.Lit., National University, Cork.

1991   *Two Lives: Reading Turgenev and My House in Umbria.*

1992   *William Trevor: The Collected Stories.*

Chapter One

Introduction

From some perspectives William Trevor might seem to be a British author: he lives in Devon, on the southwest coast of England; his publishers are two important British firms, Penguin and the Bodley Head; he has been awarded an honorary CBE by Queen Elizabeth II for his valuable services to literature. His work usually occupies a foot or two of shelf space in major bookshops throughout the United Kingdom. And his speech is accented by an urbane mix of various regions of Britain. Even so, William Trevor remains an Irish author – Irish by birth and by owned identity. That simple fact is essential to any full appreciation of his fiction.

In a 1976 interview with Jack White on Irish television (RTE), Trevor stated that Irish history is "the only academic subject I've ever been the least interested in" and described himself as a young man being "very, very nationalistic, intensely Irish."[1] Going on to consider the transition from his early work as a sculptor (in his teens and twenties), deliberately using Irish motifs, to his early work as an author (in his thirties), wherein Irish elements are not immediately apparent, Trevor speculated that he "must have used something up": contrary, he says, to standard advice given fledgling authors, he began by writing about what he did not know – England – rather than about what he did know – Ireland. Yet it is clear, throughout this early interview and in subsequent ones, as well as throughout Trevor's fiction itself, that his fascination with Irish history, Irish motifs, and his whole Irish heritage did not actually get "used up" but rather went underground for a time, only to manifest itself later as a profoundly important component of his mature work.

Born in 1928 as William Trevor Cox, in Mitchelstown, County Cork, Trevor spent his childhood in various towns in the south of Ireland, moving frequently because of his father's work as a bank official. In his RTE interview Trevor speaks at length about his vivid memories of the towns and the countryside in which he grew up and his own youthful activities there: Youghal, Skibbereen, Enniscorthy; the seaside, the fishermen, people being drowned; his going to school for the first time; "the enclosed claustrophobia of small town life" that, he says, permeates so much of his fiction; his going often into Cork to the pictures ("Clark Gable in *Too Hot to Handle*, then tea at the Savoy"); his wandering off on his own, lost in the usual childhood fantasies; his immersion in books (all of Dickens, Edgar Wallace, Agatha Christie). Because of his living as "a migrant inside Ireland" (to use Jack White's phrase), and belonging to a minority religious group (Protestant), Trevor says he early developed the sense of being "outside looking in," so that when he came to be a writer, he took up his role "as a spy." Throughout the interview, however, Trevor gently resists White's tendency (more implicit than stated) to see him as not really rooted in Ireland, perhaps not really Irish. Yes, Trevor agrees, he lived in many separate spots in the south, but they all seemed similar to him; he had a sense of continuity. Yes, "the minority thing" of being a Protestant has stayed with him, but his schooling also included the (Roman Catholic) Christian Brothers. Yes, his early fiction did focus on England and the English, but as a people and a place quite different from his own, as oddities ("I found English people . . . their rules, laws, and obsessions very interesting"). And, yes, as a matter of fact he does, even now, feel foreign in Devon, yet he experiences no conflict because "the Devon countryside and people are very like the south of Ireland where I grew up." The touchstone is always, ultimately, Ireland.

After a childhood of frequently interrupted and patchwork schooling – with some stability supplied by two years at Sandford Park School and two years at St. Columba's College in Dublin – Trevor attended Trinity College, Dublin (getting to know the city very well, especially, as he told Jack White, its night people), and was awarded a B.A. in history in 1950. His subsequent move to Northern Ireland and then to England (where he taught history and art at various schools between 1951 and 1955) in no way constituted a rejection of Ireland, no Joycean or Beckettian deliberate expatriation. As he explained to me after his reading at the Book Fair at the Edinburgh Festival in 1985, he left quite simply because there were no jobs available for sculptors in Ireland but there were in England.

Of his career as a visual artist Trevor told Jack White that he became seriously interested in sculpting at age 16 while at St. Columba's and remained a sculptor until 1960. He exhibited his work and earned his living as a professional sculptor in England, chiefly with work on churches, using Irish motifs taken from his intense study of the Book of Kells (he carved four saints from the Book of Kells for a church in Rugby, "which is rather nice – a piece of Imperialism I rather like"). His fascination with Irish crosses and other structural and decorative forms in Celtic art, along with his own intense nationalism and "desire for art to reflect the past," led eventually to his decision to give up sculpture because, as he explained in his RTE interview, "my sculpture had become wholly abstract" and "I just didn't like the look of it."

The "humanness" absent from his later sculpture was perhaps, he speculates, rediscovered in his writing. In 1958 he published his first novel, *A Standard of Behaviour*;[2] in 1964 his second novel, *The Old Boys*, won the Hawthornden Prize. Since 1965 he has lived by his pen, publishing a novel or volume of short stories every year or two and winning most of the significant literary prizes.

The Irish strain in Trevor's artistry may have gone underground during the early part of his writing career but nonetheless remains discernible. Particularly interesting is the fact that Trevor himself finds Irish elements in work that on the surface seems not to be Irish at all. As Trevor talks on videotape with Jack White about characteristics of his use of language, he illustrates its Irish cast by citing one of his English characters (the fey/pathological adolescent nemesis Timothy Gedge, from the entirely English *The Children of Dynmouth*). Replying to White's question as to whether his work contains echoes of Ireland, Trevor first responds with an emphatic "Oh, yes"; he goes on to indicate that not only does he have a number of short stories with Irish characters or settings, as well as a novel that is "wholly Irish," but even his English, French, and American characters "speak in an Irish way." He amplifies this assertion by stating that he inevitably writes "Irish patterns of speech" and notes that there is something characteristic about "the way the Irish decorate a phrase, make it slightly funnier than does the more down-to-earth English person." Such language patterns are "a technical thing," he says, but not something he does for special effect; quite simply, "It's the only way I can write." Although Trevor has mitigated this "Irish speech" somewhat, even here in this mid-1970s interview he affirms that his use of the English language has a specifically Irish form to it. This, he says, accounts for some critics finding his characters' speech eccentric or odd, not realizing the Irish cast he has inevitably given to his non-Irish characters.

Climaxing this relatively long portion of the interview with his single specific example, Trevor points out that Timothy Gedge in *The Children of Dynmouth* "speaks with the ring of a Cork boy." Whether or not Timothy's unusually frequent use of personal names in direct address ("D' you ever go to funerals, Kate?"/ "Funerals?" / "When a person dies, Kate");[3] whether or not his repetitions of key nouns ("I'm looking for a wedding-dress. I have an act planned with a wedding-dress" [100]) and his building his paragraphs incrementally using such repetitions, with key words often placed oddly in the phrase ("You didn't mind me looking in at the window, Stephen? Only I was passing at the time. Your dad was packing his gear up. He took the wedding-dress out of the trunk and put it back again. A faded kind of trunk, Stephen. Green it would be in its day" [101]); whether or not that "only" and "green it would be" are distinctively or exclusively "Irish" is not the point: what is important is that Trevor *hears* Timothy Gedge speaking with the ring of a Cork boy, despite his English surname, origin, and milieu. Elsewhere in the interview, responding to the question as to which novel is his favorite, Trevor states, "I'm very fond of my Dublin book, *Mrs. Eckdorf in O'Neill's Hotel*," which White agrees "has a strong smell of Dublin about it." Persistently, the strong smell, the ringing echo of Ireland – these permeate Trevor's sense of his work and his working.

Just as Trevor first wrote about England from the vantage point of an outsider, so later he began to write more and more about Ireland only after the years spent in England, Switzerland, and Italy had provided necessary distance, allowing him "to look back from someplace else." The word *back* is important in that assertion, indicating as it does an affirmation of his sense of continuity with his homeland (and not foreignness, such as he feels with England). The linguistic link was always there. Then, later, that abiding fascination with Irish history began to surface once again, prompted perhaps by the renewed Troubles in Northern Ireland from 1968 on. Certainly Trevor's increasingly frequent use of Irish settings, characters, and political issues dates from about that time, culminating in his masterpieces of the 1980s, *Fools of Fortune*, "The News from Ireland," and *The Silence in the Garden*.[4]

The gardens featured in Trevor's latest novels provide important images for all his work and function as the chief recurrent metaphor, at once a lost Eden and a possible Paradise, a whole flourishing and blighted world. And very often that garden is Ireland. By a conceptual "system of correspondences," frequently expressed through a rhetorical strategy of "significant simultaneity," this metaphoric equation of Ireland and garden, with all its attendant images and related themes, shapes Trevor's entire body of fiction into a remarkable coherence. That polished coherence with its interesting complexity is the subject of this book. Through careful examination of Trevor's fiction, through close reading of the published texts, this study discovers the various elements of complexity and artistry that make Trevor's work such an elegant whole, centered on the metaphor of the garden and the important ethical question of whether that postlapsarian garden is essentially waste or can be reclaimed.

The intellectual framework of all Trevor's fiction is provided by his "system of correspondences." According to the concept that dominates his work, past and present are actually the same moment; apparently separate realms (the public and the private, the political and the domestic) inevitably overlap. The various elements of space and time are intrinsically interrelated, together constituting an elaborate and powerful set of relationships, a system of correspondences, that shapes his world. This conceptual system – with its chief recurrent metaphor, the garden – is well illustrated by an important short story, "The News from Ireland," and by one of his most powerful novels, *Fools of Fortune*.

Trevor's system of correspondences raises a significant question: What is the origin of evil in such a world and how does it operate? Trevor invokes an ancient theory (that Adam's sin in the primal garden, Eden, taints all his descendants) but transforms it by the way his characters participate in their own wounding. In Trevor's account of the genealogy of evil, sin originates not only in the past but also continuously in the present, each man his own Adam, inheriting Original Sin and contributing to it capriciously, even unwittingly. Children are particularly interesting to him, simultaneously both victims and victimizers, making evil a game they are unwilling to relinquish, playing it into adulthood and old age. A variety of short stories and novels, spread across the whole of Trevor's career, illustrate these points, showing how personal, domestic, public, and political realms are mutually affected by any given act of cruelty or violence, however trivial.

Nationality and the violence it occasions are an important aspect of the political issues Trevor's later work regularly addresses. The linkage between political violence and personal cruelties develops gradually throughout Trevor's work, emerging finally as a concatenation of suffering that binds together all persons from all times and all places. Only in the last half of his writing career do nationality and national allegiance become an explicit issue, focused sharply on Ireland. The earliest fiction of this Anglo-Irish writer is set almost entirely in England with English characters; most of these novels and stories of the 1960s are comic in manner, grotesque in characterization and plotting, and generally apolitical. From the 1970s on, humor is softened by pathos; more Irish characters and settings are used; and political and domestic problems interconnect. In the 1980s and early 1990s all but one of the novels and most of the stories are Irish in setting, characterization, and subject matter; events and manner of presentation are usually serious, the tone often despairing. The earlier work shows Trevor perfecting his craft and developing those distinctive techniques and configurations of thought which ultimately lead to *Fools of Fortune* and *The Silence in the Garden*, an odyssey that moves through the city back to the garden, back home to Ireland, from a comic view of life to a much darker one in which the mutual correspondences between public and private realms are seen as some of the chief conduits of evil.

The philosophical problem of evil and specific political evils associated with nationality are joined in Trevor's fiction in a shocking metaphor: child murder used as an emblem of colonial exploitation. To highlight Trevor's treatment of this difficult subject, it is useful to juxtapose *The Silence in the Garden* (1988) with two other novels containing similar material, one by an American of very different background, Toni Morrison's *Beloved* (1987), and the other by a fellow Corkonian, Mary Leland's *The Killeen* (1985). Though child abuse and murder have occasionally been mentioned in fiction, they are rarely described in any detail; by contrast, these three novels, written within a few years of one another, are surprisingly horrifying in their explicitness. *Beloved* is, however, ultimately optimistic, while the two Irish novels significantly show a much more diffuse stain of guilt and responsibility, a more negative view of the future as a place necessarily scarred by present evils.

Summary statements about Trevor's often shocking subject matter and the interconnected evils he depicts can make his work seem sensational. But Trevor's writing is, to the contrary, subtle and finely crafted; he makes skillful use of a variety of rhetorical strategies to establish the workings of his system of correspondences and its chain of evil. Among the more important strategies are his persistent visual images, implied puns, literalized metaphors, incremental references, and significant names. *Persistent visual images* serve to show personal and political worlds mirroring each other, as illustrated in the story "Attracta," with its parallels between the peaceful schoolteacher in County Cork and her former pupil murdered in Belfast. *Implied puns* supply a single word that ramifies from its obvious denotation in context to the analogous meanings it suggests throughout the rest of the text, as in the story "Beyond the Pale," where deceptions in the plot are mirrored by deceptions in language. *Literalized metaphors* function in *Mrs. Eckdorf in O'Neill's Hotel*, for example, to indicate the reciprocal power and folly of both words and images. *Incremental references* – repeated items, such as trees, orchards, and fields – take on additional weight and meaning as they recur throughout Trevor's work, beginning initially as isolated references and then, through repetition and association, gradually acquiring the density and resonance of a symbol, suggesting various points of correspondence to other elements in Trevor's world and supporting his major metaphor of the garden. Finally, *names and naming* constitute profound indicators of identity, everything from obvious tags to inner sources of power, showing the extent to which even language participates in the sense of linked relationships that pervades Trevor's fiction.

Genre too is made to serve Trevor's system of correspondences. Trevor alters the traditional *Bildungsroman* to make it a political novel as well: the protagonist's process of maturation in both *Fools of Fortune* and *Nights at the Alexandra* is affected by political events that shift his quest away from the traditional goal of social integration and toward discovery of and reconciliation with his deepest self.

Novels by John Banville and Brian Moore provide useful contrasting examples of contemporary *Bildungsromane* with similar concerns.

The question inevitably arises as to whether Trevor's view in his fictional world is optimistic because of his frequent comic elements or is pessimistic because of his focus on what seems an endlessly multiplying series of evil events – or, to put it another way, using Trevor's own metaphor, whether or not the garden can be redeemed, reclaimed. I conclude this book by considering the extent to which Trevor's work provides resolution for the intricate evil it explores originating in the Garden of Eden and permeating the many gardens found in his short stories and novels. From the beginning of his fiction to his latest stories, such as "Lost Ground,"[5] Trevor has included three kinds of persons – some comic, some tragic – who in various ways both manifest evil and transcend it: children, celibates, and holy fools. In the 1976 novel *The Children of Dynmouth* the paradoxicality of Trevor's response to the problem of evil is most explicitly presented: apparent monsters are not outside the community but part of it, just as the snake was part of Eden; at every point goods and evils touch and mirror each other; loss may be gain; the same earth is both garden and wilderness. Placing this work against another contemporary Irish novel – Jennifer Johnston's *Shadows on Our Skin* (1977), set in Belfast and dealing with specific, recognizable political violence – helps highlight the paradoxicality of Trevor's view, a view that itself can provide redemption for that wilderness/garden of Ireland with which his work is preoccupied.

Chapter Two

The Garden and Trevor's "System of Correspondences"

When Mr. Erskine, the Pulvertaft's estate manager, begins courting Miss Heddoe, the English governess, in "The News from Ireland," he invites her "to stroll about the garden" and boasts that he "reclaimed the little garden [that surrounds his own house], as the estate was reclaimed."[1] In the Ireland of 1848 this vast walled demesne of hills, lakes, trees, shrubbery and flower gardens, orchards and kitchen gardens contrasts starkly with the famine outside. Thus in purely secular terms this estate is an Eden, a garden of abundance in the midst of want. Any poor governess would find so elevating a marriage as this offered her to be socially and economically its own kind of paradise. But Trevor allows these obvious metaphors to go unstated and instead introduces allusions to the original Eden through his reference to the Legend of the True Cross (connected ultimately with the Tree of the Knowledge of Good and Evil growing in the center of Paradise). By associating a typical Irish estate and actual historical events with the Garden of Eden and the central Judeo-Christian myths about sin and redemption, Trevor has combined in this one important short story a configuration of themes and ideas that appear in virtually all his fiction.

Behind each of Trevor's gardens lies that original garden, all of them connected by a conceptual system in which not only gardens but also all people, events, points of space, and moments of time are related to one another. The garden is one of Trevor's chief recurrent metaphors. His "system of correspondences" is the operative principle of that world, that cosmos, in which the garden occurs.

Trevor writes not only about his fictional gardens, characters, and events but even about political and historical matters from what could be called a cosmological perspective: events remote from each other in time or space are linked in such a way as to suggest that the apparent barriers of past and present, as well as of physical distance, are illusory, that connections exist among the various parts of his universe that make it a cosmos, an orderly (though often damaging) series of mutual interrelationships. According to the concept that dominates his work, past and present are, actually, the same moment; apparently separate realms (e.g., the public and the private, or the political and the domestic) inevitably overlap; all the various elements of space and time are intrinsically interrelated, comprising an elaborate and powerful "system of correspondences" which shapes the world. Such a habit of mind is indicated by the metaphors Trevor uses to describe the relationship between Irish myth and the Christian story: "The convolutions of ancient myth, the honeycomb of anecdote nestling within the major plot, the layers of fresh invention: all of it, when it was at last recorded, created an effect not unlike the elaborations of the decorated gospels."[2] This mode of thought is very like the academically familiar one described by E. M. W. Tillyard in *The Elizabethan World Picture,* though not so neat and regular: not now kings and suns and eagles and whales all conjoined by their rulership of their respective realms but English and Irish, lovers and haters, planters and dispossessed, the well-fed and the starving, each aspect of the complex, multicentury Anglo-Irish history exerting strange and powerful influences on various counterparts.

And although now, in the twentieth century, there are those who see political and moral spheres as quite different, in Trevor's system of correspondences (as also indeed in that medieval and Renaissance one) questions of good and evil are unavoidably bound up with political and secular issues. If the king was wicked, inevitably the land declined and the people suffered. So too now, in Trevor's world, the immoral behavior of individuals necessarily wounds the whole social fabric, and, conversely, rottenness in the body politic has its inevitable analogue in private lives and personal character. In Trevor's fiction the relatedness of microcosm and macrocosm is not a quaint concept from the past but a fact of human life in the present, a fact to be taken seriously.

It is in this light that the observations of the butler in "The News from Ireland" must be seen, as he waits on the current occupants of the reclaimed estate, the reclaimed garden: "Serving them in the dining-room, holding for them a plate of chops or hurrying to them a gravy dish, he wishes he might speak the truth as it appears to him: that their fresh, decent blood is the blood of the invader though they are not themselves invaders, that they perpetrate theft without being thieves" (10). These nineteenth-century residents of the big house, the Pulvertafts of Ipswich, are both innocent and guilty because the intervening years since Elizabeth granted their family the land have not mitigated that usurpation, despite their personal sense of duty in caring for estate and tenants. Their aged and poor Irish Protestant butler, Fogarty, is not simply a crank as, reflecting on history, he considers the various invaders to be "visitors": "the Celts, whose ramshackle gipsy empire expired in this same landscape, St. Patrick with his holy shamrock, the outrageous Vikings preceding the wily Normans, the adventurers of the Virgin Queen" (9). Such linkage and juxtaposition virtually annihilate time, implicate all groups in responsibility for the current distress, and deny any group, whether an invading people or a single resident family, intrinsic claim to the land, whether this particular garden or all Ireland. Yes, Fogarty *is* a crank, but he is also a vehicle for a concept that dominates all Trevor's fiction.

A closer look at "The News from Ireland" will help illustrate this point. Set in an Irish estate in 1847-48, the narrative shows private and public worlds held severely apart and yet impinging on each other irrevocably. The public is the world of famine; the private is the world of privileged domesticity (drives in the estate park, picnics, music lessons, weddings in the garden). Both worlds are flawed, perhaps in some essential, irreparable way. Although the English family, the Pulvertafts, who now inhabit this estate are aware of the suffering "outside," although they give alms, distribute soup, and even contrive a program of work for the neighborhood, they live a lie. As their Irish Protestant butler has said to himself, they perpetrate theft without being thieves. The lie they live is quite simply their assumption that this estate, this garden, is theirs; that they can live safely within its walls; that their obligations outside are a matter of charity and not justice. Trevor uses the presence of a stranger, the most recent visitor, to establish a norm of values in the story: the new English governess is horrified by what she sees, by the Pulvertafts themselves, by their inherent lack of honesty, a lack so profound that they are unaware of it. The butler aids her critical perspective by telling her the news of the starving peasant child with the

stigmata (the wounds of Christ in its hands and feet). Either explanation of this phenomenon shocks her: if the wounds are authentic, it
is a sign not to be ignored; if the wounds were inflicted by the parents as a strategy of survival, that too is an event to be reckoned
with. She cannot understand why the big house has no interest.

For the reader, of course, this child is clearly an emblem of the
peasantry itself, crucified by the ascendancy, the poor crucified by
the rich. And within the world of the story the child also serves as an
explicit emblem, a focus of discontent for the starving masses and for
the butler, who tells the governess his dream that one day descendants of these hungry people will destroy this estate, burning house
and gardens. But she does not heed the warnings given her, to act
on her outrage and leave the estate to its decay, to avoid participating in its immorality; instead she becomes an accomplice. Her critical
perspective as a stranger, allowing her to see both public and private
worlds irrevocably interconnected, gives way to the same lie the
Pulvertafts live. "I do not know these things" (43), she says with
determination to the butler, denying awareness of the observations
that had earlier troubled her. She turns her back on the public
world; she chooses the private world and the illusion that she can
live well and safely in its garden. She accepts the estate manager's
proposal despite the butler's vision of his house in flames.

At the center of her corruption is a lie, the kind of lie that makes
ordinary life possible. It is innocently exemplified in the story by the
piano recital of one of the Pulvertaft daughters: "She really plays it
most inelegantly," the new governess observes to herself. "Yet in the
drawing-room no frown or wince betrayed the listeners' ennui" (12).
Such polite deception keeps everyone in the story, not only the butler, from speaking "the truth as it appears to him" (10). There is a lie
in the way the governess takes her meals: before returning her tray
to the kitchen, the butler flushes down the toilet what she does not
eat so that the cook will not be offended. And there is a lie in her
marriage: not love but considerations of social position and compromise sway her decision.

The story is in fact full of lies, just as these two worlds, public
and private, are full of flaws. The works project of the Pulvertafts,
though intended to be beneficial, is a lie that insults the workers, a
road that goes nowhere. The old abbey is now "a lady's folly, a
pretty ruin that pleases and amuses" (43). The stigmata itself is

called a lie by the big house, wishing to dismiss it, and – with that complexity Trevor often gives to his deceptively simple details – the lie-calling is itself a lie, missing the real truth of the child's wounds, whatever their source.

But how is one to live in such a world, go on with ordinary piano lessons, marriages, and strolls in the garden? Only by doing what the governess has done – weep into her pillow, be sick at heart, write in her diary her news from Ireland (her diary: a private, not a public, medium), and then learn "to live with things" (46). Yes, of course, Trevor's story condemns her with this concluding line. And yet not entirely. "The wickedness here is not intentional" (43), the butler had said. That does not make it any less wicked but does mitigate the guilt and point to the difficulty of solution.

Where is the source of the evil? As always in Trevor's work, far, far in the past. In response to the butler's news about the child's stigmata the governess tells him the Legend of the True Cross: that a seed falling into Adam's mouth sprouted from his body when he died and grew into a great tree on which, centuries later, Christ was cruci- fied (11, 21f). This ancient legend presents a classic paradigm of the kind of thinking that is behind the correspondences inherent in Trevor's fiction. It is not enough that the act of original sin in the Garden of Paradise and the act of redemption centuries later in Palestine should both have been merely *associated* with trees. No, these trees must themselves be related to each other, intrinsically connected, just as the Savior and the Sinner are connected. Jesus is called the new Adam because there is a profound metaphysical con- nection between him and the first Adam (as Saint Paul puts it in 1 Corinthians 15:22, "For as in Adam all die, even so in Christ shall all be made alive," and several verses later Paul underscores the equa- tion between the two by explicitly calling them by the same name, one "the first man Adam" and the other "the last Adam").

Christian tradition, liturgy, and poetry extend this equation: "As sin and death had entered the world by the Tree in the Garden, so by a Tree the redemption of the world was achieved. Nay, the Tree of the Garden had been miraculously preserved, and from its wood, by the poetic justice of God, was formed the Cross, that Tree which bore a better fruit for the healing of the nations."[3] These common- place notions of Christian theology and piety need no elaboration here. But it is important to note that Trevor himself suggests by his repeated reference to the Legend of the True Cross that he wants his readers explicitly to associate such correspondences with the events in this story. Indeed, the governess herself seems to recount her telling of the legend to the butler as if it were a correlate of his story of the starving child (11), as if this religious legend and that political event were intrinsically connected, just as in another context she matches story with story "because the subjects seemed related" (39).

In the public world of famine a child is marked with the wounds of Christ. In the private world of domestic privilege and fruitful gardens the governess speaks of the cross on which Christ died. These two events of present starvation and past crucifixion are no more remote from each other in time and space than the events of Christ's passion and Adam's sin. In fact, the whole point of that ancient Christian legend is to annihilate time and space, to show the cross of salvation and the tree of transgression to be significantly one. And now, by this same mode of thinking, this starving population in nineteenth-century Ireland is also one with Christ crucified, not in some vague, poetic, metaphoric sense but quite powerfully, intrinsically one.

The conjunction of these two stories – about the stigmatic child and about the True Cross – clearly establishes this connection between various supposedly separate worlds in Trevor's skillfully structured narrative. So too does the grim pun accompanying these accounts. In its etymology the word *starve* means "to die" and is thus found in many medieval poems and carols that refer to "Christ who starf on rood." The word eventually became restricted to one specialized form of death, the meaning we use now, "to die from lack of food." Hence the pun makes all the more appropriate Trevor's association of starvation in Ireland with the death of Christ, through references to stigmata and the True Cross. The pun even seems to reinforce Trevor's implicit system of correspondences by showing that language itself partakes of the process.

It is precisely this kind of association, with its implied complex of correspondences, that at times makes Trevor's work seem grotesque to some modern readers; often in reviews his characters and situations are described as too bizarre to be generally appealing. But the point is that these seemingly odd conjunctions are in fact pertinent: that there does exist an old and abiding tradition, a view of the universe asserting that acts in one realm reverberate in another, that, for example, the physical damage of one person is re-created in the spiritual damage of a second, or vice versa.

What is striking in all Trevor's work is how frequent and elaborate these various connections and analogues are, so pervasive that it does not seem an overstatement to call them a *system* of correspondences. One of his earliest stories, "The Original Sins of Edward Tripp," presents its titular character as feeling the present so dominated by the past that his own earlier childish mischief in Ireland and the recent horrendous murder of eight nurses in Chicago become kindred events; the sister with whom he shares this vision declares, "we know about the deceased. They're everywhere, Edward. Everywhere,"[4] and she means that quite literally. In the much later story "Beyond the Pale" Cynthia, the English visitor who "is extremely knowledgeable about all matters relating to Irish history,"[5] makes her companions uncomfortable by discerning the past alive in the present of the Antrim coast where they so blithely holiday: " 'Can you imagine,' she embarrassingly asked, 'our very favourite places bitter with disaffection, with plotting and revenge? Can you imagine the treacherous murder of Shane O'Neill the Proud?' " (704). When a suicide occurs at their idyllic hotel, she will not let its implication be ignored: the violence, terrorism, and murder that precipitated the suicide are not "beyond the pale" of this garden resort but a symptom of its very existence, a present manifestation of evils going back to "the Battle of the Yellow Ford . . . , the Statutes of Kilkenny. The Battle of Glenmama" (704), and so on through a long recital. Their landlord's furious rejection of her associating past events with present realities is itself unwittingly phrased in terms that suggest connection: "You are trying to bring something to our doorstep which most certainly does not belong there" (708). Yes, this is a metaphor, but one that in context seems almost palpable: a real "something," a real "doorstep," just as there was and still is an actual "pale" holding back the starving from the well fed, protecting the complacent from the desperate, suggesting, deceptively, that private worlds of vacationing adulterers can be kept discreetly separate from the grander cruelties of history.

In addition to correspondences involving time and space are many other components of Trevor's system, ones related to plot, characterization, setting, imagery, theme, narrative technique – in fact, to all the various elements that help make up fiction. For exam-

ple, it is not accidental that references to love and war are often juxtaposed in *Fools of Fortune*; these are not simply "standard thematic
abstractions" of literature (though, as "love and death," they are
also that), but their repeated, varied, and complex conjunction
shapes this novel and helps constitute its point. Early in the narrative
Willie notices that "all around us there seemed to be this unsettling
love,"[6] and then he begins the next section of his memories with the
observation that "the men of the village came back from the war"
(32). This juxtaposition of love and war is presented but not
remarked on and indeed would not necessarily be noted in retrospect by the reader were there not so many other instances of it, not
only of the actual words *love* and *war* but of incidents related to
them. For example, gazing out a window one night as a young boy,
Willie "pretended that a Black and Tan was lurking among the mass
of rhododendrons" and that he apprehends him with his father's
shotgun. But in the next moment what he actually sees is an erotic
scene between Tim Paddy and the Sweeney girl, private, so they
think, in the bushes (37).

The boy then and the aged narrator he has now become make
no conscious connection between the subject of his fantasy and
what he really witnesses, but the novel demonstrates that there is a
most important connection, that one is virtually an emblem of the
other. Both violent attack and erotic congress, in these two particular scenes, are shrouded in darkness, attempting concealment in
"the garden," or at least in the bushes that grow in that garden; both
sets of actors intend something good from one point of view and
something bad from another (the Black and Tan would protect the
English hold on Ireland, good or bad, depending on one's
allegiance; Tim Paddy and the Sweeney girl would have their
pleasure for the moment but thus betray their real interest in other
people); and both events are frustrated, as in fantasy the soldier is
apprehended and in real life the erotic tumble is interrupted by the
arrival of others. More important than these similarities of detail is
that both events are witnessed and recounted by a character who
will grow up to become a person for whom the fantasy of "war" will
overshadow even the actuality of "love" and whose mix of these two
realities will literally become incarnate in his own child, conceived in
love and born into war.

Although the connection in Willie's mind between love and war is not a conscious one, the reader begins to notice that such conjunctions occur again and again, page after page, that Willie will soon refer to some element of war after having considered some aspect of love, or will move on to thoughts of love after having referred to an event of war. The revolution of 1916 is juxtaposed with the fact that Johnny Lacy was a rake (18); announcement of Kitty's forthcoming marriage and Willie's sisters' giggling talk of their wanting to marry Mr. Derenzy are followed immediately by further reference to the conflict of 1598, the rising of 1916, and the Great War currently on in 1918 (20-21); Tim Paddy yearns to go to war for the sake of the wine and the scented women (22); war's folly is juxtaposed once again with the heroic charity of the beloved wife, Willie's great-grandmother, Anna Quinton (29); memories of unsettling love are followed immediately by references to the men back from the war (31-32); "There's talk of a wedding" (38) is followed by "grey-faced Doyle had been murdered" (39); and when Doyle's involvement with the Black and Tans is discussed, young Willie's only question is whether "Doyle had been married" (42).

The issue in this succession of examples is not that a logical or obvious connection has been established between love and war but that Willie, the narrator, has repeatedly conjoined them in his own process of telling his story. The associations say something about him. Most compelling of all in this regard is that in his own moment of trauma – his family murdered, the house in flames, himself on the grass burned and in great pain, pretending to be dead so as not to be shot – at this terrible moment the eight-year-old boy thinks again of the various loves that have preoccupied him earlier:

> Through the fever of this nightmare floated the two portraits in the drawing-room, my dog-faced great-grandfather and plain, merciful Anna Quinton. I seemed to be in the drawing-room myself, gathering up my school books and placing them in the corner cupboard. After that I was in the dog-cart, asking my father why Father Kilgarriff had been unfrocked . . . [reference to one of the several "unsettling loves"]. I would understand such things, my father said, when I went away to school: that was why I had to. I would understand the love of Mr Derenzy and Aunt Pansy, and the different love of Tim Paddy and the Sweeney girl. (43f)

The image that ends this nightmare vision – "Geraldine's drawing of Doyle hanging from the tree" (44) – once again juxtaposes thoughts about love with those of the violence that attends war. Indeed, this entire section of Willie's narrative is bracketed by such references, beginning as it does with the question, "Would we have loved one another then in whatever way it is that children love?" (23), and concluding with the horrible visual image of the execution that precipitated the massacre, an event that even years later continued to sear that love.

These opening sections of the novel, filled as they are with frequent examples of Willie's tendency to ally memories of love and war, set a pattern that continues throughout. Not only do these associations reveal something about Willie himself, betraying a profound disturbance of his soul that his narrating voice does not present directly or try to explain; they also begin to suggest from their sheer quantity that there may indeed be a correspondence between the loves that are described and the state of war in which they founder.

All these elements of correspondence make *Fools of Fortune* paradigmatic of Trevor's fiction at its most complex: across time and space, from the Norman origins of Willie's Irish family to the English brides who over two centuries merged with and helped shape the estate and its life, across experiences of love and of hate, through the involutions of the old Willie's narrative of himself as a boy and then as a man, through all the juxtapositions of historical events, such as the ancient Battle of the Yellow Ford and the current war in Europe – through all these the novel builds a series of patterns and connections asserting that events and persons are not isolated from each other despite spatial or temporal separation. Things unspeakable, "beyond the pale," cannot be kept at bay with physical, social, or psychological barriers. The "body politic" is indeed one body, and the health or decay of each member affects the others. Original sins, whether by Adam or Edward, committed in any garden, generate evils that persist, marring the fortunes of all, always and everywhere.

Chapter Three

The Genealogy of Evil

Trevor's analysis of the evil permeating human history does not simply link adult suffering with childhood misfortunes or trace twentieth-century blight back through the ages to an original sin in a garden of Eden. Such commonplace chains of evil are transformed by the revelation that his characters participate in their own wounding, that the originator of sin is not one man only in the past but each person along the way. Childhood trauma is never merely something inflicted from without, something inherited, some physical or psychic mutilation in which the child is simply an innocent victim. The trauma often involves a game in which the child is a significant player.

A paradigm of this process is presented in the early story "The Original Sins of Edward Tripp," which by its title suggests a comparison between the chief Judeo-Christian explanation of the origin of evil (Adam's Original Sin in the Garden of Eden) and the particular forms of evil manifest in this story, an analogy both chilling and comic. Adam and Edward could not be more unalike: the first man, a being of preternatural perfection, as father of humanity his decisions affecting billions of descendants; Edward, an eccentric nonentity, father of no one at all, taken up with trivialities. The Fall of Adam was presented by the author of Genesis as profoundly serious; Edward's fall is grimly comic.

Such parody of a significant myth is part of the humor of the story as a whole. Adam's and Edward's transgressions both occurred in gardens, but whereas Adam's expulsion was from Paradise, Edward's was from neighborhood society. Adam's punishment involved his being subject to death; Edward's, in being subject to fantasies. Adam's sin, according to some interpretations of the myth, awakened him to the complexities of sexuality with his daughter-sister-wife, Eve; Edward's sin doomed him to protracted celibacy with his sister, Emily. Adam's sin was a great fall; Edward's sin was a little trip.

Remembering his "original sins" as an adult, Edward begins with an event set in the family garden: "From her own private flower-bed he had pulled her pansies, roots and all, when he was five years old; and with a pair of scissors he had cut through the centre of the buds of her roses. 'I have played a trick on you,' he used to say, sidling close to her."[1] Nasty this little boy may be, but tormenting his nine-year-old sister is not quite in a class with man's first disobedience; his are venial sins, not mortal ones. In the Catholic theological system Trevor often invokes even an infinite number of venial sins do not add up to one mortal sin, and yet in this story they do. Edward's little tricks become deadly precisely because he and his sister play a game that makes them so.

At the heart of this game lies a tenacious holding on to past wrongs: "Edward remembered the past and he knew that his sister was remembering it too. . . . Edward often felt strange in the house now, feeling the present dominated by the past, remembering everything" (70). He sees his "baby tricks" and "cruelties in their thousands" as having "fallen like a blight upon her nature, . . . embittering the whole" (71f), dominating the life they have led together into their forties. At first it seems to the reader that Emily is mad – she imagines murders everywhere in their neighborhood and sends Edward to cut down the women she thinks are hanged in adjacent houses – but such conventional spookiness is not Trevor's goal. He turns the story in a more startling and more revealing direction as Edward hysterically tries to explain the situation to an 82-year-old neighbor: "My sister is not unwell. My sister pretends, exacting her revenge. God has told me, Mrs Mayben, to play my part in her pretended fantasies. I owe her the right to punish me, I quite understand that. . . . It is all pretence and silence between my sister and myself. We play a game" (76). The words *game, play*, and *acting* are used several times by Edward, underscoring the deliberateness of what would otherwise seem like simple madness. And the deliberateness is the point of the story.

Edward's feeling "rotten with guilt" (76) and his sister's vengeful acting of madness seem disproportionate to the "little tricks" of childhood that precipitated it all. Her being marked forever and his atoning forever (72) are states they have knowingly chosen and fostered. This behavior constitutes a childhood game carried into adulthood, a way to prolong that childhood and avoid adulthood, avoid marriage and the making of a new home. Since their parents' death when they were adolescents, they have continued to live in the same house, eat the same food, and play the same game ("Only the toys have gone" [77]).

Under the "pretended fantasies" Edward and Emily symbiotically share lie the real fantasies that betray their arrested state. Edward has, of course, unsettled Mrs. Mayben with his crazy confession, and although she nervously managed to persuade him (and his ham knife) to leave her house, he daydreams about his visit quite differently: "She placed a hand on Edward's shoulder and said most softly that he had made her feel a mother again. He told her then, once more, of the pansies plucked from the flower-bed, and Mrs Mayben nodded and said he must not mind. . . . 'Come when you wish,' invited Mrs Mayben with tears in her eyes. 'Cross the road for comfort. It's all you have to do'" (78). This sympathetic, comforting, forgiving woman may have been a mother to him in his dream, but in fact the actual Mrs. Mayben[2] dismissed him by saying she was "too old to take on new subjects" (78). After entertaining his idealizing dream during lunch, Edward then turns to another fantasy: "His eyes moved to his sister's face and then moved downwards to the table, towards the knife that lay now on the polished wood. He thought about this knife that he had carried into a neighbour's house, remembering its keen blade slicing through the flesh of a pig. He saw himself standing with the knife in his hand, and he heard a noise that might have been a cry from his sister's throat. 'I have played a trick on you,' his own voice said, tumbling back to him over the years" (78). Once again Trevor comes close to the edge of conventional storytelling, only to turn away from actual murder and to the nursed thought of murder. These two fantasies – the loving mother, the destroyed sibling – fuel the game Edward and Emily have chosen to play during the 40 years they have competed for the same territory.

That territory may be the flower bed, destroyed by malice; it may be the mother, lost to death; or it may, from another perspective, be Ireland itself. This is the only story in Trevor's first collected volume to seem to be set in Ireland. The repeated reference to "Dunfarnham Avenue" suggests an Irish town, just as the presence of large engravings "featuring the bridges of London" and the collected

works of Kipling and Scott and *The Life of a Bengal Lancer* suggest a
British orientation.3 The mutual attachment and hatred that control
Edward's and Emily's lives have clear political analogues, just as their
family struggle mirrors struggles between groups in the larger social
unit that constitutes the nation of which Dunfarnham Avenue is one
part.

Throughout his *A Writer's Ireland* Trevor stresses the mix of
peoples that make up Ireland, emphasizing the various waves of
invasion to clarify that no one group is the "real" Irish, underscoring
and defending diversity. He dismisses as "glib" the view that writers
like "Somerville and Ross and Elizabeth Bowen were somehow not
quite Irish, not properly or dedicatedly so."4 He refers to the
"double colonialism" of Ulster, reminding his readers that Ireland
colonized Scotland before the loan was returned "with interest" in
the seventeenth century (171). He stresses that there were English as
well as Irish Catholics needing Daniel O'Connell's emancipation bill
(73). And he quotes with approval David Marcus's analogy concerning the genesis of the Irish short story as a "mixed marriage":
"Ireland's most renowned expert on the modern short story, David
Marcus, agrees that [George] Moore was indeed its father. He offers
Somerville and Ross as the mother. No literary union, he argues,
'could have been more fruitful of promise, for father and mother
emerged from the two widely-opposed cultures (Catholic and
Native/Protestant or Anglo, and settler) which had become the con-
stituents of the Irish family'" (143f).

The Tripp family of "Number Seventeen Dunfarnham Avenue" is
also an Irish family made up of strongly opposed members, a brother
and a sister whose present, like Ireland's, is dominated by the past
and who consequently spend all the time and energy of their life
locked in a deadly game. That they are not victims of outside forces
is indicated by the fact that their enterprise is indeed a game, a play
in which they themselves are the principal actors. But if not victims,
neither are they victors, nor "fruitful of promise," nor anything else
positive. Like the Ulster Trevor explores in a later story, "Beyond the
Pale," and like the Munster of "The Distant Past," this Dunfarnham
Avenue household turns its violence against itself.

When in "The Distant Past" the elderly Middletons discuss
recent bombings in Belfast with the butcher, Driscoll (who as a boy
50 years earlier had attempted to shoot British soldiers in their

house in Munster), he remarks that it is "a bad business"; "We don't want that old stuff all over again."[5] Miss Middleton's quip that "We didn't want it in the first place" makes the butcher, her brother, and herself laugh: "Yes, it was a game, she thought: how could any of it be as real or as important as the afflictions and problems of the old butcher himself, his rheumatism and his reluctance to retire?" This relegating of the Anglo-Irish War to "a game," making national independence of lesser importance than individual aches and pains, is not simply the apolitical view of an aged Protestant spinster puzzled by her lowered status in the Republic of Ireland. The word *game* also connects the issues of this story with those of "The Original Sins of Edward Tripp." In both stories activities that damage participants and their society (whether family or nation) are seen as games, structures of pretense that control behavior and allow destructive acts that would otherwise be abhorrent.

That the players are themselves responsible for the game is as clear in "The Distant Past" as it is in "The Original Sins of Edward Tripp." The hostility that prompted Fat Driscoll and two farmers to lock the Middleton family in an upstairs room and wait downstairs to massacre some expected British soldiers (who never arrived) continues to be fueled, despite the fact that Driscoll and the Middletons share a drink and joke about the past 50 years later. The aged Middletons protest in their Protestant church when prayers are no longer said for the Royal Family; they stand up when "God Save the King" is played on the BBC; "and on the day of the coronation of Queen Elizabeth II they drove into the town with a small Union Jack propped up in the back window of their Ford Anglia" (63). Although their Church of Ireland rector considers them an anachronism and the townspeople are amused by them (" 'Bedad, you're a holy terror, Mr. Middleton!' Fat Driscoll laughingly exclaimed, noticing the flag as he lifted a tray of pork-steaks from his display shelf " [63]), their public gestures of loyalty to the crown constitute their moves in the old game, however innocently those moves are made. Visitors to the now prosperous tourist town are impressed by the fact that "old wounds could heal so completely, that the Middletons continued in their loyalty to the past and that in spite of it, they were respected in the town" (65f). But "healing of old wounds" is the wrong metaphor: "time-out" is more exact, because the game resumes on both sides in 1967.

The Middletons grew up on an inherited rural estate, Car-raveagh, a once prosperous and important establishment now in extreme decay: "They blamed for their ill-fortune the Catholic Dublin woman [for whose favors their father had mortgaged his property] and they blamed as well the new national régime, contriving in their eccentric way to relate the two. In the days of the Union Jack such women would have known their place: wasn't it all part and parcel?" (61f). Although this merging of the public and the private – new gov-ernment and old mistress – does not stand up to logical scrutiny, it works well as a game rule: the government and the mistress are both Catholic, both "illegitimate," both ruinous to the old estates, and both therefore deserving of resistance. Yet the Middletons are aware that the game they play is hurtful and deliberate: "Alone in their beds at night they now and again wondered why they hadn't just sold Car-raveagh forty-eight years ago when their father had died: why had the tie been so strong and why had they in perversity encouraged it?" (66). They may soften the Anglo-Irish War by calling it just a game, they may think of their "worship of the distant past" as "no more than a game," but those words *perversity* and *encouraged* betray their own culpability in all that happens.

When the Troubles begin in Belfast and Derry, the Middletons once again become "the enemy" : "Slowly the change crept about, all around them in the town, until Fat Driscoll didn't wish it to be remembered that he had ever given them mince for their dog. He had stood with a gun in the enemy's house, waiting for soldiers so that soldiers might be killed: it was better that people should remember that" (68f). This resumption of hostilities infects even the Catholic priest, who had often befriended the Middletons but now turns his back when they drive into town. Thus both sets of oppo-nents in the peaceful, independent south take up their old positions to play out a game from the past.

Trevor ends his story on this melancholy note: "Because of the distant past they would die friendless. It was worse than being mur-dered in their beds" (70). He might have added "childless" to "friendless," since the Middletons have seemed to love "the remains of Carraveagh more than they could ever have loved a husband or a wife" (61) and, like Edward and Emily, have remained celibate and without issue. These two early stories suggest that childlessness is an apt metaphor for the results of personal cruelty and colonial exploitation, a concept developed at length in the later novel *The Silence in the Garden*, where another childhood game played out in a garden allows appalling behavior, and where the evil that begins in childhood becomes mortal for a whole family because of their deliberate participation in it.

These brothers and sisters doomed to sterility, these old families that thus come to an end, and the childish games that direct and appear to excuse damaging behavior (*"They did not realise. Children often don't"* [184] is the rationalization of one character in *The Silence in the Garden*) – all these examples of evil are only segments of a much longer chain. But tracing the links that form a chain of relationships is not the same as accounting for its existence in the first place. What is the origin of evil? Although this question has exercised philosophers from the beginning, no ontological or ethical system seems to provide a thoroughly persuasive answer. In the Catholic system that provides the context for Trevor's thought, theories repeatedly stumble against the problem of accounting for both God's goodness and his omnipotence and omniscience. As Archibald MacLeish jauntily put it in his play *J.B.*, "If God is God He is not good, / If God is good He is not God."[6] The power of the Book of Job lies precisely in its probing of the inexplicable mystery reconciling suffering and evil with goodness and justice. The same inexplicable mystery empowers the secular myth of *King Lear*, where both fathers are saved from despair by salutary falsity (the contrived miracle of Gloucester's "fall" and the blessed error of Cordelia's "breath": perhaps, after all, the gods do not kill us for their sport and perhaps, after all, all sorrows are redeemed [5.3.266-68]). Shakespeare's oxymoron describing Gloucester's death – his heart "burst smilingly" (5.3.200) – is as apt a paradigm as any for the contradictions inherent in attempts to reconcile good and evil.

But if there is no satisfactory *account* of the origin of evil, there are nonetheless multiple ways of responding to and dealing with the evil itself. Edgar's heroic efforts to save Gloucester from despair invoke a blessedness beyond present suffering, a blessedness independent of "facts" (there is no cliff, there is no fall, and yet the old man believes he has been saved miraculously – and so *is* saved). Neither Edgar nor anyone else in the play questions the value of salvation based on deception.

Trevor's fictional characters grappling with the problem of evil are no more successful in finding an answer than are the real philosophers and writers who preceded them (and some, most notably Miss Gomez and Mrs. Eckdorf, like Lear and Gloucester, find their comfort in untruths). One of the most vehement expressions of outrage against God for allowing evil to afflict man in the first place is voiced by Miss Samson in the novel *Elizabeth Alone*. Although badly disfigured, Miss Samson has been deeply religious all her life, positive in her attitude toward God, her fellow man, and her own plight. But after discovering in the diary of her religious mentor that he lost his faith just before dying, after brooding on this information while hospitalized herself, she finds her own faith destroyed and cries out to Elizabeth, "It isn't fair! . . . Why does He make it so hard for people? Why create His silly world in the first place? What kind of a thing is He?" She then goes on to catalog evils suggesting that God is either not benevolent or not omniscient-omnipotent: "He plays that ugly little trick on us. He gives us human cruelty. And people throwing bombs about. Your friend drinking whiskey and gassing himself. Little Mrs Drucker abandoned as an infant to a home. Miss Clapper's parents not caring a fig about her. Your own father, Mrs Aidallbery, whom you didn't like. And Arthur born backward and multiple sclerosis."[7] Her harangue is both grotesquely comic and painfully serious. The spray of saliva on Elizabeth's face as Miss Samson shrieks, the jumble of items (mixing "whom you didn't like" with "gassing himself"), the trivializing idioms ("not caring a fig," "throwing bombs about"), the quick little puns ("fig" and "clap"), the awkward lack of parallelism ("born backward and multiple sclerosis") – all these are grotesquely, painfully comic. And yet Miss Samson's grief is real, the items she lists constitute terrible suffering for the individuals involved, the indictment *is* a serious one. And the central question remains, "Why does He make it so hard for people?" This is not merely the hysterical outburst of a disfigured and disillusioned woman; it is, phrased variously and perhaps more impersonally, one of the major questions of all philosophical systems.

Elements in Miss Samson's harangue are consistent with passages elsewhere in Trevor's work probing the nature and genealogy of evil. God's "little trick" is the cosmic equivalent of Edward's little tricks. The trivializing language – *little*, *trick*, and *plays* – suggests that God is no more "grown up" than a malicious little boy, with no more vision or care than young Edward Tripp had. Indicating that the gift of "human cruelty" is the ugly little trick God plays on mankind emphasizes the subsequent role people have in propagating their own suffering. Furthermore, in Miss Samson's view "floods and earthquakes" and "marriages . . . in which everything goes wrong" are on a par, equally personalized forms of evil because "He permits all that" (279). Whatever "thing" He is, He is not a just referee in the game Edward and Emily Tripp, the Middletons, or the Rollestons play.

Miss Samson is only one character in the novel, however, and certainly not to be taken as Trevor's spokesperson. But she does belong to a number of characters throughout Trevor's work who lose their faith in either God or goodness: Mrs. Eckdorf, Miss Gomez, Penelope Vade, Cynthia Strafe (and later Julia Ferndale). In these earlier novels and stories this loss tends to be expressed explicitly; in later works the losses and disillusionments center on human relationships, rather than religious or philosophical considerations of God or the good, and are not usually stated outright by given characters but instead manifest in their choices and fates (Willie in *Fools of Fortune* cannot allow himself to enjoy family life after his act of revenge; the governess in "The News from Ireland" errs in thinking she can live an ordinary married life after the famine; Tom in *The Silence in the Garden* lives solitary).

Solitariness, either imposed or chosen, is an important element in Trevor's renditions of mundane evil. The novel in which Miss Samson's outburst occurs is essentially a study in being alone, as both its title, *Elizabeth Alone*, and its last line, "She was happy enough alone, she said" (288), suggest. The plot in this novel is quite simple: four women of different ages and from different backgrounds share the same London hospital ward; become intimate during that time, confiding in and caring about one another; and then return to their separate worlds and particular sufferings or losses when they are discharged. Their reasons for being hospitalized are thematically significant: three have hysterectomies and one needs care during a difficult pregnancy. (In Trevor's world, where both children and sterility are such important topics, these medical needs take on special meaning, pointing as they do to either the impossibility or the danger of fruitful intimacy.) Of the three women hospitalized for operations, Miss Samson is the oldest, unmarried and childless; Elizabeth Aidallbery is 41, divorced and the mother of three daughters; and Sylvie Clapper is probably in her twenties, has a current boyfriend, and needs the hysterectomy because of past sexual activities and an incompetently performed abortion. The three each have their own form of aloneness and ways of coping with it. Miss Samson feels keenly that because of her terrible disfigurement no man will ever love her, but she was content managing a boardinghouse for people from her church, who made up a kind of family among themselves, until her subsequent loss of faith alienated her from them. Elizabeth is beginning to feel bereft of the people she loves (two of her children are "rowdily growing up," the third has "gone off with a Jesus freak," and her mother is "packed away in a Sunset Home" [260]); because she had "never been much good at being alone" (260) she probably would have married her devoted childhood friend, Henry, despite not loving him, had he not gassed himself while drunk. Sylvie, emotionally abandoned by her parents, needs a lover and so blinds herself to her lover's infidelity and dishonesty in order to stay with him, and even goes through the motions of becoming a Catholic so that they can marry.

All three women have made compromises or entertained falsities to shield themselves from loneliness, with varied results: Miss Samson's failed faith has dropped her into a hell of suffering; Elizabeth's frustrated willingness to marry a man she did not love has left her alone though possibly "happy enough"; and Sylvie's multiple self-deceptions have gained her a jolly but unreliable Irish husband in Liverpool. During the course of the novel all three women have experienced loneliness as their own special affliction of evil. Their fourth companion in the hospital ward is a young woman who has had many miscarriages (induced partly by systematic persecution from her mother-in-law); this time she manages to deliver the baby safely but must live forever with the alienation occasioned by her husband's admission of early sexual practices that humiliate him and shock her. It is significant in this novel that the sterility-to-fertility rate is 3:1, and that the successful birth is only reported, the child and its parents never subsequently shown. Instead, the final and therefore conclusive scenes of the novel focus on the physically and emotionally marred Miss Samson, with her bitter protest against God, and on Elizabeth herself, "happy enough" but alone.

As with Trevor's other fiction from this period, *Elizabeth Alone* is both comic and tragic. Serious events, such as Henry's failed life and muddled death and even Miss Samson's anguish, are portrayed with hilarious details. Like *The Boarding-House*, *The Love Department*, *Mrs. Eckdorf in O'Neill's Hotel*, and *Miss Gomez and the Brethren*, this novel shows lonely and eccentric people managing to cope with the evils that plague them while simultaneously contributing to those evils and perpetrating further evil on others. The Dickensian quality of many characters keeps the overall effect amusing, even when situations are grim.

This paradigm so prevalent in the early novels also helps shape *The Children of Dynmouth* (1976) and *Other People's Worlds* (1980), though both of those novels are darker and more dreadful than their predecessors. Just as *Mrs. Eckdorf in O'Neill's Hotel* and *Miss Gomez and the Brethren* seem like companion pieces, so too do *Elizabeth Alone* and *Other People's Worlds*. Like Elizabeth, Julia Ferndale is an attractive cultured woman in her forties, with daughters by a marriage that ended several years previously (though in Julia's case through sudden widowhood, not divorce). And like Elizabeth, Julia is brought painfully to face the essential solitariness of her life. In this later novel, however, devastating loss of faith in a benevolent deity is suffered not by a secondary character, a Miss Samson, but by the central character herself as she experiences malevolence at the very heart of what she thought was love.

In *Other People's Worlds* Trevor once again traces his typical line of evil from childhood abuse through that child's later adult perpetration of abuse on others. The "psychopath"[8] Francis Tyte (very like Septimus Tuam in *The Love Department*) is the chief example of this phenomenon. Sexually abused when he was 11 by a homosexual lodger in his parents' home, he grows up unable to feel affection for anyone, unable to imagine that others have any feelings or needs, focused entirely on himself, lost in his own compensatory fantasies. He is, of course, an actor, both professionally and in his private life, always wearing a touch of makeup, always "onstage." He readily charms and exploits women, and once persuaded a woman to bear him a child just from his passing whim of wanting to know what it is like to be a father; he stays in touch with the mother, Doris, and the child, Joy, because it is convenient to have a place to stay when he is in London, and he keeps them enthralled but also at bay by an elaborate series of lies about himself. Doris becomes a dreadful alcoholic, and Joy, at 12, is a dreadful adolescent. This segment of the plot presents a truly horrible case history of urban distress but also is frequently comic in its details (like Mrs. Tuke in *Miss Gomez and the Brethren*, Doris is a sloppy drunk whose self-deceptions and affectations are at times hilarious).

Although Joy's inability to read at age 12 is continually blamed on her school (which, with its various fads, such as taking elephant tranquilizers, also seems both dreadful and blackly funny), the name of that school connects it with her father: Tite Street Comprehensive and Francis Tyte have both failed her. A nightmare Joy has midway through the novel clinches the implied connection between school and father and personal damage, and indicates that she is permanently scarred with his "image": "She dropped off to sleep and dreamed that she was back at Tite Street Comprehensive, where Clicky Hines had persuaded her to have the face of her father tattooed on her stomach. He'd even persuaded her that he could do the job himself. . . . She woke up with a jerk because the drill thing he was using had got out of control and was cutting her open when it should have been putting the blue in the eyes" (121). Such lethal disfigurement at the very center of her being has actually occurred, beginning with the irresponsible procreation, continuing through a childhood where both mother and father are either physically or emotionally absent, and culminating in the shock of her father's publicized bigamy and her mother's drunken murder of her father's first wife. All these events are either directly or indirectly the result of Francis's deeds, Francis's self. He was a damaged child, and now as an adult he damages others, including his own child, Joy.

"The child was the victim of other people's worlds and other people's drama, caught up in horror because she happened to be there" (219) – these are Julia Ferndale's thoughts, as the novel ends with her musing about Joy: "The child should not have been born but the child was there, her chapped face and plastic-rimmed spectacles. She was there in the garden and the house, while time went on and the seasons unfussily changed" (220). Like Corny and Tom in *The Silence in the Garden*, like Edward and Emily in "The Original Sins of Edward Tripp," and like Timothy in *The Children of Dynmouth*, Joy is yet another child whose personal damage is juxtaposed with the tranquil beauty of a garden and its gentle cycle of normal change.

Julia's role in the novel prevents its being a simplistic exploration of a cliché about disturbed parents producing disturbed children. As in Trevor's other work, evil here is also shown to be a cultivated phenomenon, not merely imposed. And it is Julia's understanding of this process that is the real focus of the novel, not the black comedy of Francis Tyte's bigamous marriage to her, or of Doris's cracked mind, or of Joy's damaged life.

Initially presented as an "innocent," a person who since girlhood has been taken advantage of by the various lame ducks she befriends (a judgment her own mother and both her daughters share), Julia takes on stature and nobility toward the end of the novel. Francis in his narcissism *talks* about forgiveness (and by this he means he forgives the people whom he has injured, never realizing he has done the damage, not they [216f]), but Julia is a person truly able to forgive. This contrast raises the question of whether her apparently foolish kindness represents character weakness or unusual magnanimity. When Francis on their unconsummated wedding night indicates he has married her bigamously because he thought marriage to him was what she wanted, then asks for her jewels and money before deserting her, she gives him the jewels and cashes her traveler's checks for the required amount, even supplying a statement that these are gifts. Repeatedly in the novel Julia says yes when common sense indicates she should say no: she accepts (and pays for) the dog Francis had ordered before their wedding; she allows hysterical Doris and dropout Joy to visit her at her lovely home in Gloucestershire, even giving Joy the run of the house; she brings Joy to see the aged Mrs. Tyte, her grandmother, in a nursing home in London, because there is no one else to do it. When Francis writes for more money, she sends it. Mere foolishness? or heroic, saintly giving coat as well as cloak?[9] Is Julia another of Trevor's holy fools?

In deploying elements of good and evil in this novel Trevor has given his narrative a number of twists. He shows all the characters caught up in illusions in one way or another, then disallows illusions as an excuse for cruelty. He presents Julia as a woman easily taken advantage of, then shows her behaving with extraordinary responsibility. He lets her terrible experience with Francis destroy her faith in

God, then allows her to feel that Father Lavin's prayers have, after all, saved Susanna Melody's life (whom drunken, jealous Doris had threatened to kill). Then in yet another twist he reveals that Julia's efforts to save Susanna are mocked by the fact that Doris has indeed committed murder (with, of all grotesquely comic things, a teapot), but it is Francis's first wife who has been bludgeoned to death, not the suspected girlfriend, Susanna. Thus prayer is mocked, and Julia is left with her grief, her despair, and the rest of her life to live out.

Julia's despair began after her desertion by and disillusionment with the man she so passionately loved; she then finds herself wondering if God too is an illusion, "my bearded cloudy God who saw me through my childhood and my widowing" (178f), just "a fog of comfort to be lost in" (179). Like Miss Samson, she suddenly finds life to be a catalog of horrors as she, in an apparent non sequitur, reminds Father Lavin of Pentecostal missionaries whose children were murdered before their very eyes: "They stood in a row. When the sun reached a certain point in the sky they were clubbed to death. A week ago a legless man in Arizona was tormented by teenagers until he died. In Birmingham a husband killed his wife with a knife because she wouldn't cook his bacon right. Bombs explode everywhere" (179). For her all of this is associated with Francis, with "his whole terrible world" (181), which makes Calvary seem remote, "just another distant act of violence" (181). This cry of anguish to Father Lavin is much like Miss Samson's to Elizabeth, or Kate's to Mr. Featherstone in *The Children of Dynmouth*, and none of these spiritual counselors is able to offer a satisfactory answer, leaving their confidants bereft. But unlike the aged Miss Samson and the young Kate, Julia moves beyond her lost faith to struggle with evil in whatever way she can. One of her chief insights is that Francis was responsible for himself and for his actions. His various stories – both true (that he was sexually abused) and false (that his parents died in a railway crash) – were designed to gain pity and to provide excuses. Yet in response to Doris's litany of blame – "I blame that lodger. . . . I blame the old parents" (163) – Julia realizes that "Francis Tyte had blamed other people when he should have blamed himself, that the blaming should not be continued" (163). By not allowing Francis's horrific childhood to excuse the man he has become, by not explaining away what she realizes is deliberate cruelty (144), Julia begins to understand how evil functions through human actions.

Even the irony of the murder Julia goes out of her way to try to prevent, a murder that indeed occurs but with a different victim, exposes yet another fact about evil: its permanence. (As Francis's father says years later of the abusive lodger, "He's dead now, but he hasn't taken his evil with him" [192].) The link between individual human actions and the abiding permanence of evil is expressed in a well-known colloquialism Doris so vividly remembers Francis using that it seems his voice is present in the room with her: "Again he referred to Constance Kent.[10] Again he spoke of Rowena Avenue and the dressmaker's house, and the whispy grey moustache of the debt-collector. 'Tit for tat,' he said" (159). This "tit for tat" principle is what moves evil along through time, from one person to another. For Francis his early homosexual seduction by the debt collector who lodged in his parents' house has left him with a lifetime of "repayment," which includes seducing as many people as he can, not sexually but with his lies and fantasies; the currency of this repayment is hatred, expressed by either petty thefts or personal cruelty; and the energy for the work comes from violent fantasies:

> He stopped in his walk, indulging his dislike, listening to the shrill voices, the late-night cries of people determinedly having a good time. He wouldn't have cared if all of them had been shot down dead, if gunmen had appeared from the Mayfair doorways and opened fire in the orange street light. He imagined the bodies scattered, reminding him of the bodies in the train crash, and the victims of the terrorists the director [of his TV program] had referred to, and the victim of Constance Kent. (85)

Francis's fantasies include the imagined violent murder of his wife in Rowena Avenue (104f), a murder Doris actually does carry out, since she is hardly a person in her own right but seems "a figment of his pretense which had somehow acquired reality" (118). Thus "tit for tat" not only serves to perpetrate retaliations but spreads an infection of evil to people not directly involved in the original equation. "Tit for tat" is shorthand for the game rules that operate in "The Distant Past," "Attracta," *Fools of Fortune*, and *The Silence in the Garden* – all those many stories of Trevor's which show what happens when ancient wrongs are not forgiven and forgotten. And in the phrase introducing Francis's fantasies – "indulging his dislike" – the word *indulging* damns the whole process of cultivated resentments by pointing up its deliberateness.

Francis is clearly a moral monster, unable to face his own culpability yet profoundly responsible for horrors that occur – a man unable, really, to forgive. But is Julia – morally sensitive and genuinely good-hearted, taking responsibility for the welfare even of strangers – also responsible for the evil in this narrative? Does she participate in its perpetration? Readers who see her gentle accommodation to the demands of others as a weakness, a fault, will no doubt answer yes. But beyond that the text offers another indication of her involvement. The images at the center of her experience of religious despair first came to her at a moment of great happiness: "a group of missionaries of the Pentecostal Church had been assassinated in Africa. They had been made to watch the killing of their children first, and then they had been killed themselves. She didn't know why she thought of that again, something that had horrified her for a moment while she prepared for her wedding" (137). Wedding and horror had been allied in her consciousness but, like other elements in the narrative, were "pieces from a forgotten jigsaw puzzle, the elements of a pattern . . . scattered, lost in a confusion that Julia wasn't even aware of" (48). She is "guilty" of not seeing, not understanding. At the end of her experience of loss – loss of husband, loss of God, loss even of family and friends because she is so much different from them now – when she is entirely solitary, she sees and understands connections that had been obscure. Francis's commonplace "tit for tat" is balanced by her insight into yet another cliché: "surely God's creatures are all connected" (179). With something near the madness of an Ivy Eckdorf, she takes this metaphor quite literally; however, although her childhood God has been destroyed and she is left alone, she nonetheless feels keenly the connectedness among these creatures, her fellows.

The novel ends by showing Julia having been crushed by evil yet rising above it. Fantasies, television, movies, alcohol, drugs – all have supplied vehicles of escape for various characters in various ways thoughout the novel. Julia's attempt to absorb herself in the passionless language of legal documents (which she types at home to make a living) in order to deaden her pain does not work. She finds she cannot "pack God and Francis Tyte away" (220). This phrase on the final page of the novel does not suggest that she regains her faith in the sense of returning to her childhood's comforting beliefs. That was Eden, and she is very much in a postlapsarian world now. God is coupled with Francis Tyte: both have failed her. Yet she finds she continues to love Francis: "she had begun to love him for what he should have been" (195); she still pities him and still longs "to forgive because it was her nature to" (217). And for God she perhaps also has pity and forgiveness, even though "the very thought of prayer made her feel as cold as ice" (216); she will at least "continue to go to mass, for it would be too much like a gesture never again to practise her Catholic faith" (216). She seems somehow to agree with the judgment of those who witnessed what she suffered: "It wasn't fair, the verdict was, though some said also that fairness was neither here nor there" (216).[11] In the colloquial world of ordinary people the assertion "that fairness was neither here nor there" may be as satisfactory a way as any to reconcile good and evil, beneficent creator and malevolent events.

Although in the fatigue of despair Julia agrees with her mother's earlier judgment that "her compassion made a victim of her" and agrees too with Father Lavin's observation that "she sought connections which didn't exist" (216), Julia continues with both her compassion and her sense of connection. Like the ending of *Mrs. Eckdorf in O'Neill's Hotel*, *Other People's Worlds* ends with a focus on stories, narratives. The novel itself is a story about several stories and several kinds of stories: within the reality of the novel itself Francis's life makes up a story, as do Doris's and Julia's lives; the television account of Constance Kent's life is yet another kind of story, a grisly nineteenth-century murder, providing entertainment for a twentieth-century audience, just as this novel provides entertainment for its readers. The parallel between the stories of Francis's childhood abuse and of Constance Kent's abuse, as well as their mutual need for revenge, makes a neat piece of literary contrivance, interesting for the author to construct, interesting for the critic to discuss, and reassuring to the reader that fictional worlds, at least, are wonderfully coherent, full of dreadful events made a pleasure to enjoy vicariously. Thus once again Trevor nests the realities: in his fictional world there are fictional worlds (movies, daydreams, and this particular television program, based on a "real" murder that through dramatization becomes a fictional one). How far does the reader have to back out of the story to find what is real?

Trevor's narrative supplies an answer, at least with regard to something that is real enough. Watching the television program in which "an unbalanced girl revenged herself," Julia realizes that Constance's story is merely "a glossy diversion,"[12] whereas "it was the child's [Joy's] story that mattered" (219). However real Constance Kent may have been in her time, she is long dead and has now become a fiction. But Joy is very much alive and therefore amenable to change. The meaningless image of Constance Kent on the television screen gives way to another image in Julia's mind, one that belongs to possibility and the future: "Mistily, a scene gathered in her mind, seeming like a family photograph: an old woman and a child, a middle-aged priest and a middle-aged woman, a spaniel asleep in the sun" (219). This odd collection of beings can become a family, through Julia's powers of forgiveness and her belief in connections: her own tough-minded mother and Francis's delinquent child; herself and Father Lavin, the parish priest who has loved her for years (present as a frequent guest, not as a lover); and, completing the idyllic scene, the dog Francis irresponsibly ordered but did not pay for. She sees this vision as a family portrait, and so it will become because she cannot deaden her feelings, cannot "pack God and Francis Tyte away," and cannot doubt there being some purpose in her world. She lives in "a plain house," but she knows it should be "made the most of" (220). Violent crimes may happen, but they are not "gorgeous" (as films or fantasies make them). "Four people [sitting] ordinarily beneath a tree" is perhaps as much good as mankind ejected from an ideal garden can now find. Julia's musings and the novel end with the affirmation that "in spring there were mornings of sunshine" (220).

Unlike Edward and Emily Tripp, unlike Francis Tyte, Julia will return good for evil. Although this provides no philosophical answer to the problem of the origin of evil, it does indicate a possibility about the future of evil, suggesting as it does that a chain of evil connections could be replaced with one of good. Thus even if a perfect Garden of Paradise cannot be regained, ordinary overgrown gardens can be weeded and perhaps reclaimed, offering pleasant refuge to motley groups of people whose altered fates, according to Trevor's system of correspondences, could change the course of nations.

Chapter Four

English Settings, Irish Characters

Nationality and the violence it occasions are an important aspect of the political issues Trevor's work regularly addresses. But the link between political violence and personal cruelties, emerging finally as a concatenation of suffering that binds together all persons from all times and all places, develops gradually throughout Trevor's work, and only in the last half of his writing career do nationality and national allegiance become an explicit issue, focused sharply on Ireland. It seems, in fact, as if the young Anglo-Irish author needed time and distance to develop his view of his native country, learning to deal with it as he learned his craft of writing.[1] Only after working his way through a variety of English settings did Trevor begin to position his stories firmly in Ireland. Only after developing comic-grotesque English characters and a few stereotypical Irish ones did he begin to create the strong, serious Irish characters of his later fiction.

Although the entire body of Trevor's work exhibits a striking consistency in its thematic concerns (e.g., complex correspondences between elements of good and evil; gardens, children, and cruelty; sterility, celibacy, and madness; the comfort of lies and the hazards of truth-telling), the earlier fiction is distinctive in its use of national settings and character types and in the mode of their presentation. During his first decade of publication, which corresponds roughly to the 1960s, Trevor sets his work for the most part in England, usually in urban areas, with his principal characters English. *A Standard of Behaviour* (1958) deals with "swinging" London society; *The Old Boys* (1964), with aged English public school alumni; *The Boarding-House* (1965), with solitary eccentrics in London; and *The Love Department* (1966), with lonely hearts in Wimbledon. His first published collection of short stories, *The Day We Got Drunk on Cake* (1967), is in setting and characterization almost entirely English. All these novels and most of the stories are comic in manner and tend to be more grotesque in characterization and plotting than is true of the later work.

From the 1970s on, the humor is softened by pathos; more Irish characters and settings are used. In the 1980s all but one of the novels and most of the stories are Irish in setting, characterization, and subject matter; the events and manner of presentation are usually serious, sometimes even "tragic," the tone often poignant or despairing. Both the first novel, *A Standard of Behaviour,* and the most recent, *The Silence in the Garden,* contain similar concerns and develop through similar motifs and structures (e.g., both are *Bildungsromane* or variants thereof), but the journey from 1958 to 1988 has brought about significant differences in characterization, setting, kind of event, and narrative tone and effect. The earlier work shows Trevor perfecting his craft and developing those distinctive techniques and configurations of thought which ultimately lead to *Fools of Fortune,* "The News from Ireland," and *The Silence in the Garden,* an odyssey that moves through the city back to the garden, back home to Ireland, from a cheerful view of life to a much darker one.[2]

Although *A Standard of Behaviour* contains several violent events of a genuinely serious nature (date rape, suicide), its real concern is with the unnamed narrator's gentle progress from schoolboy loves to heterosexuality, from youthful misery through bohemian experimentation, erotic success, and lost love followed by new love. The plot tends to be episodic, each incident a kind of dramatized joke (a small fat priest interested in working "among the aggressively sceptical"[3] attends a nudist party). The narrator's own attitude toward his story is wry (Mrs. Lamont's guests at the nudist party are described as "the gay young things of twenty years ago" [58], lumps and sags thus neatly implied, not described). His own friends are portrayed as amusingly silly, campy, London-sophisticated in behavior and idiom ("I think Nigel is a very fine chap and one day will be a genius" [34]). Aside from a comic rich German patsy and a Latin señorita (both part of the narrator's drinking crowd), as well as a minor unidentified Irishman who jumps the betting queue at the races (35), all the characters are English. Nor does one reference to the narrator's ordering a bottle of Guinness (41) offset the gallons of Sassenach cocktails consumed throughout the novel. Aside from a two-page holiday in Paris, all the scenes occur in England, mostly London. This first novel written by a Corkonian in his late twenties, resident for five years in England, is slight, amusing, and very, very English.

Trevor's next novel, *The Old Boys,* is entirely English in its setting, characterization, and attendant details. Aside from mention of "an Irish maid,"[4] there is no reference to anything Irish (and even that one phrase by its very specification reinforces the feeling of Englishness). This novel moves beyond the narrow confines of *Bildungsroman,* with its focus on individual development, to state that (in the opinion of one character) the old boys' school is "the world in miniature" (17) and to show through a comic narrative how hilariously true this fatuous assertion actually is (or if not *the* world at least *a* world).

Literary devices employed in this novel will become a hallmark of much of Trevor's subsequent work: the use of comic tag names (Mr. Nox is a noxious spoiler; Mr. Swingler, a swindler; Mrs. Strap, a bossy charwoman) or tag behavior (the aged retirees Messrs. Sole and Cridley amuse themselves by seriously responding to advertisements for things they could not possibly buy; Mr. Swabey-Boyns petulantly corrects people who shorten his name to Boyns); the use of comic ironies and reversals (the sins of the son are visited on the father, as the arrest of Jaraby's dropout, child-molesting, budgerigar-breeding, rejected son destroys Jaraby's highest goal in life, to be elected president of the Old Boys' Association of his public school); and, most distinctively, that special technique of Trevor's, "significant simultaneity."[5] This last device is only occasionally and mildly comic, as when the central heating salesman and the bossy charwoman sit in different bars of the same pub in Barking, strangers to each other but having interacted earlier with some of the same crazy "old boys": "And though they met before the night was out and walked together through the rain, they did not discover that there was a conversation they might have had" (185). Trevor is always fascinated by such hidden connections and often weaves them into passages of epic, or shaggy-dog, proportions. This particular connection between Mr. Harp and Mrs. Strap occurs in a chapter describing a rainy night and the activities of various people on that night, some of whom are known to each other and some of whom are not (and, unlike the salesman and the charwoman, never will be), yet the very rain itself seems to establish connection:

The rain spread from the west. It fell in Somerset in late afternoon; it caught the evening crowds unprepared in London. A woman, glad to see it, walked through it in a summer dress. A man in Putney, airing his dog, lost his dog on the common and died in October of a cold that had become pneumonia. The umbrellas of the cautious, a handful only, moved smugly through Knightsbridge. Seagulls darted on the river; elderly tramps huddled around a tea-stall near Waterloo Bridge, talking of winter doss-houses. Women whose place was the streets stared at the rain morosely from windows in Soho, wondering how the change would affect their business and guessing the worst. People with rheumatism said it would affect their bones and recalled the pain that the damp air presaged. (184)

Such a passage is not simply a post-Renaissance filling up of a commonplace, a set piece for atmosphere, a rhetorical gambol. All these Londoners begin to seem genuinely related to one another because they live forever in the same paragraph, because their only begetter has chosen to create them thus juxtaposed. Their lives touch, whether they know it or not. The rain is more than random drops of water: here it is the medium in which they fictively live. The rain is significant; the rain has consequences. A man drenched in the summer will die in the autumn; prostitutes will lose business; bones will ache. As Trevor goes on to develop other paragraphs, with other named characters rained on by the same rain, the chapter seems to confirm what the headmaster had earlier in the narrative rather pompously asserted, that this is indeed a little world: the school, the rainy evening, the city, the novel.

With *The Boarding-House* these devices begin to approach tragicomic brilliance. The boardinghouse too is the world in miniature, filled with eccentrics and misfits whose lifelong process of development has led them far beyond the wry promise of young love that ends Trevor's first novel and well into the thicket of errors and misunderstandings that humorously complicates his second. This third novel is a fuller one, not merely in being actually longer[6] but in making even more effective use of these devices, especially in making the characters, though comic grotesques, entirely believable. Even the plot in which they move, though it deals in implausible events, becomes believable because it has such clear overall shape, such persuasive balance. As in the previous two novels, the scene is London, but the focus is narrowed to a group of people whose only real relationship is that they live in the same boardinghouse, have been brought together because the proprietor, Mr. Bird, is interested in observing characteristics they all share: loneliness and an inability to tell the truth. Hence the fact that Mr. Bird is a "tireless collector of people"[7] makes this group of eccentrics believable because they so clearly belong to a project within the novel itself. And the plot of the novel, though at first seeming merely episodic – another series of jokes – is suddenly locked firmly in place when its end links back to its beginning: the novel opens with Mr. Bird's death and concludes with his comic apotheosis in a second death.

This circular shape and this collection of people make the boardinghouse seem a world in miniature, its inhabitants presenting a broad spectrum of types and eccentricities. For example, Mr. Scribbin, the railway enthusiast, alone in his darkened room plays his train records for solace: "he was conscious of a certain peace, a peace that was complete for Mr Scribbin when the room was filled with the echo of wheels moving fast on rails, or the sounds of shunting and escaping steam. . . . The train crashed through the room, the sound bounced from wall to wall, the rhythmic roar of fast spinning wheels dominated his whole consciousness" (194). By repeating detailed instances of these various sounds throughout the novel, Trevor changes a pathetic obsession into a comic one: "Class A4 Pacific 60014 hissed its way out of Grantham station, increasing its steam for the ascent to Stoke summit" (70), indicating how immediate and how precise these sounds are for Scribbin, and "when it was difficult to return to sleep he rose and listened to *Narrow Gauge on the Costa Brava*" (130), suggesting that these hisses, whistles, and clickety-clacks are in a class with the Goldberg Variations.

This particular "tag" characteristic becomes increasingly funny through frequent repetition (and by the irony of the extent to which Mr. Scribbin's method of achieving peace becomes everyone else's disturbance), until finally it begins to stand for obsessive behavior of any sort, for all those repeated activities that make life bearable and stave off the sense of impending chaos. This white Englishman's obsessiveness has its counterpart in the life of Mr. Obd, his black Nigerian housemate, who is also crazily devoted to an ideal. For 12 years Obd has faithfully loved an English girl (whose simple kindness at the Society for the Promotion of Commonwealth Friendship he has misunderstood), bringing her expensive flowers daily, writing her long letters, unable to hear no for an answer however clearly

said. These passages too, through frequent repetition, become pro-
gressively funnier, climaxing in a scene of hilarious exaggeration
when Isabel Tonks returns to Obd 12 years of unopened letters.
"One thousand two hundred and forty-eight letters" (230), he
laments, while the reader laughs at the imagined storage problem for
poor Isabel all these years. And so the novel continues, with vignette
after vignette, a series of shaggy-dog stories involving eccentrics
whose cartooned outlines quickly swell to Dickensian fullness, characters as real and as amusing as Wemmick and the Aged.[8]

The various comic vignettes – Miss Clerricot's nonadulterous
weekend with Mr. Sellwood; Major Eele's fling with Mrs. le Tor;
Nurse Clock's donation of clothing to Mrs. Trine – are all separate
events; despite their common elements (such as mix-ups and errors),
the jokes are self-contained. But three characters bind these dis-
parate parts together: Mr. Bird, who brought all these people
together in the first place and whose detailed *Notes on Residents* is
frequently quoted by the omniscient narrator, and Nurse Clock and
Mr. Studdy, to whom Mr. Bird willed joint continuance of the
boardinghouse and whose intrinsic hatred for each other supplies
the action that destroys the boardinghouse and severs all these characters from one another for the future. Here for the first time, in the
person of "S. J. Studdy (53)" (85), Trevor supplies a major character
who is Irish.

Studdy is as comic and Dickensian as all the other inmates of the
boardinghouse, a small-time con artist, hilariously unsavory. He is
described in Mr. Bird's *Notes* as "a species of petty criminal, with his
hair-oil everywhere and his great red face. Yet how can one not
extend the hand of pity towards him? Anyone can see that poor old
Studdy never had a friend in his life" (85). Whatever pity Mr. Bird
may have felt is thoroughly diluted for the reader, however, by
Trevor's nicely chosen series of comic tags that define Studdy's character in action. The straight pin he carries in his lapel because he
longs to jab Nurse Clock in the knee is emblematic of the trivial
petulance of his feelings and the childish inefficacy of his plans; each
time he fingers the pin (which he self-importantly considers "the
small weapon" [192]) his pettiness is underscored. Though he temporarily discards the pin when he and Nurse Clock join forces to
exploit the boardinghouse, he finally allows himself to use it during
the confusion at the end of the novel. But his "weapon" is no dag-

ger, only a pin, and his action, like himself, merely a foolish irritant. Trevor raises the issue of Irishness early in the novel. In altercation with a publican, Studdy jeers, "You Irish are all alike," and the publican counters, "It is you who are the Irish one, Mr Studdy. There's no Irish blood in me at all," to which Studdy merely replies, "There is Irish blood everywhere" (38). The omniscient narrating voice then goes on to describe Studdy as "a red-haired man" wearing in his left lapel "a small religious badge, the emblem of the Sacred Heart" (another indication of his Catholicism is his making the sign of the cross when he sees Mr. Bird's corpse [13]). Year-round, even in very hot weather, he wears "a thick, black, double-breasted overcoat," which suggests Beckett's Irish derelicts as well as the typical peasant convinced it is always better to be well bundled up. These stereotypical indicators of the Irish (red-haired, Roman Catholic, pugnacious, and dirty) find confirmation later in the occasional use of Irish idioms and structures ("Sure, what harm does it do the old soul?" [75]). Trevor's comic climax of Studdy's Irishness comes in one of his confidence tricks, persuading a feisty, bedridden old woman (one of Nurse Clock's patients) to wear a "potato charm" around her waist to cure her ills. Although he regularly defrauds this old woman (e.g., by loosening wires in her radio, then taking it to be "fixed" and pocketing the repair money), the potato charm is pure mischief, the triumph of an Irish stereotype over Nurse Clock's reign of established medicine.

Studdy with his sleazy tricks is nicely balanced by his opponent/partner Nurse Clock, whose high-minded benevolence masks her own forms of extortion: not money but physical and emotional subservience. Her own feelings of inferiority (52ff) are assuaged by the controlling power she exerts over her aged patients (e.g, she delights when "Bishop Hode, a man in his time of education and power, had been incontinent in the airing cupboard" [202] and she can console him, instruct him, and lead him to the bathroom as a mother would a child; his shame is her pleasure). Nurse Clock's sadism is just as manipulative as is Studdy's small-time thievery, but she stands upright while he slinks; she is antiseptically clean, in light clothing, while he is dirty, in black: they are a neatly balanced pair. That Mr. Bird should have left the boardinghouse to them jointly constitutes part of the comedy of the narrative.

Mr. Bird himself is made up of contraries. Is he angel or devil, benefactor or malign destroyer? Early in the novel he is presented as a self-made messiah: "He in his time had sought these people out, selecting them and rejecting others. He sought them, he said, that they in each other might catch some telling reflection of themselves, and that he might see that happen and make what he wished of it. 'I rose from my desk, most down-trodden of men. I smote adversity to make myself a God to others'" (20). And elsewhere: "I have kindled some comfort in their hearts; I have created a great institution in the south-western suburbs of London. Such has been my work and my vocation. . . . I am Thy servant, O Lord; in Thee do I exist. . . . I will fear no evil" (35). The biblical echoes in this language, along with events in the plot (e.g., after his death Mr. Bird first appears to his most lowly disciple, the scullery maid, just as Christ appeared to Mary Magdalene), combine to make Mr. Bird seem like a savior. But other passages suggest heartless meddling ("Mr Bird said he had studied the condition of loneliness, looking at people who were solitary for one reason or another as though examining a thing or an insect beneath a microscope" [104]). And his leaving the boarding-house to the joint care of Nurse Clock and Studdy seems perverse ("'What a thing for Mr Bird to have done,' said Rose Cave, 'to have thrown those two together. What on earth was he thinking of?'" [252]). His use of lies and his description of himself as "not unsubtle in these matters" (44) ally him with the devil, the subtle serpent, the Father of Lies.

The narrative too bears out this suggestion of split character by linking Mr. Bird's death with Mr. Obd's. The opening line of the novel is "'I am dying,' said William Wagner Bird on the night of August 13th" (7), and the last lines are "They thought of Mr Obd, and Mr Obd died in the moment they thought of him, and did not feel a thing. And William Bird, called Wagner after a character in a book, died again as his boarding-house roared and spat, and his people watched in Jubilee Road. They stood alone and did not say much more, as the morning light came on to make the scene seem different, and the sun rose over London" (287). Between these balanced moments of night and morning, with their death of a white man, death of a black man, one landlord, the other tenant, between this symmetrical beginning and end, the novel uncoils itself as a tragicomic study of related lonelinesses, interconnected isolations.

And through it all runs the central puzzling issue of Mr. Bird's benevolence or malignancy: has his establishment of the boardinghouse itself been a terrible perversity, a combining of emotional derelicts in order to "observe" them, influence them? Has his clear "fostering" of them been an act of charity to save them from something worse, or a diabolic act, preserving them in their misfortune? Has the failed lawyer, Mr. Tome Obd, been given a refuge from racial discrimination in this alien London, or has he been seduced from returning to his African tribe where, the novel speculates, he might feel more at home? Since it is he who at the end of the novel burns down the boardinghouse, with no loss of life but his own, and since it is he who ends what Mr. Bird had begun, thus killing Mr. Bird a second and, one assumes, final time, the nature of Mr. Bird's relation to Mr. Obd is important. And since Mr. Obd is associated with visions of Bird in glory, a kind of Christ Pantocrater, the issue of Bird's holiness or malignancy is crucial.

The description of Mr. Bird's apotheosis is interestingly ambiguous: "And had Mr Obd been with them [the other people of the boardinghouse watching the fire] then he would have glanced into the night sky and said that he saw there the floating form of William Wagner Bird, displayed in the darkness like a neon advertisement. But the others saw nothing: not Mr Bird in golden raiment, playing a trumpet or seated on a chair in glory. They thought of Mr Obd, and Mr Obd died in the moment they thought of him, and did not feel a thing" (254). The verbs in "would have glanced . . . and said" suggest that this vision was perhaps something Mr. Obd was actually seeing at his moment of death, in the house rather than outside with the others, and that their failure to see this golden image of glory results from their mundane living state. But since he was in fact *not* with them and did *not* glance up, perhaps he saw nothing and the gaudy spectacle is mere narrative speculation. However real or imaginary this vision actually is, it verbally unites Mr. Obd, at the moment of his death, with Mr. Bird, blazing in the sky like a deity: dark and light are thus united, soaring above a city that begins a new day.

This conclusion, however, does not have the stirring effect of a dream by Martin Luther King. Instead, because of its mode of presentation it provides a highly comic conclusion to a very funny, and painful, novel. Mr. Obd's death itself, though dreadful as suicide, is hilarious as a parody of ritual sacrifice. The primitive man (for so he has been presented) arranges a blazing pyre on which to consummate his frustrated love, on which to climax his ruined life, and none of the self-superior English observers (themselves potential victims) understands what is going on. He is seen bearing his package of fire lighters from the hardware store "proudly in his arms" (244), that "proudly" suggesting priest or king or warrior. The inmates notice that "there is a smell of petrol," that "the potatoes taste queer" (246); one observes, "Here's a firelighter in with the laundry" (244), and another even sees Obd saturating the cushions in the television lounge (247). Obd's openness, thoroughness, and proud carriage all contrast with the dreadfulness of the deed and the obtuseness of his housemates: the shock of that contrast is inescapably comic in context. As noble African Obd prepares a fire; as Invisible Man he gets away with it. His painless death (drugged with aspirin) becomes a showy triumph. The simple black alien ousts the condescending locals by making their home his pyre.

Studdy and Obd are the only two colonials in this novel. The Irishman simply walks away after the building burns, wearing a suit taken from Mr. Bird and cherishing the "small weapon" of his petty vengeance: "To the end of his days he carried a pin in his lapel to remind him of the night of the fire, of the moment when in front of everyone he had driven it deep into Nurse Clock's arm" (253). Studdy remains the redheaded, red-faced, dirty, pugnacious, petty criminal, the Irish misfit. Obd, however, magnificent in his revenge against the city that has rejected him, triumphs in glory with Mr. Bird: neither one an angel or a devil, but comic blends of both, on so grand, so improbable a scale as to be funny.

Trevor's next novel, *The Love Department*, also involves London, a group of eccentrics, and a trio of beneficent/malignant outsiders. Like the previous novels, it also presents painful and destructive events in a comic light. All the participating characters are English except for the "enemy of love,"[9] Septimus Tuam, who is Irish.[10]

Some of the eccentrics have the cartoon quality of characters in *The Old Boys* and *The Boarding-House*: Mr. and Mrs. Clinger bring their pet monkey with them to a dinner party; the self-confident, unwittingly absurd charwoman announces, "I myself am a Mrs Hoop" (214); lecherous Linderfoot, whose wife is bedridden, flirts with every female he encounters, invariably saying, "You have lovely hair" (132); and once again repetitions effect humor. But in this novel Trevor also includes conventional characters whose behavior and situation are quite ordinary and whose plight is made to seem more poignant than comic: despite their name, the Balsovers are not a grotesque pair who have made a balls-up of their marriage but a fairly typical suburban couple who have drifted apart into boredom but who eventually reunite after both realize how deadly his career is and how spurious her extramarital love affair is. The effect of this mix of realistic and cartoon characters is much like that of a Disney movie combining human actors and animated ones. Given the subject of this novel, such a contrast is especially appropriate.

The novel deals with loneliness, as did *The Boarding-House*, and with the fantasies that alleviate it. Fantasies are, of course, cartoons of real desires, a kind of lie, and Trevor explores in comic form the disastrous effects of entertaining such lies and the sometimes equally disastrous effects of truth-telling. At the comic-grotesque end of the spectrum are the adolescent raptures of ancient Mr. Beach for "a Mrs Hoop" and the hero worship that attractive Miss Brown accords the sexless (and eventually toothless) cad Mr. Lake; somewhere in the middle lies the menopausal romancing of Blanche FitzArthur, histrionically playing her lover and her husband against each other (but wisely choosing husband when the blue chips are down). At the far end of the scale, cast with a live actress, is Eve Bolsover, suddenly midsummer madly in love with one of the cartoons, a bloodless fantasy, Septimus Tuam. As effectively as any Titania enchanted by the juice of "a little western flower" called "love-in-idleness" (*A Midsummer Night's Dream*, 2.1.166ff), Eve suddenly perceives this short, dark, hatchet-faced con man as *beautiful* and is willing to give up home, husband, and children to marry him.

With *The Love Department* Trevor has constructed a much more ambitious plot than in any of his previous work. Eve's love for Septimus and the outcome of her enchantment form only one of several important lines of action in the narrative; it is paralleled by a series of similar minor lines (Mrs. FitzArthur's simultaneous involvement with Septimus, Miss Brown's with Lake) and is connected at various points with other, different ones (Lake's project to ruin Mr. Bolsover's career and take over his place on the board, Mrs. Hoop's plan to trick Beach out of his money). Another major line of action involves Edward Blakeston-Smith and his attempt to "act his age," to move from an infantile and overliteral perception of the world, seeing billboard characters as actual threatening giants, to some sense of peace and community with others, which he eventually achieves after leaving the provincial monastery where he had been recovering from his paranoia, moving through a series of comic ordeals in London, and returning finally to the monastery to become Brother Edward, praying for all the lonely people he had encountered in the city. During that urban interval he works for Lady Dolores Bourhardie, whose "vocation was the preservation of love within marriage" (14) and whose pursuit of the enemy of love, Septimus Tuam, constitutes yet another major thread of action.

The nexus of these various plot lines is in the Love Department itself, the office of the magazine for which Lady Dolores writes her weekly page giving advice to the "ten million lonely women in England" (14) who write to her about their troubled marriages. From several of these letters she has learned about Septimus Tuam, the scourge of Wimbledon, whom she hires Edward to try to locate, childlike Edward whose activities affect the Bolsovers, the FitzArthurs, and even Mrs. Hoop and Mr. Beach. Through these three – Septimus Tuam, Edward Blakeston-Smith, and Lady Dolores Bourhardie – all the other characters and their fates connect.

Lady Dolores is herself one of Trevor's most brilliant Dickensian characters, impossibly grotesque and utterly believable. "She drank some whiskey, soaking it into the icing of her chocolate cake" (97) – this is the only food the short, fat, rough woman is ever known to take, and she takes it repeatedly throughout the novel; aside from cigarettes and long baths, she seems to have no other sensual pleasures or activities: she lives in her office, married to her work; she lives to capture Septimus Tuam.

The structure of events leading to this capture is wonderfully comically complicated, made up of a Rube Goldberg/Heath Robinson web of loves and hates. Mr. Beach loves Mrs. Hoop, who hates Eve Balsover and admires James Balsover (and for this reason Mrs. Hoop tells James of Eve's affair with Septimus, which precipitates their decision to divorce and sends James off to the country to live the simple life he has desired during years of boring corporate success and also sends Septimus away from Eve and toward his fate). Miss Brown loves Lake, who hates James Balsover (Lake, who covets James's job and whose plot to destroy him goes awry when Lake dumps Miss Brown, who then crushes Lake's false teeth, which Lake tries to replace by borrowing Beach's, unsuccessfully, leaving Lake to testify before James's board toothless, while James simultaneously decides to resign his job and divorce his wife, paving the way for Septimus's abandonment of Eve and final progress toward his fate). Mr. FitzArthur loves Mrs. FitzArthur, who loves Septimus Tuam (Mrs. FitzArthur's trip to New York to decide between her husband and her lover gives Septimus time and place – the FitzArthur home – in which to court Eve; Mrs. FitzArthur's eventual dismissal of Septimus sends him angrily out into the rain and his fate). James Balsover, despite boredom, loves Eve, who loves Septimus (Eve's affair with Septimus constitutes the focus of Edward's investigation, which leads – via a pair of yellow gloves given Edward as a reward by Lady Dolores – to Septimus's fate). Cutting in a straight line like a pointing arrow across this multipincer plot is the single-minded obsession of Lady Dolores to wreak vengeance on Septimus Tuam for acts against marriage: her passionate hatred supplies the initial motivating force that finally leads to his fate.

And what is that fate? To be killed by a man incapable of killing, to be killed – unwittingly – by Edward, third member of that trio of beneficent/malignant outsiders.[11] Lady Dolores, Septimus Tuam, Edward Blakestone-Smith – all three are outside marriage, outside the ordinary, mundane lives of the other characters (whether "real" or "cartoon"). All three can be seen as joint emblems of good and evil, Lady Dolores in her worthy goals (to alleviate loneliness, to protect marriages) and her destructive methods (her personal inhumanity and virulent hatreds directed obsessively against a person whose death she finally causes).

Septimus and Edward constitute an even more interesting manifestation of combined good and evil mirroring each other. Both connnect birth with death: Edward "had dreamed in the night that he was being born . . . and he had felt [his mother] slipping away from him as she died" (221), and Septimus tells Eve that not only did he nearly die when he was born but he "should have dropped dead from [his] mother's womb" (171). Both feel intrinsically flawed and doomed, Septimus hating "the whole of womankind" and feeling "with the [unspecified] flaw in his nature" destined to fail in his relations with them (238), and Edward flawed by feeling three years old, incapable of adulthood (8) however much he tries to disguise his "shortcomings" (16). The one has characteristics of a stereotypical angel; the other, of a devil: Edward has "light-blue eyes, with red cheeks and fair golden hair" and smiles with pronounced unworldly innocence (15), while Septimus is dark, "hatchet-faced" (34), and remarkably ugly (162). Mrs. Hoop's comment that Septimus is "an angel of the devil" (198) points with unintended theological accuracy to the connection between good and evil that both Edward and Septimus display in their parallels, since indeed devils are angels, fallen angels, and since any angel could have fallen. Edward and Septimus also share a naive single-mindednesss in behavior: Edward is bent on growing up by conquering the man who preys on married women (154), Septimus is bent on hoarding the money he heartlessly cons from married women (30), and neither appreciates any subtlety in the issues involved (Edward blurts out to Eve, "God save your marriage. This is a slippery man: stick with your husband" [189], as if such bald advice would make any difference, and Septimus, when he later breaks with Eve, having got the money he wanted, can think of her only as "this woman" [226] and "seemed not to be able to distinguish what the meaning was" [230] of her tearful words to him). This naïveté that characterizes the two men is described in Septimus as "a dimension missing" (171); he seems like a man "out of a black and white film," colorless, someone who would "make a good priest" (150); that all these observations are Eve's just before she falls in love with him indicates the strength of this flat man's enchantment. He is a man who feels nothing (28), who thinks nothing (50), who does not dream, who is austere and orderly (143), and yet who can in an instant shift from seeming ugly to seeming beautiful, without any words or promises causing a sensible woman to imagine romantic scenes, "a quiet wedding, attended by a handful of friendly Arabs" somewhere in the Middle East (171), an impossible Rubáiyát idyll.

Although the parallels between Edward and Septimus could be multiplied, these few examples serve to indicate how clearly they mirror each other, how markedly they share a mix of traits, good and bad. These many similarities make their one prominent difference stand out significantly: Edward is English and Septimus is Irish.

Edward's Englishness is established directly in a single sentence: in reply to a man's question as to whether or not he is a foreigner, "Edward said that he was English" (94). The questioner, an ordinary "man in the street," speaks contemptuously of foreigners, especially ones who "pass for natives. 'You cannot trust a soul,' he added. 'The Irish brought an empire down' " (94). Edward's identity as someone who "belongs," someone who is trustworthy because he is English, is thus clearly distinguished from dangerous interlopers such as the Irish.

Septimus Tuam's Irishness is more delicately established. He is never referred to by the narrating voice or by other characters as Irish. But he has a "Celtic voice" (156), and he sometimes uses typical Irish phrasings (" 'Well, now,' said Septimus Tuam to a hovering waitress, 'I'll have a coffee, bless you' " and "It is most unsettled, the weather we're getting" [32]; "God guide you and send you safe" [79]; "What bother is it, for the Lord's sake?" [82]). His name is a distinct pointer: Tuam is a town in Galway and strikes people in England as an odd surname ("Ridiculous" [204], James says). In Irish *tuam* means "grave mound,"[12] an appropriate family name for someone described as "a young man of great paleness and gravity" (24) whose mission involves destruction. A scattering of other references to the Irish appear throughout the novel: a letter to Lady Dolores from "Joe from Bantry" is thrown away as inconsequential; a touching letter from Mrs. Sweeney is judged by Edward to have been concocted by "two Irish labourers" (22) in a pub; Harold, the bartender, is Irish (197); "West Indians and Irishmen" are linked as undesirable colonials and separated by a comma from others in a list of construction workers that includes "Londoners and men from Yorkshire and Wales" (181). None of this is of any special importance except to continue the suggestion of prejudice against the Irish blatantly stated by the man in the street in conversation with Edward.[13] But the reference to Ireland that does pertain significantly to Septimus and his role in the novel is found in Trevor's subtle verbal echo of Joyce's story "The Dead."

Instructing Edward in his task, Lady Dolores remarks that "Love falls like snow-flakes, Mr Blakeston-Smith; remember that" (37), and indeed he does remember that image as he goes out among people, "all over England [where] marriages were cracking. . . . Love came and went and left a trail" (38). Lady Dolores's phrasing is often odd, stilted, and full of bizarre clichés, but this particular image, remembered frequently by Edward (and thus presented often to the reader's attention), seems unusually odd until echoes of Joyce's

"The Dead" begin to be heard. Then the contrast implied between the two narratives strikingly points up the comic nature of Trevor's story, the ultimately comic nature of Septimus Tuam's role. The snow that falls "all over England," like that "all over Ireland,"[14] falls on the living and the dead alike, but in Trevor's novel the reference is not to people really living or really dead, as it is in Joyce's story, but to those whose marriages are living or dead, marriages with a certain cartoon or sitcom quality owing to the network of loves and hates described earlier. In "The Dead" Gretta's nostalgic grieving for an idealized love is melancholy, distanced by time and retelling, seriously and tenderly romantic in its details (the pale young lover, standing ill in the rain, dying for love), whereas Eve's idealizations of Septimus are comic, all too present and therefore subject to the narrator's satiric eye, and silly in their details (a man who washes suburban dishes then whisks his beloved off to an exotic Middle Eastern wedding).

However flawed the Conroy marriage, it holds; however outside his wife's cherished first love Gabriel stands, he is able to hear while she speaks of it. If they do not touch that night, they nonetheless share a realization of separateness and loss. The evening's dinner party, with its varied moments of seriousness and comedy, provides a larger social world into which this poignant conjugal moment fits; then both public and private events are swallowed up by the city itself, Ireland itself, and the quiet snow that falls on everything. The imagery and the cadences of Joyce's last sentence emphasize the melancholy of the final scene and cast a grave shadow back over the liveliness of the party too: "His soul swooned slowly as he heard the snow falling faintly through the universe and faintly falling, like the descent of their last end, upon all the living and the dead" (224). Trevor's story, however, by focusing on love, not death, on actions, not ends, is essentially comic in conception, a comedy that is intensified by the cartoonlike nature of some characters, the chirpiness of their descriptions, and the trite fantasies that lead to folly. By thinking of Septimus Tuam as someone out of a black-and-white film, Eve not only senses his flaw but also idealizes him ridiculously (her imagining a desert wedding suggests Rudolph Valentino). But to associate Septimus with "The Dead" by repeated reference to the snow that falls all over England, to imagine him in the bedroom scene or even at the party, is to show him for the caricature he is, both as a lover and as an Irishman.

Pitting Edward against Septimus is to pit England against Ireland, but not in any serious political sense. Septimus is a shallow cad, but Edward is an infantile fool. They both have a dimension missing. That Edward finally "kills" Septimus is no victory but rather the climax to a comedy of errors. Turning his back on the assassination he thinks Lady Dolores wants him to perform, leaving London behind him, riding his bicycle in the rain back to the monastery, Edward throws away the yellow gloves Lady Dolores had given him as reward for his service; a man stoops to rescue the gloves, and a taxi swerves to miss that man and hits Septimus Tuam, who just happens to be there at that moment. Thus Edward has unwittingly succeeded in killing Septimus by failing to kill him; he is, as one witness affirms, "innocent" (246). And Trevor's narrative once again shows the profound, hidden, and sometimes comic consequences of contiguity in time and space. All the elaboration of Lady Dolores's plan, all the intricacies of plot climax in this one amusingly involuted accidental death.

The novel ends as it began, with Edward back in the monastery, now as Brother Edward well on his way to becoming "the patron saint of middle-aged wives" (258). Yet though the dark Irish devil of Wimbledon is dead and presumably the women of England are now safe in their marriage beds, Lady Dolores – sustained by chocolate and whiskey – persists in her obsession, sure that Septimus Tuam will "rise from the dead repeatedly and often" (261). Thus the three unmarried outsiders continue their strange triumvirate, animated cartoons playing beneficently and malignantly with real marriages. The sufferings of the *enamorados* is real enough for their world to be called "a vale of tears" (262), but the distortions and complications of their fantasies plunge them into situations of sheer farce. That mix of real pain and hilarious event, that tragicomedy, marks most of Trevor's early fiction. And although some of his best rogues and devils are Irish, they remain caricatures, no more actual villains than Edward is a hero.

Two novels that serve as a bridge between the early work and that of Trevor's next two decades, when his stories become more frequently set in Ireland and are increasingly more painful in their subject matter, read like companion pieces: *Mrs. Eckdorf in O'Neill's*

Hotel (1969) and *Miss Gomez and the Brethren* (1971). Both take place in a major city, and that city constitutes "a world": the one, Dublin; the other, London. Both have as main characters women who become religious fanatics and whose craziness is clearly linked to childhood trauma and parental loss. Both women are concerned with speaking the truth, and both oversimplify what the truth is and are overconfident about their access to it. Both women are obsessed with the need to order life, to control their own life and all the world. Both disdain sex, the one by indifferent adolescent promiscuity and the other by frigidity. Both dress in distinctive and "skin matching" clothes, the Caucasian Mrs. Eckdorf all in cream and the Negro Miss Gomez all in black.

Both novels contain paragraphs in which points of the city are located at a particular moment in time, and the thoughts, words, actions, and dreams of various characters are described, these repeated juxtapositions suggesting hidden bonds of unity among them all, a significant simultaneity. Both novels also contain exercise books in which personal feelings and experiences are, significantly, recorded. Both novels contain frequent instances of self-deception, through such aids as romance novels, movies, drugs, and alcohol. And both novels are painfully funny.[15]

The points of similarity could be further elaborated, but what is important for this discussion is the comic mode and treatment of the Irish in these two companion novels, which serve as the pivot between an early, almost exclusive concern with English settings and characters and a growing increase of Irish ones.

The Dublin of *Mrs. Eckdorf in O'Neill's Hotel* has all the variety of Joyce's *Ulysses* and might be seen as a parody of it, or a similar though less ambitious invoking of the city as a grid of spaces and lives, interlocked and interacting. All the characters are Irish except for an Englishwoman (formerly married to a German and now living in Munich), Mrs. Eckdorf, and a salesman from Liverpool, Mr. Smedley, both visitors to Dublin. The rest represent a variety of careers, ages, and personalities: prostitutes, publicans and barflies, priests, clerks, businesspeople, housewives, maids, and porters. Though they are all Irish, their number and variety make that Irishness incidental. Mrs. Eckdorf may be charmed by "them," and Mr. Smedley increasingly irritated by "them," but it is these two English visitors who are the foreigners, not the Irish. And both these visitors come to grief in

Dublin, Mr. Smedley by the farce of his search for a prostitute and Mrs. Eckdorf by her religious crisis; he flees the country, personally and financially embarrassed, and she flees reality, remaining forever in a madhouse. The humor of this novel ranges from the broad farce of Smedley's losing his trousers, through various mix-ups and errors typical of comedy, to the ironic "happy ending" of Ivy Eckdorf's paradisical lunacy. If national identities are of any consequence at all, it is the English who are the oddities and whose actions raise hilarious havoc both for themselves and for others. In this novel for the first time in Trevor's fiction the Irish constitute the unexceptional norm: they are the insiders; the English, the outsiders. And this is altogether a darker novel, despite the humor, at times almost grim in its exposure of the compromises, lies, and fantasies that make life bearable.

Miss Gomez and the Brethren, published two years later, may at first glance seem simply a return to Trevor's earlier preference for English settings and characters. Most of the novel takes place in London, and most of the characters are English. The characterization has much of the same distinctive cartoon quality, the Dickensian tags of appearance and behavior; the plot has comic elaborations and involutions of the sort found in *The Love Department*. But an important difference exists in mood. There seems to be more at stake. The novel is still funny but is not primarily a series of jokes. The Irish characters, marginal in the earlier stories, count for more here. The main character, of course, is neither English nor Irish but a Jamaican black woman, Miss Gomez. Against the major conflict – Miss Gomez versus London – the Irish characters appear sensible, admirable, and triumphant – even the comic ones.

A one-line remark by a man in the street in *The Love Department* becomes a plot event in *Miss Gomez and the Brethren*. He claims that "The Irish brought an empire down" (94), and in this later novel they are in a sense shown actually doing so by razing whole neighborhoods. A crew of demolition workers leveling London – or at least the area where most of the action of this novel takes place – is composed of colonials from all over the world but "mainly from the provinces of Ireland";[16] prominent among them is the brawny, sweaty, red-haired Atlas Flynn from County Cork, who does his part not only destroying buildings but also seducing the English publican Mrs. Tuke. Although he does not manage to take her dancing to the Emerald Isle Club, he is often successful in taking her to bed upstairs at her own pub; Beryl's pretended resistance is no match for Atlas's attractions. In her own thoughts she may scorn him as dirty Irish and deceive herself about why she succumbs to him (with perfect Sartrean bad faith pretending she does not know what is happening), but by naming her Beryl (emerald/beryl) Trevor suggests her essential affinity with the Emerald Isle's Atlas, despite national differences. This 28-year-old Irish laborer is utterly besotted with this fat, middle-aged Englishwoman, not only because he likes his women big but also because he and she are made of the same stuff and share a sexual earthiness (which he acknowledges and she denies). But in the narrative the Irishman appears a more admirable character than the Englishwoman. Though both are comic adulterers, his activities are straightforward, his passion and admiration openly expressed; not a moment of self-doubt or doublethink mars his pursuit or his possession. The comedy of that pursuit and possession comes from the grotesque nature of its object and Atlas's splendid erotic blindness in finding Mrs. Tuke desirable: the comedy of a Bottom in pursuit of his female counterpart.

Mrs. Tuke, however, is a comic adulteress whose chief point of humor lies in her deliberate self-deceptions. She immerses herself in "true romance" novels about doctors and fantasizes and dreams about being gallantly courted by "Dr D'Arcy, or Dr Finlay or Dr Tom Airley" (51). But coarser impulses sometimes intrude:

> Sometimes Dr D'Arcy turned into one of the Irish labourers who were at present working on the surrounding demolition. Usually it was a labourer called Atlas Flynn, whom she'd seen looking at her a couple of times when the men came in for their lunchtime refreshment, a big coarse-looking fellow with arms like oak-trunks and curly red hair full of grease that had a smell of a herbaceous border. She felt uneasy when Atlas Flynn looked at her like that, admiring her bulk and comparing it maybe to his, saucy with his eyes when he'd had two or three glasses of beer. . . . Mrs Tuke gave a small shiver, recalling the pleasant dreams that sometimes turned into nightmares. A sewer ran through Eddie Mercer [a former lover], as she knew to her cost, and she suspected that a sewer was the end-all and be-all of the red-haired Atlas Flynn. She drank some more of her gin and peppermint, trying not to think of any of that. (51)

Mrs. Tuke's preferred drink is emblematic of her sexual life: she likes strong spirits but pretends they are sweet nothings, a delicate little peppermint cordial that a lady would sip, no scent of heavy alcohol. Such a concoction allows her to drink herself "innocently" drunk, her body ready for some brawny laborer while her mind manages "not to think of any of that."

Mrs. Tuke denigrates her various lovers at the same time that she "unwillingly" enjoys them; her scorn centers on social class (in her estimation Eddie Mercer was "no better than a coal-heaver really" [51]). But her ultimate point of contempt, directed against everyone – lover or not – whom she considers foreign, has to do with race and nationality: she lumps Irish and blacks together ("Atlas Flynn, of course, was an exile, just like Gomez, and so was Alban Roche, and all the Irish boys who came in at lunchtime" [58]); she considers them all either children or savages. Nasty as her prejudice is, its stupidity is also often funny (she considers Miss Gomez's eye-glasses an affectation: "Ridiculous having glasses, imitating white people" [47]). Her virulent attitude toward foreigners is echoed by London at large: when a man from Nigeria has car trouble, other motorists consider him inept because he is black (" 'Typical,' a man in a Vauxhall Victor remarked to another man and the other man agreed" [124]); even gentle Mr. Tuke feels "London was different now, with foreigners everywhere, Chinese and black people, the Irish and the Italians" (102).

This prejudice, which is expressed by various people every few pages throughout the novel, is directed primarily at the Irish and at blacks. In addition to Atlas Flynn, whose very name suggests the extent to which he is a cartoon character, is another important Irishman, one who is more complex and who triumphs over attempts to make him into a mere stereotype, though in his case the stereo-type in question is not "Irish laborer" but "sex maniac." Alban Roche becomes a suspect in the supposed murder of Mrs. Tuke's daughter, Prudence (born of imprudence with Eddie Mercer), when Miss Gomez in religious frenzy prophesies he will commit this evil deed and when Prudence in fact disappears. Alban's calmness and dignity – and lack of cooperation – in dealing with the police result from his knowing all along that Prudence is away cleaning the house he and she will move into, along with the pet shop he has inherited and to which they are both devoted. But this happy ending is not revealed until late in the novel. Meanwhile the reader fears some-thing dreadful has happened as all London follows the sensational

search, hoping for the worst. Alban Roche is, of course, a likely suspect, since he has been in jail for "two months' detention under psy-
chiatric observation because of his repeated illicit presence both
outside and within the women's changing-rooms of the Swansdale
Badminton Club" (35). In one extreme view of this fact Miss Gomez
considers Alban an incurable agent of evil, his next victim already
designated, and she feels her own divinely revealed mission is to
forestall the murder. Another view of the undeniable fact that Roche
has been a Peeping Tom is the one Trevor actually supplies for his
plot: the sneaky-salacious effects of Alban's repressive childhood and
hatred of his mother simply fade away when he meets the right girl,
and if he does not live in complete happiness ever after, neither does
he become a murderer. This normalizing of Roche's character avoids
stereotype and also accords well with Trevor's demonstration in
other novels that "monsters" are not necessarily monstrous.

Roche may not be a sex maniac, but he is Irish, and certain
aspects of his Irish upbringing have made him the temporary misfit
he is at the beginning of the novel. Although Miss Gomez occupies
most of the narrative attention for the whole of the novel, Trevor
devotes as much space to important scenes in Alban's childhood as
he does to hers (and no other character is supplied with so exten-
sively described a background).[17] His boyhood in County Cork is
marked by Catholic education, first with the Presentation Nuns and
then with the Christian Brothers, learning fine penmanship and
conjugating Irish and Latin verbs; it is also marked by going to
church and to the cinema with his widowed mother, being flooded
with her love yet tormented by the conflict between his pure love for
her and his growing lustful fantasies about other women: "When he
looked at her he prayed that he would never be alone again in his
bed with girls, nor see Claudette Colbert naked before him, nor the
woman stepping into the bath. He wanted her to keep him always
close to her as she had when he'd been a child" (74). After her
painful death from stomach cancer, he suddenly realizes that "he
had disliked his mother" and hated as well the town, its buildings
and people, his teachers, and his church (76f). Yet running away
from this home, he cannot leave his mother behind; he brings a
trunk and two cardboard boxes full of her personal possessions with
him to London (77f), where his fantasies of "bad girls" dressed in his
mother's clothes and jewelry and his spying on the women changing

at the badminton club are simply extensions of his earlier conflicted feelings about sex. Only when he and Prudence, in bed after making love, share stories of their painful childhoods is he able to let the hatreds go (216). In his London fantasies his mother's clothes had fit Prudence Tuke perfectly (79); now she becomes the woman who will take his mother's place and heal the wounds his mother made.[18]

The Irish details of Alban's childhood had been stressed, but now, in London, allied with Prudence, national identity is no longer an issue (he is not the English girl's "Irish lover" as Atlas is her mother's "Irish lover"). Freed from his mother's damaging possessiveness and religious idealizations, he is now simply an ordinary young man who happens to have inherited a pet shop from the widow he worked for in London, a quiet young man with a quiet girlfriend, both of them loving animals and sharing a dream of breeding squirrels and jerboas, selling "clawed frogs and geckos and axolotls and toucans and fruit bats and chameleons" (218), an exotic but not impossible fantasy. In its own way this lesser plot line concerning Alban Roche is a mini-*Bildungsroman*, from which the young Irishman emerges ready for life, a man.

Thus the two important Irishmen in this novel – the one a cartoon character, the other more complex – both come off better than their English antagonists. Atlas Flynn enjoys his grand passion heartily without a second thought; Mrs. Tuke, however, bound to a passion she eschews, is both comic and contemptible in her self-deceptions. Even after moving to a posh pub in a new neighborhood and resolving to get rid of obviously inappropriate Atlas Flynn, she continues to succumb to his charm: "She told him she'd set the police on him if he ever dared to return, but he insisted on arguing with her and in the end she couldn't help giving a laugh because of the way he put something" (243); this "laugh" always leads to bed, and the "couldn't help" constitutes her ongoing rationalization. Alban Roche triumphs too, not over just one English person but over the whole of London: he is not the sex maniac all readers of the London papers were hoping to discover; instead, he is united with a loving and redeeming young woman, despite efforts by her parents and Miss Gomez to keep them apart, and he has financial independence dropped in his lap by the kind gift of Mrs. Basset, for whom he had worked, who wills him the pet shop and the animals to which he is devoted. He may still be a bit odd – preferring animals to people

(217) – but he has what he needs for his life, and he gets on with it. Mother and Ireland are left behind; England and the London police have not managed to destroy him. His final interview with furious Inspector Ponsonby, who had mistreated him during the investigation, shows Alban triumphant in dignity and moral character: "He spoke softly and without aggression, displaying no resentment that Inspector Ponsonby had searched his property without a warrant" (197).

The chief object of prejudice in the novel is, however, Miss Gomez in particular and blacks in general. Although Ponsonby is furious with Alban Roche for not being a sex maniac, it is Miss Gomez he blames for the fiasco: "It was this black woman who had started the thing about the youth's eyes, repeating to the girl's parents what she'd imagined she'd seen there. As far as he could see, it was the black who had been the cause of everything, because of some dotty religion" (197). Mrs. Tuke even goes so far as to accuse Miss Gomez of breeding the wild cats that terrorize the demolished neighborhood and kill Mr. Tuke's dog, Rebel: "Negroes didn't understand about domestic pets any more than they understood about normal food. She'd heard of cases where they kept cats and dogs just in order to cut them up and tin them. They didn't mind what they ate; they'd tin you as soon as look at you, most of them" (230). The many expressions of prejudice, which range from Inspector Ponsonby's mild disdain to Mrs. Tuke's mindless virulence, are nicely turned back against their English perpetrators by an ironic twist in the plot. As Inspector Ponsonby (official representative of orderly British life) interviews Miss Gomez, who is responsible for the falsity of his case, he begins to feel attracted toward her, has the growing sense that he has met her before, then suddenly remembers having visited her, as a client, when she was a prostitute: "He raised his head and looked at her and he knew that she'd recognized him also. He had a sudden desire to stay with her, a feeling that he wouldn't mind her talk about religion and that in time he'd even grow to love her simplicity. He thought he'd like to marry her, and immediately realized that the thought was laughable and eccentric. He tried to smile, to give some slight sign that he wasn't above remembering her, but he could not. 'Good-bye,' he said, and went away" (204). Like Mrs. Tuke with Atlas Flynn, Inspector Ponsonby is conflicted about his attraction to someone he considers inferior and dismisses it as "laughable." Yet that very attraction betrays something about his prejudice, his inability to acknowledge the worth of what he desires: a personal equivalent of the ambivalence essential to colonialism, in its double movement toward acquisition and denigration, the former being justified by results of the latter. (And, of course, the very word *denigration* specifies the particular prejudice in question.)

As a black colonial Miss Gomez represents the "darkest" extreme of both Atlas and Alban. Blacks and Irish have been coupled in remarks made by various voices in the novel; although both have a right to presence in the civilizing mother country, they are nonetheless scorned as "foreigners" by their English rulers. The Irish may be only "children," as Mrs. Tuke says, but blacks are "savages," thus even worse morally and culturally. By centering the novel on Miss Gomez, Trevor shows what it is the English fear from natives of their colonies and what the effect of colonization has been on those natives: they disrupt English society when they enter it, and they themselves are disoriented, even to the point of madness.

But this novel is not a tract on colonialism. Trevor moves the issue beyond politics and into the larger realm of the problem of evil. As always, he shows the origin of evil to be found in childhood mutilations, physical or emotional, which then set off a chain of other, related evils. This Miss Gomez who is responsible for the sex-murder fiasco in London began her life in Jamaica, where she grew up in an orphanage, the only survivor of a fire in which "ninety-one people were burnt alive" (10). Although she was only two and a half at the time of the disaster, it haunts her, making her incapable of feeling affection or believing in God: "She felt as a shadow among real people, which was what she'd meant when she'd described herself as nothing: it was a feeling only, but Miss Arbuthnot hadn't quite understood that. Miss Arbuthnot hadn't understood that peculiar feelings had as much potency at the heart of them as any other feelings. Miss Arbuthnot betrayed no sign that she admitted the existence of feelings at all. What use was talk about love?" (13). In the orphanage she is destructive and alienated; with indifference she allows the janitor, Mr. Kandi, "small, elderly liberties" (14), then runs away first to Kingston, then to London, buying her way with her body.[19] Although "she didn't know why she wanted to go, being aware only that she wanted everything to be different" (14), Trevor makes it clear that what she wants is love, and ironically in London she will find it, spuriously offered by the Church of the Brethren, based back home in Jamaica.

This circle of flight and return traces the issues of love and belonging that trouble Miss Gomez (and everyone else in the novel in various ways) and that also trouble the phenomenon of colonialism. The orphanage that was intended to help Miss Gomez was founded on guilt, not love, by a white woman whose family had made money in the sugar business: "Miss Arbuthnot was the last of her family's line, a righteous woman who believed that in the past her family had exploited the natives. As best she could, she sought to make amends but did not always find it easy" (8). Thus a member of a family that does not "belong" in Jamaica tries to provide a home for children who, though orphans, do belong. And one of those children, at least, despite the colonizers' efforts, feels bereft of any feelings of love or belonging and must go to the alien "mother country" to find what she lacks. Miss Gomez's feeling of homelessness makes perfect sense, of course, because of her orphaning, but Trevor, by linking her alienation to Miss Arbuthnot's colonizer's guilt and ineffectual love, points to a context larger than personal deprivation.

The fire that so troubles the young girl was set by someone whom Miss Arbuthnot dismisses as "demented" ("A wretched man, my dear, who truly didn't know what he was doing") but whom the girl insists was sane, his motive being deliberate malice: "There was nothing wrong with his mind, Mr Kandi said. He was all misshapen: he had an incurable disease of the bones" (11). By thus explaining the cause of the fire Trevor points up that every evil has an antecedent evil (but does not deflect his story by providing an infinite regress of antecedents for the incurable disease). What is important is establishing the fact that one evil leads to another, ruthlessly damaging children physically or emotionally, children who then grow up to damage others, and so on perhaps ad infinitum. (As Miss Gomez explains to Sergeant Grove, the mothers of Alban Roche and Prudence Tuke, as well as her own substitute mother, Miss Arbuthnot, all damaged their children because of their own fears of loneliness: "These three women passed cruelty on, down into other people's lives" (165).

The linearity of these linked evils strikes across Miss Gomez's experience of circularity. The novel begins with her in Jamaica as a child and ends with her back in Jamaica as an adult; in the meantime she has moved from atheism and a feeling of nonexistence to faith and a strong sense of identity and purpose. She firmly believes that her prayers and those of the Brethren intervene to turn evil to good (203); thus she has faithfully scanned newspapers for stories of disaster and sent that information to her church so that the Brethren can pray for criminals and victims of all sorts, especially for their deliverance from loneliness. Like a novice who has passed probation, Miss Gomez returns to Jamaica to deliver herself and all her money to the Church of the Brethren, which she had never seen but only learned about from an ad in a London paper. The church, predictably, is nonexistent, a confidence trick perpetrated by a derelict, ganja-smoking Englishman (who has absconded with the loot shortly before her arrival and whose own life history exhibits a chain of evil going back to childhood damage [251f]). But despite such disillusionment, her faith continues: "There was a heaven in which the incurable man [who started the fire she survived] now was, in which he had been given an explanation for the nature of his worldly existence. That was a place in which all explanations would in time be made, to Alban Roche and Mr Tuke, to Prudence and to Mrs Tuke. . . . There would be madness everywhere . . . if there was no dream of heaven to come true, where order was drawn out of chaos" (255).

As in so many of Trevor's novels and stories, this comforting faith is of dubious validity. Miss Gomez is clearly a disturbed person, something of a fanatic, something of a comic grotesque. When she leaves the site of her disillusionment about the Church of the Brethren, she immediately notices the signboard for another church in Kingston and carefully marks its address and phone number. Thus Trevor ends the novel on the amusing note of folly continued. Yet as is often the case in Trevor's work, this faith that is folly also has its positive aspects: Miss Gomez has gained a structure of meaning for her life; what was chaos now has pattern; in particular, death, that greatest evil, now makes sense as part of God's mysterious plan.[20] Folly, which is the butt of comedy, is here tempered by another view, one suggesting the value of being a "holy fool," a fool for God's sake.[21] Hence the novel ends with paradox and is itself paradoxically both serious and comic.

One of the central motifs in *Miss Gomez and the Brethren* concerns the transitoriness of things. Miss Gomez's parents perished in a fire; a whole London neighborhood is being razed; marriages, both happy and unhappy, do not last forever; old women die in their sleep and young girls take overdoses of drugs; an Alsatian dog is massacred by cats. Prudence, in bed with Alban, suddenly realizes "that her parents must once have loved as they did now" (217), yet even with that dreadful object lesson before them she and Alban are able to slip into a "harmless pretense that the idyll [of abiding happiness] waited for them in Tintagel Street and would for ever continue, that they could count on permanence when all around them permanence failed" (218).

The failure of permanence, the threat of chaos, the prevalence of loneliness – these are grim issues treated here more seriously than in any of Trevor's earlier work except *Mrs. Eckdorf in O'Neill's Hotel*. Both these early novels are hilariously funny and yet at the same time are clearly set in that vale of tears to which Adam was exiled, that wilderness which replaced the garden. Here the Irish characters come off well – saner than Mrs. Eckdorf and more realistic in their goals than Miss Gomez; in various ways triumphant over the English and less personally damaged than other colonials; no longer mere joke-Irishmen or cartoons but substantial persons to be taken seriously. In Trevor's later work the derelict garden will often be Ireland itself; the chain of evil will be made up of Ireland's history and the generations of its people – Celts, Vikings, Normans, English and Scots, colonizers all.

Chapter Five

Child Murder and Colonial Exploitation

The philosophical problem of evil probed by all of Trevor's work and the specific political evils associated with nationality that occupy so much of his fiction are joined in a shocking metaphor: child murder used as an emblem of colonial exploitation. To highlight Trevor's treatment of this difficult subject, it is useful to juxtapose *The Silence in the Garden* with two other novels containing similar material – one by an American of very different background, Toni Morrison, and the other by a fellow Corkonian, Mary Leland. Morrison's *Beloved*[1] uses child murder as a metaphor both for the damage done to the self and the damage done to the race by the experience of slavery in the United States. Trevor and Leland also use child murder to represent the experience of oppression, but in their novels, *The Silence in the Garden*[2] and *The Killeen*,[3] the scene is Ireland. Originating in two quite different countries that have both experienced colonialism, rebellion, and independence (and through it all the oppression of one people by another), these novels depict a shocking event not often found in literature, an event that functions as an apt metaphor for these experiences but in the Irish novels is handled differently from the way it is treated in the American novel. Trevor, Leland, and Morrison have all constructed parables of oppression, but whereas Morrison focuses on the individual deed and the wound given to the original victim, Trevor and Leland show a much more diffuse stain of guilt and responsibility.

In the American novel the child dies directly by its mother's hand; in the two Irish novels the affected children die as the result of a series of events involving many people. But in all three novels the deaths are vivid, explicit, and of great importance in themselves. One has only to consider the infanticides in *The Heart of Midlothian* (1818) and *Adam Bede* (1859) to appreciate the significant difference in these contemporary novels; both Sir Walter Scott and George Eliot use infanticide as a plot event that seriously affects the heroine's life, but it is the heroine we see, not the child, who is for all the world like those empty bundles clutched to the bosom of a live actress in plays where infants somehow figure but do not need to be cast. The murder, or purported murder, is distanced by being briefly reported, not vividly described; even the pathetic eyewitness account at the trial and Hetty's own confession to Dinah in *Adam Bede* focus on Hetty's feelings and behavior and not on any violent act as such, for the murder is a "gentle" abandonment.[4]

In the Trevor, Morrison, and Leland novels the mode of the child's death is particularly horrible and involves mutilation, actually or symbolically. In *Beloved* Sethe cuts her baby daughter's throat with a saw, nearly decapitating her; and when Sethe nurses her youngest child (named Denver) soon thereafter, the infant drinks in her sister's blood along with the milk because Sethe is drenched with that blood. In *The Killeen* the illegitimate child, Thomas, is taken home by his uncle to be cared for by the child's grandmother, who secretly tortures Thomas, burns him, starves him, attempts to cut off his genitals, and eventually, despite the uncle's attempts to protect the boy, successfully hates him to death. In *The Silence in the Garden* the role of the mutilated child is doubled: the young Corny Dowley is frequently hunted like an animal by four other children threatening to kill him; while they do not actually shoot him then, his feet are badly cut from his attempts to flee on the island where they all live, and his spirit is irrevocably damaged. Later, as an adult, he is actually shot and killed, not by them but by others as a direct result of events leading back to this early terrorization. Still later a second child, Tom, a boy from another generation, mirrors Corny's fate, being terrorized not physically but morally, dealt a psychological blow as fatal as the bullets that killed his prototype.

To prevent her children from being returned to a state of slavery the runaway slave Sethe had attempted to kill them as the sherrif and her former master approached; she was unsuccessful with all but one, the little girl whose throat she cut with a saw. Since then, after her time in prison, Sethe has lived in the same house, with her surviving children, haunted by the ghost of that slaughtered baby and ostracized by the community. When a fellow escaped slave finds her 18 years later and tempts her back to a normal life of love with him, the invisible ghost is apparently exorcised, only to turn up the next day embodied as a young woman who is the age that baby would have been had it lived and whose name is the same as that inscribed on the baby's tombstone: Beloved. The arrival of this being is presented with details that suggest birth and infancy: Sethe's "water" breaks when she sees the woman; the woman has skin that looks absolutely new, smooth feet, unwrinkled hands and face; she wants only to drink, not eat, and is weak and passive. Like an infant, she appears apparently ex nihilo, and remains as if she belongs there and nowhere else. That she is indeed Beloved returned is soon clear to her younger sister, Denver; only gradually becomes clear to Paul D., Sethe's lover; and only much later becomes clear to Sethe herself. Much about this spirit, Beloved, is malignant: she seems to be present as the lost child seeking its mother and desperate for her love, but so voracious is that hunger that she begins to consume Sethe, until by the end, just before she is driven away a second time, she has supplanted Sethe, growing large as Sethe shrinks, ministering to Sethe as if Sethe were the baby. Initially Denver had been at pains to protect Beloved from Sethe (lest Sethe "do it again"); toward the end of the novel, however, Denver is trying to protect Sethe from Beloved.

This rough and only partial summary makes the novel seem merely ghoulish and sensational. But in fact it is elegantly written and subtle in its effects. That Beloved is not "simply" a ghost is made clear in part by her name itself and by the biblical passages cited[5] and echoed in conjunction with her name, especially "My Beloved is mine and I am his,"[6] suggesting the union of God and man, salvation that comes by "incorporation," use of the personal and individual as emblem of the whole, the secular erotic for the ecstatic divine. There is psychological resonance too for the name: Beloved may be "the other" but it is also the self, as Paul D. tries to help Sethe realize ("You your best thing, Sethe" [273], he tells her) and as the ghost's vestigial footprints reveal, since they fit anyone who steps in them (275).

This story of Beloved is a story about the experience of slavery, physically and spiritually. Slavery has subjected Sethe to the worst kind of damage, the worst possible mutilation: self-mutilation. As Sethe says repeatedly in the novel, in killing Beloved she has killed her best part. Her intention had been to save her child, but in fact she murdered it. And the nature of the haunting makes it clear that the murder has been both blessing and curse: Beloved loves her mother, but she also tries to strangle her. Beloved is the embodiment of Sethe's guilt, her self-hatred. She can now no longer embrace her child, because that lost child will devour her. Although Paul D. tries to get Sethe to realize that her best part is herself, the self she is *now* when slavery is over, that scar of self-mutilation/child murder marks her nonetheless. Beloved, as an incarnation of both the loves and the evils of the past, is her constant companion, her ghostly shadow, her other self.[7] It is significant that what drives the ghost away the second time is Sethe's attempt at a second murder. But this time she seizes the ice pick not to kill the child (again) but to kill the white man who she thinks is coming to take the child; here for the first time she turns her hatred not toward herself (embodied in her child) but outward toward the evil that threatens them both. That such formulas of psychic strength are not unambiguous is indicated by the irony of Sethe's mistaken target: she attempts to stab the white man who has worked hardest to abolish slavery and to protect and foster her own freedom. When Paul D. and Stamp Paid later nervously joke about Sethe's being crazy ("Every time a whiteman come to the door she got to kill somebody?" [265]), they point up this irony, but their humor does not condemn her, for they acknowledge that her target was indeed a generic evil, not a particular person. By fighting back Sethe has freed herself from her consuming hatred, personified in Beloved. Now the way is open for love: Paul D. returns to care for and, it would seem, restore her once again to life.

Only one child was murdered; the others live. Denver, who drank Beloved's blood along with her mother's milk, has long since freed herself from the ghost of Beloved and is ready for life: at the end of the novel Denver turns away from the past and toward the young man who calls to her (267), suggesting by her delight that love and the possibility of newly made children await her. The narrating voice concludes the novel by proclaiming, "This is not a story to pass on" (275). Old hatreds and persistent mutilations do not have to mark subsequent generations, despite hovering ghosts. Exorcism is possible; the future can redeem the past, both for the individual and for the race: "*I will call them my people, which were not my people; and her beloved, which was not beloved.*"

Although Morrison's novel is line-for-line bloodier than either Trevor's or Leland's, the sense of deliverance, the tone of quiet, and the sheer gentleness of the language that ends the novel corroborate the catharsis suggested by the events that conclude the plot. No such relief is offered by either *The Silence in the Garden* or *The Killeen*.

Although Trevor's novel, like Morrison's, can be read as a parable about oppression (the personal story standing as an emblem for national, racial, and cultural events), there is much more indirection in his manner of presenting it. Both novelists make use of gradual exposition and a variety of voices and narrative forms, relating the full horror of the murderous event only near the end of the novel, luring the reader with a mystery to be revealed. But that event itself in Morrison's novel presents the evil clearly: Sethe has been so maneuvered and so maddened that she participates in the destruction of her "own best part" and can free herself only when she turns her violence against her oppressor rather than against herself. But in Trevor's novel the issues blur: the children who hunt young Corny are both innocent (because young and thoughtless) and guilty (carrying as they do the marks of an ancient, senseless impulse to evil); they are both victimizers and victimized (they mutilate Corny psychologically, and they suffer the permanent effects of this mutilation when his attempt to kill them, in adulthood, goes awry and kills an innocent servant instead, leaving them guilty survivors, effectively sterilized). Yet if this were all, one might see the novel as fairly straightforward. But Tom's role in the novel takes events far beyond poetic justice, suggesting how entirely insoluble some problems are, how entirely unredeemable some evils and unfair their effects, how permanent some scars.

Tom is born illegitimate because his father was blown up by the bomb Corny intended for the Rollestons just a week before the marriage was to take place. This chance, gratuitous evil has altered Tom's life radically and unredeemably. He is forever stained, contaminated by his parents' sin. He is in fact seen as that sin incarnate, a source of contamination himself; consequently, people – even his grandmother – avoid touching him. Tom grows up accepting that there is something wrong with him: no amount of his touching the holy clay of the holy well he tends will ever make it safe for anyone else to touch him. The dying Mrs. Rolleston's farewell hug does not counteract Sister Conheady's shrinking from the slightest brush of

fingers. Tom is essentially isolated as a child and holds himself emotionally aloof as an adult. Although Esmeralda Coyne would, oppor-
tunistically, marry him when he inherits the Rolleston estate, he is
determined to continue the solitary life he feels his illegitimacy has
thrust on him.

Tom will never marry; Tom will never have children. And this,
ultimately, because a group of children harmed another child a generation past. Here is the form of Trevor's insoluble equation of evil, a
line of carnage (186) that stretches from the arrival of the first Rollestons in the seventeenth century, *"with slaughter in their wake"*
(188), to the cruel hunting game of the twentieth century, with its
consequent revenge, bloody reprisal, and final sterility for all
involved. None of those who as children hunted Cornelius Dowley
themselves have any children: John James has a fruitless comic-
bathetic secret liaison with a local widow; Villana breaks her
engagement with the man she loves and 10 years later marries a
much older admirer with the understanding that they will not have
children; Lionel quietly looks after the farm, ignoring the silent devotion of Sarah.[8] The victimizers remain childless, but so too do the
many victims of their cruel game: Cornelius Dowley dies as a young
man, unmarried; Kathleen, the Rolleston maid who was in love with
him, nurses her loss into old age. Brigid, the other maid, who was to
have married Lichy, Tom's father, has only the one illegitimate child,
and both her line and Lichy's come to an end with Tom's celibacy.
Sarah, who might have had a life with Lionel, is left to dependency
and spinsterhood.

That these sterilities are related to the Rolleston children's
wicked game is indicated by the fact that Villana and her cousin
Hugh, who as children had been among the hunters, break their
engagement the same week that their prey, Cornelius Dowley, is
shot. Why the engagement was broken puzzles various characters in
the novel (and is presented to the reader as a mystery to be solved):
when the fatal game and its eventual success are finally revealed,
they are understood as something that "accounts for" Villana and
Hugh's turning away from each other: *"For how could their children
play in that same garden and not ever be told of what had festered
so horribly in a wound?"* (187). This postlapsarian, festering,
wounded garden is one in which there can be no children at all

anymore. Physical sterility is the fitting emblem of moral evil and its mutilating, rotting effects.

The estate mirrors this sterility. As the novel ends, Carriglas is in a progressive state of ruin. Like the ancient fallen abbey and the even older pre-Christian burial mound on the island, it too will become a "tourist attraction," a fragment of the past, dead to the present. Tom will take no steps to modernize the estate or recoup the family fortunes; he will let Carriglas return to its original clay, as, in time, so will he, dying childless.

Reflecting on the three Rolleston children who preceded him and whose cruelty damned a household, Tom is also aware that their subsequent lives have been a deliberate act of expiation: "their punishment of themselves seems terrible, yet a marvel also" (204). Only one of the group of hunters has escaped guilt and expiation, and that is their cousin Hugh, who went to England, married an English girl, and has had three children. But he is a shadowy figure, absent since his engagement with Villana was broken, not seen, not heard. Only by leaving Ireland has he been able, apparently, to avoid the consequences of his early participation in evil; he has cut his ties to his homeland, to his family, to his own past. If any furies pursue him abroad, they are not acknowledged in this novel.

Carriglas is Ireland in miniature. Its island history is one of successive waves of invasion, dispossession, and cruelty. As in so much of Trevor's fiction, there is the suggestion that expiation is necessary, but however marvelous was the Rolleston self-punishment, it did not keep the evil from passing on to the next generation; it did not save Tom his psychic mutilation. The best to be hoped for is return of the "garden" back to its original state of wilderness. There is no hint of a future, no hope of redemption and new life: *"Absence has gathered in the rooms, and silence in the garden"* (204). Tom, immured in his darkened house, is (like Lavinia at the end of Eugene O'Neill's *Mourning Becomes Electra*) deliberately buried alive.[9]

A similar pattern of inherited evil is found in *The Killeen*. The child who is murdered is emblematic of a whole line of mistreated children. Thomas's parents were themselves ill-used by the adults in their youth: a resentful mother denied Margaret education and was grim, scolding, and unloving; Margaret's father was kind but feckless, unable to protect her against cruelty. From this grudging home Margaret went to the city to work as soon as she was old enough, and there, lonely, she was "ruined." Her lover, Earnan, was an Irregular on the run, cousin of a famous hunger striker, Maurice Mulcahy, whose family and especially whose maiden aunts are presented as rabid nationalists; the narrating voice implies by its scornful tone ("blood relatives of . . . hero and martyr . . . their political lineage was impeccable for eternity" [40]) that this form of violent national-ism is despicable and suggests that the young people groomed for it by their elders are misled and misused. Indeed, a servant in the "martyr's" household refers to his aunts as "a couple of old harpies" (62) responsible for his death. These two modes of child abuse, physical and psychological, have their roots in various kinds of hatred, some of it intensely personal (Margaret's mother's malevo-lence) and some of it generalized and dignified as ideology (Earnan's aunts' nationalism). Both modes of abuse and many kinds of hatred are directed against Thomas, Margaret and Earnan's bastard child, whose inevitable fate is suffering and early death.

Neither hereditary line allows Thomas a future. And in both cases old women are the ones responsible for his fate. The first plan for Thomas is that, as a bastard, he is to be given up by Margaret and cared for by a woman selected by Earnan's aunts; their actual plan, however, is not to foster the child kindly in the country but to school him to be an Irregular, a martyr if necessary, "fodder for the fight" (95). But Margaret, worried about his future, steals him away, giving him to what she hopes is the safety of her family. Nevertheless, her own childhood experience is repeated when her mother physically and emotionally tortures the child, and her brother (like her father, kind but limited in his effectiveness) is unable to prevent Thomas's death.

The lengthy graphic descriptions of the physical abuse to which Thomas is subjected are dreadful (see 124-27), but no more dreadful than those of the horrible slow death Maurice suffers because of his ideological indoctrination (see 87-90). Although Maurice is an adult when he dies, his fate nonetheless was engineered in childhood by the training his aunts gave him: he carried a bomb in his pocket that they placed there (79). Thus as killers of Irish youth Margaret's mother and Earnan's maiden aunts all seem malignant versions of Yeats's image of Ireland as crone, delivering her young men to death. But they provide no later apotheosis, no transformation of them-

selves into beautiful Cathleen ni Houlihan, no renewal of their young
men in glory.

The parallel couples in this novel and their children show life in
Ireland as unremittingly destructive. Margaret and Earnan, Julia and
Maurice have the briefest possible relationship, their potential for a
loving life together destroyed by ideological fanaticism and political
violence. Both women, although from different classes (at one point
Margaret is a servant in Julia's house), have the same fate: to be
abandoned by their child's father, to be manipulated by those in
authority over them, and to find their hope of a future only in
flight – Margaret to England and Julia to France. Dessie, who marries
Margaret and takes her to the job waiting for him in England,
expresses as part of their joint motivation to get "well away from that
crowd [of killers]" (106f). But Margaret's bastard child is left behind.
Julia, rich and cosmopolitan, is able to save not only herself but her
son, Patrick: "They'll never get him" (89), she told her starving, hero-
martyr husband; the aunts will never turn Patrick into another Maurice, never educate him "according to their political and religious
precepts" (94). The only salvation lies in flight, which is part escape
and part exile.

Margaret's brother and sister supply yet another example of similarly damaged lives. After witnessing the cruelty visited on
Thomas – not only the physical torture but the moral ostracism,
culminating in the priest's refusal to give the child a Catholic
burial – Michael realizes he can no longer live among such people.
He likens the experience to a mutilation: "The child who was dead
was like a branch of his own body; he had been offered to the community when there was no request to be made, no special treatment
needed. And he had been rejected" (131).[10] Michael too, in order to
live with some sense of personal integrity, must leave his homeland.

Mary, Margaret's and Michael's sister, remains behind to care for
their mother. And she, like the dead Thomas, is sacrificed to that
mother's need. Her fate, like Nora's in John Millington Synge's *The
Shadow of the Glen*, is to marry a landed man not for love but for
expediency, and in words echoing Nora's she laments, "I never knew
how old he was, not till the night I married him did I know how old
he was, how old" (136). But unlike Nora, she does not escape.

The last words of the novel – "the cravings of her own body had
been driven underground by the urgent hungers of the land"

(136) – suggest the sterility that also concludes *The Silence in the Garden*. There are no more children; the young have been killed or have fled. In Trevor's novel the garden has become a silent waste-land. In Leland's, the hills and woods and fields reduce to a burial ground, unsanctified, a *killeen*. Unlike Morrison's novel with its exorcism and promise of new life, Trevor's and Leland's studies of the physical and psychological effects of colonial exploitation end with mutilation and sterility.

Such destruction of children and termination of family lines in sterility compose a theme that appears frequently in Trevor's work, especially in the later novels and stories. His latest collection, *Family Sins*, has a particularly horrifying lead story in which two family lines terminate in a bloody murder, not only physically destroying the young adults who would have propagated the next generation but also emotionally destroying their parents. The cause of this violent destruction is rooted in oppressions that are both political and social.

"Events at Drimaghleen" is made up of a scene, the residue of an event, followed by a series of "explanations," narratives in which characters in the story attempt to account for what really happened. This writing a story about telling stories, this probing of what is "true," is a frequent occurrence in Trevor's work, but the immediate events and explanations often fit into a larger context. Here the central event of a double murder and suicide on a poor farm in Ireland is bracketed with opening references to other appalling events in Irish history and with concluding references to curious newspaper readers in England and all over Europe. Thus this single act of rural violence is shown to reach back into the past, forward into the future, and far beyond its own obscure townland.

The event itself elicits two opposed explanations: the official one deduced by O'Kelly of the local Garda (with which the people of Drimaghleen concur) and a sociologically trendy one constructed by Hetty Fortune of an English newspaper's Sunday supplement. In the first a possessive mother, eccentric and insanely jealous, shoots "her son's sweetheart rather than suffer the theft of him," and he, wrenching the gun from her, shoots her, "by accident or otherwise," then in horror at what has happened, kills himself.[11] In the second version the sweetheart, Maureen McDowd, idealized by the supplement as *"a saint by nature and possessing a saint's fervour,"* is seen as making up *"for all the sins she had ever resisted,"* by killing the interfering mother, the feckless lover, and finally herself (24). The first explanation results from an assessment of a particular Irish woman made by her Irish neighbors, who condemn her possessiveness and her violent deed, seeing her as marginal to their community; along with Maureen's parents, the whole community puzzles over "the cruelty of chance" through which a good, ordinary girl became "mixed up with so peculiar a couple as that mother and son" (16). In the opposing explanation strangers from the city of Dublin and from England make judgments that condemn the whole community by advancing a thesis about poverty, repression, and the Irish character: *"These simple farm folk* [the story reads] *of Europe's most western island form limited rural communities that all too often turn in on themselves"* (27). Various tricks of the media are used to enhance the Gothic nature of the crime: emphasizing rural stupidity (the Gardai are limited by *"sluggish imagination"* [22]); hinting at bizarre sexual activities and repressions (*"this extraordinary crime* [follows] *hard on the heels of the renowned Kerry Babies mystery"* [22]; Maureen, *"bitterly deprived of the man she loved," "realised she could never have him now," "this weak man whom she so passionately loved"* [24]); indicating the community to be closed-minded and vengeful (*"The Irish do not easily forgive the purloining of their latter-day saints"* [25]); and suggesting stereotypical emotional and sexual perversions through the conjunction of *"rural"* with *"turn in on themselves"* (27).[12]

Quite simply, the Sunday supplement story exploits these ordinary people who happen to live in rural Ireland, turning them into objects of interest, disallowing their humanity in the very process of seeming to sympathize with their suffering. Like the meticulously composed photographs that accompany it, the account seems "so much a picture that it invited questioning as a record" (26), or at least it seemed so to the actual people involved. This exploitation will probably continue through other newspaper articles; moreover, "Father Sallins imagined a film being made about Maureen McDowd, and the mystery that had been created becoming a legend" (27). Like Mrs. Eckdorf's photo essays, like the television program on Constance Kent, this story describes the ease with which one group can be exploited, emotionally colonized, by another. Trevor names his exploiter Hetty Fortune because she finds her own fortune in the suffering of others and perhaps also because there is something "heady" in her pursuit, something rash and violent, arousing mere-tricious excitement in herself and her readers.

In the total context of Trevor's work it is not surprising to find that the poor, exploited couple are Irish and that the invading exploiter is English (18). At stake here are not just land and physical dispossession of the sort indicated by the Rollestons' supplanting the Cantillons in *The Silence in the Garden* (41) but expropriation of the meaning of someone's life, the imposition of another meaning. In response to Hetty Fortune's description of the McDowds as *"disadvantaged people,"* Mrs. McDowd asks, "Does disadvantaged mean we're poor?" (27). The poverty is no secret, but to be labled "disadvantaged" before all those curious readers is to be falsified.

By contrasting (a) the helpless pain of the aged parents in response to the slick story that makes their murdered daughter seem to be the murderer with (b) the facile composition and contrived photographs of the Sunday supplement, Trevor indicts the distor-tions and heartlessness of public curiosity. However appalling its central event, his story itself is not Gothic but instead condemns that sort of prurience and sensationalism. The focus is on the survivors' abiding pain, which makes the Sunday supplement story "nearly as bad as the tragedy itself" (25).

In addition to the newspaper's exploitation of the events at Drimaghleen (the "theft" of the old explanation and the "plantation" of a new one, which constitute a "media colonization" of that rural townland), there were also internal, domestic exploitations of Maureen by her own parents. The tight-lipped anger with which Mr. and Mrs. McDowd respond to Maureen's absence (before they dis-cover her body), Mr. McDowd even calling her "the little bitch" (11), betrays the extent to which their daughter is a "colony" in their own lives, not an independent 25-year-old woman. The unspoken thought that possesses both parents (the first in the series of "explanations" that comprise the narrative) is "that their daughter had taken the law into her own hands and gone off with Lancy Butler, a spoilt and useless man" (10). Trevor says it all in that passing cliché: "taking the law into her own hands." What *law*? No actual civil law prevents two single adults leaving home to be married. The "law" is the parents's expectations and determinations: they will not "allow" their daugh-ter to marry a man they disapprove of; they need her to stay on the farm and help with the work.[13] In the domestic realm such paternalism parallels the modus operandi of colonists everywhere.

In some stories – such as "Attracta," "Beyond the Pale," *Fools of Fortune* and *The Silence in the Garden* – Trevor places in the foreground Ireland's colonial history and the various forms of exploitation and violence that continue it. Often, however, in other stories that history is present only in a few brief allusions. The shocking murders and various public and domestic exploitations in "Events at Drimaghleen" are introduced with reference to other "dramatic occurrences": "In the 1880s a woman known as the Captain's wife had run away with a hunchbacked pedlar. In 1798 there'd been resistance in the hills and fighting in Drimaghleen itself. During the Troubles a local man had been executed in a field by the Black and Tans" (9). Thus historical memory also juxtaposes the domestic and the political, another of Synge's Noras, along with the loaded terms "1798" and "Black and Tans." Reference near the end of the story to *"Europe's most western island"* (27) completes the picture of an Ireland belonging both to the past and to the future, to a world of exploitative colonization and a world of independent cooperation. In this context the "world that bounded the lives of the people of the Drimaghleen farms" (14) seems like a very little world indeed, its boundaries constrictions indeed. The family pressures that spoil the lives of children – eventually destroying them as Maureen and Lancy were destroyed by Mrs. Butler's "furious jealousies" (13) and the McDowds' opposition to Maureen's choice of lover – are truly family *sins*, and as sins contribute to the progress of evil from generation to generation. The actual death of children – such as the murdered Maureen and Lancy – does not put a stop to this genealogy of evil, since there is always someone in the next generation to be infected, such as Tom in *The Silence in the Garden*, who succumbs to the evil effects of Villana and her brothers' exploitative childhood game.

By using the shocking metaphors of child murder, child abuse, and that absolute negation of new life, sterility, as indicators of the damaging effects of colonial exploitation (whether at the national or familial level), Trevor helps expose an "ideologically excluded other"[14] of profound consequence. Not the "other" of some disadvantaged or maltreated group (women, children, whales, or seals) but an idea, a concept so revolutionary that no society (however idealistic) has ever truly taken it seriously. In light of this concept colonialism itself becomes yet another metaphor.

If indeed it is true that "it is at those borders of discourse where metaphor and example seem arbitrarily *chosen* that ideology breaks through" (125), and if indeed "a functional change in a sign-system is a violent event,"[15] then the insistent presentation in fiction of metaphors and examples shocking in the present and for the most part avoided in past literature perhaps suggests the advent of a new and unsettling awareness.

The unspoken premise of the ideology operative in the societies portrayed in Trevor's fiction (and implicitly condemned by that fiction) is that persons are *individual*, therefore separate and separable. Certain of Trevor's characters have questioned this premise: Julia openly with her assertion "surely God's creatures are all connected"[16] and Mrs. Eckdorf, Miss Gomez, and Imelda in various ways by their behavior. But Julia can be dismissed (and is, by her own mother and daughters) as soft and sentimental, whereas Mrs. Eckdorf, Miss Gomez, and Imelda are all mad. Ideology is unmasked not by such pious assertions or puzzling eccentricities but by the violence of a startling image that, like lightning flashes in the dark, shows what lurks just outside the window. Timothy Gedge stands there, the child who in his mix of good and evil is an emblem of the community itself, even when that community denies its *community* with him, calling him monster and attempting to reject him.

The ultimate rejection, expressed in Trevor's shocking image of child murder, is effective as a metaphor for colonial exploitation because it calls into question, at the level of feeling, the premise that a distinction exists between self and other. Villana and her brothers hunt themselves when they hunt Corny; Corny in effect kills himself when he tries to kill them; Tom is the heir not only of their property but of their lives: Tom is Corny and Villana and James and Lionel extended through time. The identity between Sethe and Beloved that Morrison expresses as a "ghost story" and the identity between Michael and his nephew that Leland expresses in the metaphor of the branch make a similar point. The child and the adult are one humanity. To reject the child, to kill the child, is to destroy the self – not the individual self but that larger manifestation of life of which all individuals are a part.

In the expressed ideology of colonialism, natives are children (as stupid Mrs. Tuke complacently asserts); the colonizer plays the role of superior adult, whose mission toward the native is education and toward the native society, civilization. But if that civilizing process results in the death of the native culture or in the mental or emotional derangement of particular natives, then murder expresses what is really happening more accurately than the gentle and positive "leading out" indicated by the word *education*.

Child murder is shocking only to the extent that an important connection is sensed between the child and the adult. That Trevor's metaphor does indeed shock is one of the more hopeful elements in his fiction. By transferring the strong feelings aroused by murder itself to social and political situations, Trevor helps alter the "sign system" (a slaughtered baby is more than just a slaughtered baby; natives are more than just natives) and generates emotional credence for an idea about humanity that at the intellectual level may be dismissed by prevailing ideologies as sentimental, impractical, utopian, or simply crazy. Thus Trevor is in the tradition of an earlier Irish author, Jonathan Swift, whose *A Modest Proposal* made sensational use of a double taboo – child murder and cannibalism – but with an important difference. Swift's satiric mode, his celebrated creation of a persona who presents the unspeakable as if it were reasonable, allows the reader to condemn that persona, thus exalting and distancing himself. Swift's elegant rhetorical maneuvers, the breathtaking strategies of his argument, are ultimately negative in effect: the insensitive speaker and his monstrous proposal are condemned by readers already sharing Swift's values. Child murder in *A Modest Proposal* is presented as a grotesque hypothesis. The exaggerated mode of its presentation prevents its being understood literally; the word *metaphor* is stamped clearly across its face.

Thus with Swift the reader is not at the "borders of discourse" but at the very center, where the prevailing ideology and its rhetoric are *used*, even though against themselves. Certain twentieth-century writers, however, by straightforward presentation of child murder as a real event within the fictional world, its details vivid but not exaggerated, thus require the reader to accept that murder as an actuality (rather than reject it as a possibility, as Swift's technique requires). Such "realism" prevents metaphor from becoming argument, avoids forcing the reader to take sides, and allows the experience of "story." There, where characters and events are simultaneously fiction and "truth," readers seem to feel the horror more directly than in Swift's satire, because they are not hurried away into judgments prearranged by the author. At the very point where the child's murder, as a choice of subject, seems gratuitous – where the reader's feelings of horror are reinforced by the realization that the terrible event is not simply a rhetorical stratagem but is (within that fictive world) irrevocable – the premise under the violated taboo begins to assert itself, not as an intellectual proposition but as a truth deeply felt. Julia in her simple way was able to verbalize it – "surely God's creatures are all connected" – and Willie, Villana, and Tom live out its implications. Hence in Trevor's fiction the murder of a child shows in the domestic realm what the colonial oppression of a people is in the political realm: both acts violating a concept so idealistic in its goal and so inconvenient in its consequences that most ideologies and most societies prefer to exclude it.

By tapping the horror attendant on child murder and associating it with social and political situations, Trevor helps a more generous view of human relationship itself begin to emerge from under the complacent exclusions of the Mrs. Tukes of this world, whatever their class: individuals are not separate; all are part of one life. The correspondences that exist throughout Trevor's universe – that govern his presentation of history and permeate his implicit ethical values and his characters' psychology – are dramatized throughout his work in various ways, but nowhere so effectively as in the resonant shock produced by his instances of child murder.

Chapter Six

Rhetorical Strategies

Summary statements about Trevor's often shocking subject matter and the interconnected evils he depicts can make the novels seem sensational. But, to the contrary, Trevor's actual writing is subtle, finely crafted, and makes skillful use of a variety of rhetorical strategies to establish the workings of his system of correspondences and its concatenation of evil. Recursions and repetitions are common to many of these strategies, mirroring in their own rhetorical way the thematic similarities and interconnections that fill his work.

That Trevor himself is given to such reduplicative thinking is interestingly suggested by his brief note to *The Distant Past*,[1] published in the Poolbeg series devoted to the modern Irish short story. Wrestling with the phrase "Irish stories," Trevor suggests several notions as he works his way toward his essential point. The category itself goes undefined, as he rejects both "using a pin to make this selection" from his work and choosing his "eleven favourites" because that "would have had a lopsided feel about it." But the considerations become more specific in his next set of rejected criteria: "If I'd chosen the ones that were superficially the most Irish, or all the ones set in a small town, or the ones about the Irish abroad, there'd equally have been something missing." Without bothering to catalog those superficialities, Trevor nonetheless suggests that clichés do not compose whatever it is that makes something "Irish"; nor is the real Ireland essentially rural; nor is the typical Irishman an exile, worker, or immigrant abroad yearning for an idealized homeland. Then justifying inclusion of the story "Miss Smith" on the grounds that it "might perhaps have come out of anywhere, but in fact is set in a town in Munster," he reveals the capaciousness of that undefined category "Irish short story." In the author's mind "Miss Smith" may indeed be set in Munster, but there is not a word, phrase, detail of event or characterization, or sentence rhythm that indicates Munster rather than Devon or Dynmouth.[2] And that is the point: these are *Irish* short stories because they have been written by an Irishman, who is no less an Irishman because he has gone to live in Devon or on the Continent, and whose work is no less "Irish" because it is part of that larger body of literature written in the English language. Although brief, this account of Trevor's method of selection for a particular anthology expands the concept of Irish literature, rather than restricting it to superficialities of subject matter and scene, clichés of characterization and language. Yet at the same time this account suggests that something distinctive and unifying about Trevor's work guided the actual choice of stories: "So I tried to think of stories that felt right together, with not too many obsessions repeated, stories that were different and yet echoed one another – though not, I hope, too clamorously." What Trevor self-deprecatingly calls "obsessions" – these repetitions and echoes – not only distinguish his fiction as a recognizable body of work but also give it a peculiar unity. The stories in *The Distant Past* indeed feel right together, and so too do the other novels and stories in Trevor's 35 years of publication. One of the special pleasures in reading Trevor's fiction lies in the growing perception of the extent to which any given story seems to contain all the others, not through tedious repetitions but in the magical way that each cell of an organism is potentially that whole organism, or that each point of a hologram contains the entire picture, a dynamic blend of unity and diversity.

Besides several recurrent themes and the chief technical device of "significant simultaneity" Trevor uses a number of rhetorical strategies that help shape and distinguish his fiction: persistent visual images, implied puns, literalized metaphors, incremental references, and tag names.

Persistent Visual Images

"Attracta," one of the newest stories in *The Distant Past*, contains elements that make up Trevor's fiction published both before and after it. Here as elsewhere personal and political worlds mirror each other and serve as mutual metaphors. The damaged child, the sterile adult, the self-deceiver and the truth-teller, the mistaken victim, the murderer as ordinary person, the ruined movie house, the solitary island, the Black and Tan conflict, the ambush and booby trap, the repetitions of history, the sense of the incomprehensibility of evil, and so on – but to list elements this way, though handy for summary, is misleading because it is reductive. Part of Trevor's skill as a writer lies in his presenting these repeated elements, motifs, "obsessions" as integral parts of the story, fresh each time; only on reflection do they seem to suggest some category or other.

"Attracta" is an emotionally powerful story, graphic in its descriptions of physical violence, penetrating in its indications of how that violence affects various members of a community. The strong visual imagery, persistent in the story and in Attracta's mind, constitutes both a technical and a thematic component of the narrative. The core of the story is the change in thinking about history and education that occurs in an elderly Protestant schoolteacher when one of her former pupils (who had been sent the head of her soldier husband by the terrorists who murdered him) goes to Belfast to join the Women's Peace Movement, is herself raped by all seven of the murderers, and then, in despair, kills herself. The schoolteacher pairs this horrific 1978 event with her memory of her parents' deaths, when she was three, in 1920. Holding the graphic details until later in the narrative, Trevor begins his story with its central fact and realization: "Attracta read about Penelope Vade in a newspaper, an item that upset her. It caused her to wonder if all her life as a teacher she'd been saying the wrong things to the children in her care."[3]

This gentle beginning, with its mild word *upset*, is followed by two calm pages of background information about the 61-year-old spinster and her quiet life in a small town near Cork. Only then does Trevor gradually reveal the horrible event, first with words from the objective news item itself, then finally through the lurid details as replayed in Attracta's imagination: "Alone at night, almost catching her unawares, scenes from the tragedy established themselves in her mind: the opening of the biscuit-box, the smell of death, the eyes, blood turning brown. As if at a macabre slide-show, the scene would change: before people had wondered about her whereabouts Penelope Vade had been dead for four days; mice had left droppings on her body" (105).

The four substantial paragraphs Trevor devotes to vivid description of the murdered man's head and his wife's death are among the
most grisly and detailed accounts of violence in his work and loom
large in the economy of the short story form. Their shocking information is juxtaposed with another story of violence, recounted without
any vivid detail, focused instead on the response of the child who
hears it. The elderly Attracta remembers being taken aside by a
fanatical Orangeman when she was 11 and told that her parents
were shot by accident in an ambush prepared for Black and Tans,
and she learns further that a couple who have for years befriended
her, Mr. Devereux being like a second father, were in fact responsible for the killing. The Orangeman's vicious report is unsettling to
the litle girl: "It was impossible to believe him. It was impossible to
visualise the housekeeper and Mr Devereux in the role he'd given
them. No one with any sense could believe that Geraldine Carey
would kill people. Was everything Mr Purce said a lie? He was a
peculiar man: had he some reason for stating her mother and her
father had met their deaths in this way?" (114). When the story is
corroborated by both her aunt and her minister (shorn, however, of
Purce's bigotry), it still leaves the little girl puzzled: "She couldn't
understand how Mr Devereux and Geraldine Carey had changed so
[from the "wildness" that made them killers]. 'Maybe they bear the
burden of guilt,' Archdeacon Flower had explained. . . . 'Maybe they
look at you and feel responsible. It was an accident, but people can
feel responsible for an accident' " (116).

This memory of learning about her parents' deaths takes up the
central section of the story (12 of the 20 pages) and is flanked by the
section about Penelope's death, already described, and the final
pages in which Attracta tries to present the two stories to her class in
a way that she feels will teach them something they really ought to
learn: "for so long she had been relating the details of Cromwell's
desecration and the laws of Pythagoras, when she should have been
talking about Mr Devereux and Geraldine Carey. And it was Mr Purce
she should have recalled instead of the Battle of the Boyne" (106).
For the elderly teacher history suddenly becomes personalized; her
own story is the one to recount. The distant past must give way to
the lived present.

But the irony of this realization lies in the fact that the present
simply mirrors the past; Cromwell's desecrations continue in con-

temporary murder and rape; the Battle of the Boyne continues through religious bigotry. Attracta has learned her lesson too late to help Penelope Vade and too late to influence her current students, who are puzzled by her reason for recounting the two stories: "'Sure, isn't there stuff like that in the papers the whole time?' one of the children suggested" (119). Even the minister, sent by the children's anxious parents to see that Attracta retires ("School was not for that, they had angrily protested" [123]), fails to appreciate what Attracta has suddenly understood, that "monsters did not remain monsters forever" (122). If Mr. Devereux and Geraldine Carey could change, then Penelope's rapists could change; there is a gleam of hope.

That history repeats itself in Ireland is not news, but Trevor gives the phenomenon new light by his startling shifts of focus, first on Cromwell, then on Purce, from historical figure to nonentity, showing not only that Cromwell's story still lives but that ordinary daily viciousness has its significance too: both stories must be told, the deeds of both great and little person must be reckoned with. Trevor gives these public and personal deeds an interesting twist. The bigotry that leads to violence always operates in terms of oversimplified categories (for Purce the outrage of the accidental killing lies in the fact that "a decent Protestant pair" [113] were destroyed, and he can imagine no reason for Mr. Devereux and Geraldine Carey to be kind to Attracta except the desire to make a Catholic of her). But the facts of Trevor's story belie these easy classifications. The terrorist couple are not both Catholics; one is Protestant. Shocked to discover how their use of violence (even for what they conceive to be a good purpose) has gone astray, they reform, dwelling together now in penitence (once adulterous lovers, they continue celibate; Geraldine lives like a nun, dressing always in black, going daily to Mass). They make what reparation they can to the bereft girl, providing presents, outings, and parties – kinder even than the aunt with whom she lives. That the whole community accepts this reformation of Mr. Devereux and Geraldine Carey – and so too does Attracta after she learns of their responsibility for her parents' deaths – suggests that responsibility for violence and the evils it generates is to be shared equally by Catholic and Protestant; by constructing a story in which the terrorists were united in a common political concern and were undeterred by religious difference, Trevor has shown the extent to

which Mr. Purce's insistence on abiding enmity between Catholic
and Protestant reflects his bigotry and not necessary social reality.

Then 50 years later, in the other atrocity Attracta ponders, there
is also a "mix" of backgrounds, only this time the mix involves the
victims, not the murderers, and has to do with nationality more than
with religion: Penelope Vade is from the Republic of Ireland, and her
husband (whose nationality is not specified) is connected with
Britain by his service in its army; thus as a couple they represent the
two nations. And although the reader knows Penelope must have
been a Protestant, since she was a pupil of Attracta's, no stress is put
on her religion or on that of her husband. Furthermore, by not identifying the murderers in any way (though readers familiar with the
actual situation in Belfast will assume they were Provos or some
other nominally Catholic anti-British group), Trevor downplays the
neat categorizations and oversimplifications that are the stuff of bigotry and focuses instead on the horror and gratuitousness of the acts
of violence themselves. Though the terrorist killing of Penelope's
husband is no different from the intended action of Mr. Devereux,
the hardened viciousness of sending the murdered soldier's head
through the post to his wife contrasts with the humanity of Devereux's repentance. And the rape of Penelope because she has
joined Belfast's Women's Peace Movement is an act of pure malignancy, showing that the terrorists have come to value violence for its
own sake rather than using violence merely as means to an end.
Since this recent atrocity suggests a world so vile as to be unredeemable, Penelope despairs and kills herself. Against this despair
Attracta is driven to try to teach her pupils that hope is possible,
change is possible. By a story from the world of her youth she tries
to mitigate the evils they accept as inevitable in the world of theirs.

History records atrocities on both sides (whether those sides be
English and Irish, Republican and Unionist, Republican and Free
Staters, Catholic and Protestant), but Trevor's story draws the lines
that define "sides" differently. The peaceable constitute one side,
the violent another, regardless of political, religious, or national
affiliation. Thus Mr. Devereux and Geraldine Carey as terrorists are
opposed to Attracta's family (even when their target is not their fellow townspeople but the foreign Black and Tan soldiers), but when
they repent, they change sides and become a substitute family for
her. In this context "Catholic" and "Protestant" are irrelevant terms,

except to bigots like Mr. Purce, with his fixed categories, ideas, and images.

Throughout this story, as is so often the case in Trevor's fiction, persistent visual images play an important part in the characters' lives and supply for the narrative yet another instance of the personal and the public mirroring each other, serving as mutual metaphors. Attracta's life as a teacher is expressed in terms of remembered faces of her pupils, as well as of pictures of persons and maps of countries that embody what she has taught ("portraits of England's kings and queens. . . . Irish heroes: Niall of the Nine Hostages, Lord Edward Fitzgerald, Wolfe Tone and Grattan. Maps of Europe and of Ireland and of England, Wales and Scotland hung side by side" [103]). The old globe in her classroom is not now and never will be out of date, because "it did not designate political boundaries." This parade of faces, this mix of history and myth, monarchy and democracy, this indication that nations must coexist "side by side" and that the world has a shape and a unity beyond the shifting lines of political statehood suggests in the introductory paragraphs ideas that will be shown more fully by the story as a whole.

References to several kinds of visual images are repeated often throughout this short story: newspaper photos, movies, televison, and the visions of imagination. Attracta's recollection of trips to Cork for shopping and films and her judgment that films now "were not as good as they'd been in the past" (104) provide the kind of detail that makes Trevor's depiction of the elderly spinster convincing; in retrospect, however, her nostalgic memory of wonderful movie houses, now in ruin, where romantic films were shown ("the dreamland of Fred Astaire and Ginger Rogers" [107]) parallels her sense of a world in ruin now, a ruin shown daily in newspaper photos and television reportage of sectarian violence.

Attracta seems to understand most keenly when her understanding is embodied in images. The newspaper photos of Penelope Vade and of her husband (both taken before the atrocities) and the house in Belfast where she went to live are supplemented by images generated in Attracta's imagination by the newspaper account of the murder, rape, and suicide, until finally Attracta has an ongoing slide show in her mind, replaying and replaying the horrors. Attracta's memory of her own horror story also involves strong visual images or reference to visual images. When Mr. Purce tells her about how her parents died, her recollection of that moment 50 years later includes the fact that the conversation took place by the monument in the center of town, a statue "of the Maid of Erin" (111). Neither the little girl then nor the brooding spinster she has become seems conscious of the irony of this image, but the reader cannot but notice that an actual Irish girl suffers because of deeds done in the name of an idealized image. So powerful indeed are images that Mr. Purce's specific warning to the young Protestant girl is not to *look* at the rosary beads if ever Geraldine Carey tries to show them to her – as if merely seeing them could contaminate her with popery (112). After Attracta tells her aunt about what Mr. Purce has told her, the aunt corroborates the information but discounts the virulence as bigotry, indicating that he *sees* things in a certain light and cannot help himself (117). For her part Attracta first has difficulty believing Mr. Purce's story because "it was impossible to visualise the housekeeper and Mr Devereux in the role he'd given them" (114); she tries to imagine the scenes and cannot (115); then after the story is corroborated, she finds she "couldn't help imagining Mr Devereux and his housekeeper laying booby traps on roads and drilling men in the hills," even when she is counseled by Archdeacon Flower that it all was in the past and should now be forgotten (116).

But in Attracta's mind images remain to haunt her and become the vehicle by which she tries to help her students understand. Telling the two stories, she urges them to visualize the details: "Can you see that girl? Can you imagine men putting a human head in a tin box and sending it through the post? Can you imagine her receiving it?" (119). And regarding her own experience "she tried to get into the children's minds an image of a baby sleeping while violence and death took place on the Cork road." Trevor devotes several pages to Attracta's vivid lesson, urging her students to try to imagine, to see the images and thus to understand. So intense is her own visualized understanding that the two stories become one and she herself experiences what Penelope Vade experiences:

> "My story is one with hers," she said. "Horror stories, with different endings only. I think of her now and I can see quite clearly the flat she lived in in Belfast. I can see the details, correctly or not I've no idea. Wallpaper with a pattern of brownish purple flowers on it, gaunt furniture casting shadows, a tea-caddy on the hired television set. I drag my body across the floors of two rooms, over a carpet that

> smells of dust and cigarette ash, over rugs and cool linoleum. I reach
> up in the kitchen, a hand on the edge of the sink: one by one I eat
> the aspirins until the bottle's empty." (121)

Perhaps without even realizing it Attracta has preached a sermon in
the best Catholic tradition to her Protestant students; her account of
Penelope Vade's death is in form exactly like meditations on the Stations of the Cross or sermons preached about Christ's death during
Holy Week: "composition of place" is the first step, with its consid-
eration of vivid details (which need not be actual as long as they
accord with the central truth of the event); then imaginative reen-
actment of the event itself, generating emotions of sympathy and love
for the sufferer and climaxing, if possible, in union with the sufferer.[4]
Having gone through Penelope Vade's experience herself, Attracta
tries to re-create it for her pupils. But they are sated with this kind of
imagery from the daily news and cannot respond with the emotions
and understanding Attracta tries to elicit. Nor indeed can their parents or their priest. Attracta is like a saint or prophet in their midst,
able to see not only with eyes but also with mind and heart. And like
a prophet, she and her message are without honor in her own
country.

Place is always important in Trevor's work; in this story Attracta's
meditations on the connection between Penelope's story and her
own occur by the sea, on a headland overlooking a bay. Walking
there in the heather, she remembers in detail her own story and
concludes with the vivid image of Penelope's horrible experience
and death (105-19). Although this central section of Trevor's narrative involves lengthy and detailed flashback to a period 50 years in
the past, it begins significantly in the present with Attracta looking
out at a "solitary island" as she combines visual perception with
speculation about life itself (105). This island, like so many others in
Trevor's work, stands as an emblem both for Ireland's plight and for
the character's: "No one had ever lived on the island because its
smallness would have made a self-supporting existence impossible."
And although when she had been growing up "she'd often wondered what it would be like to live alone on the rocky fastness, in a
wooden hut or a cottage built of stones," she concluded that such a
life would be "not very agreeable . . . for she'd always been sociable"
(105f).

There, in brief, is the problem of this story: individuals cannot
survive solitary and neither can communities; a cottage made of
stone cannot provide enough for life and neither can a heart of
stone; self-supporting existence really is impossible. Attracta's
"sociability" is not restricted to one group, such as her fellow
Protestants. Every action she takes in the narrative shows her with a
much broader sense of human connection. Her apparent "narrowing
down" of herself to identify with Penelope Vade is actually an exten-
sion of herself to all sufferers, figured forth in this one particularly
vivid image. In "becoming" Penelope and in retelling their joint stories she is attempting to change the ending of Penelope's story, with
its despair, to the hopeful ending of her own, not only for the sake of
this pupil from the past but for all the pupils she has in the present
and for all the generations to come. Attracta's act is nothing less than
a heroic effort to redeem all Ireland, to make it an island large
enough in spirit to support life.

But the story does not end on so ringing a note. The children
have not understood; nor have their elders. Attracta will be retired
with a presentation of Waterford glass, a symbol of Ireland at its best.
The clergyman and others will turn from the televison news with its
persistently hateful images to more cheerful topics (aided by tea with
"more biscuits and a slice of cake" [123]), leaving the prophet if not
despised at least rejected, watching alone as the violence on television merges with the face of Penelope Vade, all the images of suffering becoming one unified image: in the public world of Christian
culture, a crucifix; in the private world of this particular teacher, a
former pupil.

Implied Puns

Puns are not often used by Trevor's characters or by the narrating
voice. But although the pun as rhetorical caper is absent, significant
words used in the text often generate a variety of meanings for the
reader to play with, a single significant word ramifying from its obvious denotation in context to the analogous meanings it suggests
throughout the rest of the text. This is especially true in the short
stories, where the whole brief narrative can, in a way, function as a
single figure of speech. What is usually referred to as the "economy"

of the short story form, the rendering of a single impression, a single event,[5] is often facilitated by just such a structuring: a single word is provided by the text, a single note sounded, but the rest of the text reverberates sympathetically. Perhaps only half of the pun is stated outright, but its whole is implied by the story as a whole. Thus the implied pun unifies and enriches the narrative, at once contracting and expanding it, and the tension between these two movements – this gesture toward confining the story to a single word while showing its relation to multiple meanings – produces much of the emotional power of the narrative.

"Beyond the Pale" well illustrates this principle as it operates here and throughout Trevor's work. The governing word is *pale* (or the whole phrase "beyond the pale"),[6] supplied by the title and repeated six times in close succession toward the end of the 21 pages. A distraught Englishwoman, Cynthia Strafe, guest at a resort hotel on the beautiful Antrim coast of Northern Ireland, first uses the phrase as she tells a story she has just heard about an Irish couple, calling them "two people who are beyond the pale."[7] Moments later, addressing the English proprietor of the hotel, she asserts that "Murderers are beyond the pale, Mr Malseed, and England has always had its pales. The one in Ireland began in 1395" (708); she then goes on to state, "We made a sensible pale here once, as civilized people create a garden, pretty as a picture" (709). The participant narrator, Milly, also uses the term as she describes this scene: first quoting herself referring to "some pale or other" (708), then commenting that Cynthia's husband, after shouting at her to shut up, "muttered that he was sorry, but Cynthia simply took advantage of his generosity, continuing about a pale" (709). These six references, all confined to the same climactic scene, suggest meanings that reverberate throughout the story.

The narrator, Milly, on holiday with Dekko and Major and Mrs. Strafe (a regular bridge foursome), recounts an event that not only ruins the current holiday but will affect all subsequent ones and prevent any further returns to the Ireland they have visited every June for many years; within her story she quotes another one, told by Cynthia Strafe. The phrase "beyond the pale" belongs to Cynthia's story but illuminates Milly's as well.

Glencorn Lodge is "perfection" (691), a superbly restored and maintained Georgian house by the sea, exclusive in its clientele, an "idyll" (703) with "flowers . . . everywhere" (705). It is run by a couple from Surrey and visited by discriminating guests from around the world. It seems exempt from violence – so exempt, in fact, that Milly prefers less forthright words: "coming as we did, taking the road along the coast, dawdling through Ballygally, it was impossible to believe that somewhere else the unpleasantness was going on" (693); even "a particularly nasty carry-on" is diminished as a "carry-on" (693). Milly's voice itself constitutes a pale, a barrier, separating the acceptable from the unacceptable: her diction, her phrasing, her tone, her selection and explicit evaluations of details in her story – all betray where she thinks lines of inclusion and exclusion ought to be drawn. In Milly's narrative Cynthia is regularly "poor Cynthia," showing her marginality to the group (Strafe only stays with her through kindness, she says, thus putting Strafe in a good light and Cynthia in a bad one; "Naturally we never discuss her shortcomings or in any way analyse the marriage. The unwritten rule that exists among the four of us [to refrain from comment about one another] seems to extend as far as that" [696]. Hence Milly makes her long-term adulterous relationship with Strafe seem noble, two strong persons being considerate of a weak one). Milly not only rejects sectarian violence as "unpleasantness" and Cynthia as "small and ineffectual"; she is also superior in relation to Dekko (it is convenient to borrow sleeping pills from Dekko to give to Cynthia, but Milly at the same time criticizes him for "relying on the things too much in my opinion" [698], indicating her scorn of the pills by her phrase "the things" and her superiority to the people who use them by her self-aggrandizing disclaimer "in my opinion"). Even Strafe, the lover she always presents positively, whose very faults are virtues (e.g., he is *above* being punctual [698]), is diminished in her way of reporting the rituals of his lovemaking: "Actually it's all rather sweet, Strafe and his little ways" (696). Thus long before Cynthia's important story is introduced, Milly's voice has established a world in which barriers of money, mores, class, personal behavior, and attitudes separate persons into categories of acceptable and unacceptable. Long before the phrase "beyond the pale" appears in any character's mouth, its most ordinary meaning has been established in the text: in typical usage what is "beyond the pale" is not something heinous but something mildly unacceptable; the thing rejected (even if it *is* heinous) is diminished and the user of the phrase is exalted (by being able to diminish the thing rejected). Thus rhetorical stratagems attempt to control threatening experience: the incumbent wife (who inconveniently remains in place) is reduced to "poor Cynthia"; sectarian violence in which real people are really injured is trivialized as "unpleasantness"; and murder is only "beyond the pale."

Cynthia, however, tries to shift attention away from the common usage of that phrase to its more powerful origin, as she attempts to tell her story to her resisting companions. An uncouth-looking red-haired man[8] (an atypical guest, one of the "locals," Milly assumes, for whose presence Mr. Malseed even apologizes [695]) has drowned. Cynthia, who had been speaking with him for two hours before he walked out on the rocks, insists the event was suicide; everyone else thinks she is hysterical and prefers to consider the death an accident. Just as Milly's voice neatly controls her narrative, other characters too prefer tidy explanations, accident rather than suicide, which will allow them more quickly to forget, to control, this new "unpleasantness" (701) and get back into a holiday mode. Milly notes with approval that "everyone was making an effort. . . . That life should continue as normally as possible was essential for Glencorn Lodge, the example already set by Mrs Malseed" (701). Proprietors, foreign visitors, all prefer to focus on scenery and ignore "the locals," to erect a barrier of untroubled comfort between "us" and "them."

After the body has been quietly removed by the police, Milly and the others are prepared to enjoy an excellent tea of "sponge cakes and little currant scones" (701) – thus obliterating "unpleasantness." Cynthia alone insists on facing what has happened, talking about it: an act that some other narrator might present as courage but that Milly attributes to emotional weakness, Cynthia's being hysterical, perhaps even mad. (At one point in this scene Milly vividly imagines Cynthia's being taken way to an institution, an image she reports to indicate how distraught Cynthia is, not realizing that she simply betrays her own desire to be rid of the inconvenient wife.)

Cynthia's story, told her by the man who drowned, constitutes the climax of Milly's. As Cynthia recounts this narrative of "two children who had apparently ridden bicycles through the streets of Belfast, out into Co. Antrim," "two children who later fell in love" (702), she is constantly interrupted by Strafe, Dekko, Milly, and later

even Mr. and Mrs. Malseed, attempting to stop her, at first sympathetically and dismissively ("'Horrid old dream,' Strafe said. 'Horrid
for you, dear'" [702]), then more sternly ("Cynth, we have to put it
behind us" [704]), and finally with venom ("'You fleshless ugly
bitch!' [Strafe] cried. 'You bloody old fool!'" [710]). By telling her
story Cynthia broaches several pales.

The story she tells begins with an idyll and ends with violent
death. The two innocent children who once cycled from city to
country grew up, drifted apart, and became killers; the ruined Georgian house with its idyllic garden where they sought delight and
refuge, now rebuilt as a hotel for foreigners, is lost to them, just as
childhood and now life itself is lost to them. The story, interrupted
and fragmentary, gradually completes itself at the disrupted tea table:
as an adult in Belfast, the young man learns that the girl he earlier
loved is now a terrorist in London, making bombs; failing to dissuade
her, preoccupied with her violence, hating it yet sharing it, he shoots
her, then revisits the Eden of their youth, where, tormented in his
desire to understand the roots of cruelty and evil, he commits suicide. Thus death itself becomes the ultimate pale, the bourn from
which no traveler, English or Irish, can return home.

These questions about cruelty and evil torment Cynthia too,
because she sees their manifestation everywhere: "Chaos and con-
tradiction, she informed [Strafe], were hidden everywhere beneath
nice-sounding names. 'The Battle of the Yellow Ford,' she suddenly
chanted in a sing-song way that sounded thoroughly peculiar, 'the
Statutes of Kilkenny. The Battle of Glenmama, the Convention of
Drumceat. The Act of Settlement, the Renunciation Act. The Act of
Union, the Toleration Act. Just so much history it sounds like now,
yet people starved or died while other people watched'" (704). Cynthia herself watched, helplessly from the cliff, while the young man
walked off the rocks into the sea, and Strafe, Milly, Dekko, and others in the tearoom watch Cynthia as she tells her story with great
grief. But whereas Cynthia listened to the young man's story with
sympathy and "saw into" what really happened, the others focus
only on externals: if Cynthia's manner of telling her story sounds
"thoroughly peculiar," then the history she recites "really hardly
concerns us" (705), as her husband dismissively puts it. Manner and
mores constitute a pale: the young man himself was suspect from the
beginning because he did not look or behave like other guests; Cyn-

thia is dismissed because she is making a scene, speaking emotionally about subjects this well-bred group prefer to ignore. Nice-sounding names constitute a controlling barrier against the chaos of history; even the concept "history" can serve as a barrier against the realization that real people really starved and died while other real people looked on, certain that it hardly concerned them.

In the public world of society and politics the concept of history as something remote – and finished – serves as a shield, a barrier against the uncomfortable "truth" of real events. In the more private world of individual relationships lies of various kinds serve the same purpose. Thus to tell the truth in either realm is to pass "beyond the pale" of what makes "pleasant" life possible. That Cynthia transgresses in both realms indicates, once again, those correspondences which exist in Trevor's work between the public and the private. And this particular example of correspondence makes an especially strong statement.

That Cynthia should combine the worlds of "we" and "they," the worlds of public and private events, seems "almost unbelievable" (709) to Milly: "In Surrey we while away the time, we clip our hedges. On a bridge night there's coffee at nine o'clock, with macaroons or *petits fours*. Last thing of all we watch the late-night News, packing away our cards and scoring-pads, our sharpened pencils. There's been an incident in Armagh, one soldier's had his head shot off, another's run amok. Our lovely Glens of Antrim, we all four think, our coastal drives: we hope that nothing disturbs the peace" (709).[9] Like history, television news provides a barrier, separating this peace from that violence, allowing people in Surrey to eat petits fours (and people at Glencorn Lodge to eat curranty scones). To combine these delicacies with reference to a head shot off is to broach inexcusably a convention designed to reduce real events to mere objects of interest. But Cynthia goes even further, implying a connection between this supposedly distant violence and the most private part of private life. Her story ends with the sudden public announcement, " 'That woman,' she said [pointing to Milly], 'is my husband's mistress, a fact I am supposed to be unaware of. . . . My husband is perverted in his sexual desires. His friend [Dekko], who shared his schooldays, has never quite recovered from that time. I myself am a pathetic creature who has closed her eyes to a husband's infidelity and his mistress's viciousness. . . . [M]echanically I smile. I hardly exist' " (710). By addressing these revelations to Kitty, the maid, in the presence of everyone in the tearoom, Cynthia broaches yet another pale. Not only does she make public the secrets of her own group; she speaks to one of "them," one of the "wild Irish," as to an equal whose attention and opinion are important (709). And her most shocking transgression is to have spoken the brutal truth aloud.

All references to the pale have been made by Cynthia (Milly's are merely uncomprehending echoes of Cynthia's words). Attempting to shift focus away from the superficiality on which words like *unpleasantness* are fixed, Cynthia began with an ordinary phrase, "beyond the pale," with its present vacuous suggestion of mere inappropriateness, and then insisted on the historical facts underlying that phrase, the actual Pale begun in 1395, a wall of division and exclusion.[10] But although she provided this historical reference, the others ignored her allusion or did not even understand it (for superior Milly it is "some pale or other"). Although Cynthia ran through several applications of the figure, no one seemed to follow her thought: when first she referred to the Irish couple, they were apparently scorned as merely "two people who are beyond the pale," much as Milly had scorned the two Irish policemen for "their natural slowness of intellect" (699). Her next reference was more condemnatory; by coupling the explicit word *murderers* with the milder phrase "beyond the pale," she pointed up the inadequacy of all such genteel idioms (including Milly's self-deceiving "unpleasantness"). In her next reference she indicated the phrase to be a metaphor with a variety of applications ("England has always had its pales") and supplied that metaphor's original point of comparison (the barrier begun in Ireland in 1395). And in her last reference, addressed to Kitty, she indicates the goal of all pales (both the actual barrier of 1395 and its various private and public analogues), which is the creation of a walled garden – a place of beauty, comfort, and safety for a select few: "Beyond it lie the bleak untouchables, best kept as dots on the horizon, too terrible to contemplate" (709).

This image of the garden appears frequently in Trevor's work as an emblem for Ireland. By thus referring to the pale, the dividing wall, as both a physical barrier and a metaphoric one, separating the acceptable people from the unacceptable ones, the civilized from the terrible, Trevor's story plays with a phrase that has become cliché and suddenly exposes its depth of meaning. After Cynthia tells Kitty, "We love you and we love your island. . . . We love the lilt of your racy history, we love your earls and heroes," she introduces her mention of the pale with an adversative: "yet we made a sensible pale here once, as civilized people create a garden, pretty as a picture" (709). The conflict indicated by that "yet" (conflict between the inclusion suggested by "love" and the exclusion of "pale") reveals why "we people of Surrey" cannot understand anything about Ireland, past or present. The most that can be understood, Cynthia says, is that "evil breeds evil in a mysterious way."

But to know that is to know a great deal. And to say it aloud is to transgress the barriers of self-deception. To supply specific examples of "the hell [that] has invaded the paradise of Glencorn" and to admit that "we, who have so often brought it, pretend it isn't there" (710) is to pass altogether "beyond the pale." The idyllic garden of rural Antrim, the flower-filled peace of Glencorn Lodge, may indeed be pretty as a picture, but the picture is deceptive, like the "nice-sounding names" of history and euphemism, like the careful behavior of "civilized people." Innocent children can grow up to become murderers. That Milly ends her story acknowledging the truth of Cynthia's prediction that the group would never talk about what has just been said, and acknowledging as well that she would like "to batter the silliness out of [Cynthia]," corroborates that pales may be broached occasionally but not demolished: the cover-ups of language and silence remain, the hidden impulse toward brutal violence remains, the self-deceiving sense of superiority remains.

Literalized Metaphors

Playing with several well-known assertions, Trevor probes the elusive nature of truth in *Mrs. Eckdorf in O'Neill's Hotel*. As a photographer Ivy Eckdorf operates on the principle that "pictures don't lie"; a typical response to this cliché among sophisticated readers might be the counterassertion that indeed they do, through selectivity, framing, angle, focus, and quality of light, if not also through tricks and touch-ups of various kinds. In the course of this novel Trevor turns the matter another way, suggesting that some pictures (photographs

as well as other kinds of images), though not lying, may nonetheless
reveal a truth quite different from what is expected.

Another assertion, well known in Christian circles, is Jesus' new
commandment, "love one another; as I have loved you,"[11] demon-
strated at the Last Supper: just as he then washed the feet of his disciples, they too are to wash each other's feet.[12] This deed is reenacted yearly as part of the Holy Thursday liturgy and is usually taken
as a symbol of other acts of love and service to be performed
throughout the rest of the year. But in ordinary daily life no one
takes the injunction literally. In his narrative Trevor demonstrates
that Ivy Eckdorf's attempt to wash the feet of someone she loathes is
comic, grotesque, even insane; at the same time, he suggests that
could she really do it, she would be able to purge herself of the
hatred that has driven her mad. By literalizing the metaphor Trevor
shows both the power and the folly of what it expresses.[13] Both
these well-known assertions, one from the realm of photography and
one from the realm of Scripture and liturgy, indicate something
about the nature of the truth involved in various kinds of representa-
tions (visual images and gestures or behavior) and point toward yet
another well-known assertion quoted in this novel – "the truth will
set you free,"[14] the problematic nature of which permeates all of
Trevor's work.

Mrs. Eckdorf in O'Neill's Hotel is full of references to visual
images: the coffee-table books of photo essays Mrs. Eckdorf produces; the photographs of prostitutes Morrissey uses to drum up
business; the Olivia de Haviland movies with which the orphan-pros-
titute Agnes compares her life; films and "earnest television pro-
grammes" (17) that invade people's privacy; dreams, fantasies, and
visions of various kinds (everything from racing tips to divine revelations). Concerning these images, especially photographs themselves,
there are conflicting attitudes among the characters. Mrs. Eckdorf is
intent on "the documentary truth that only the probing of a camera,
enriched by compassion and perception, could supply," her conscious motive a noble one ("truth was the parent of understanding
and love" [122]). Others, however, find this "telling of the truth" in
film, television, newspapers, magazines, and books of photos to be
gratuitous meddling (" 'It does not concern you,' [her second ex-
husband] had muttered in dreary irritation" [123]). The local priest
in Dublin states outright that Mrs. Eckdorf's photo narratives are

lies[15] and that her motivation is actually pride (230). When Mrs. Eckdorf insists that her photos of Mrs. Sinnott of O'Neill's Hotel show "God moving in a mysterious way" (220), Father Hennessey counters that her explanation of what the photos mean is pure invention: "You are making an ordinary thing seem dramatic when it is not that at all. The truth is simple and unexciting: you are twisting it with sentiment and false interpretations, so that a book will sell to people" (221). The novel's narrating voice seems to share Father Hennessey's judgment when it reports Ivy's own perspective on her work in a way that indicates an irony she misses but the reader sees: "And in the end she had been proved right, for it was right, she knew, that the fears and faithfulness of poverty-dogged peasants should be seen and understood on the coffee-tables of the rich" (123).

The flaw, of course, in Mrs. Eckdorf's logic lies in the word *understood*. This is what Father Hennessey tries to show her when he argues that the explanations she evolves for the pictures she takes, the narrative implicit in her selection and organization of those pictures, is false. But in doing so Father Hennessey is faced with having to temper some passages from Scripture and some tenets of popular piety that in sermons and retreats he would routinely have urged for wholehearted embrace. Mrs. Eckdorf is seeing God's presence in a world where Father Hennessey must tell her she is seeing her own imaginings; Mrs. Eckdorf proclaims, on good authority, that "the truth will set you free" (123), and Father Hennessey must tell her she deals in lies; Mrs. Eckdorf repeatedly asserts, "We are all God's creatures. . . . We concern one another" (16), and Father Hennessey must help her see that she has simply reduced humanity to raw material for her art (219). He has no sympathy whatsoever for her desire to wash the feet of the man whom she first photographs with the prostitute and then locks, naked, in his room (while she struggles to overcome her hatred of him so that she may return to cleanse him and purge her own heart). Father Hennessey's unenviable – and unsought – task (distressing to him, comic to the reader) is to persuade a crazy woman not to take Scriptural injunctions literally, not to literalize metaphors.

Photos do not lie? What you see is what you get? In this novel, both yes and no. The plot line involves a double quest: Mrs. Eckdorf, visitor to Dublin, seeks to find the solution to the mystery she intuits

as she prepares to photograph O'Neill's Hotel and the deaf and
dumb Mrs. Sinnott's ninety-second birthday party; at the same time,
Mr. Smedley, another well-traveled visitor, seeks a prostitute, and
after repeated failures to find a pimp among a succession of outraged
publicans and men in the street ("We make do with our wives in this
town" [71]), finally ends up at O'Neill's Hotel on the afternoon of
the birthday party. Both Mrs. Eckdorf and Mr. Smedley crisscross
Dublin during the same two days;[16] both, frustrated in their search,
feel that they are in the wrong city (126, 147); and both finally consummate their search in ways they had not foreseen or desired. Mr.
Smedley, having chosen Agnes from Morrissey's collection of photos,
arrives for his appointment at the hotel only to find that she has
changed her occupation and gone to work in a convent; outraged by
the substitution of fat Mrs. Dargan, he is nonetheless badgered by
Mrs. Eckdorf into going upstairs at a much higher price than he,
Morrissey, or the delighted Mrs. Dargan had dreamed of. His clothes,
shoes, money, and airline tickets are removed by Mrs. Eckdorf and
hidden in a sideboard in the dining room (not to be discovered for
four months); he is photographed in the nude, locked in his room,
and only much later released when his cries are finally heard by Mrs.
Sinnott's drunkard son, Eugene. Thus the comic progress of Mr.
Smedley, "man of vigour" (71), whose lechery is both satisfied and
punished by the righteous Ivy Eckdorf. The photos did and did not
lie: seeking a sex object (Agnes), he does find one (Mrs. Dargan). But
photography gives the truth an unexpected twist: beginning as
voyeur, he suddenly finds himself object of the camera's eye. The
hilarious subplot of Mr. Smedley's quest serves as the occasion for
revealing the tragedy of Mrs. Eckdorf's true motivation for her own
quest and provides as well the event that drives her over the edge
into complete madness, from which she never recovers, leaving her
trapped forever in a small fragment of time and space.

 Why should Mrs. Eckdorf concern herself with Mr. Smedley at
all, when she has ample activity photographing the birthday party?
And why should she be so virulent in her emotional response to him?
As she later confesses her life to Father Hennessey, her real motivations appear: abandoned by her father, laughed at by her mother
(whose sexual liaisons shocked her), sexually solicited by a lesbian
teacher, she finds she cannot "bear the thought of other people's
flesh" (224). And so her two marriages were unconsummated (225),

and she is "incapable of having a human relationship" (226). Thus Smedley's physical desire horrifies her (as had her husbands'), and she perceives him as "degenerate" (227). During this same period she has been piecing together a story about "the tragedy from the past" that she intuits at O'Neill's Hotel, finally deducing a rape, a forced wedding, and various consequent alienations; she may be right about these "facts," but what she makes of them ultimately is a distortion (according to Father Hennessey), because she perceives the kind and loving Mrs. Sinnott in extreme terms as a saint, someone whose goodness provides the grace and whose birthday provides the occasion for all these alienated persons to come together as a family in forgiveness. The original sin of this tragedy is thus, to her, a *felix culpa* and the hotel a holy place. In the presence of such holiness (as she perceives it) Mrs. Eckdorf feels impelled to take to its limit her professed belief that "we are all God's creatures," to purge herself of her loathing for Mr. Smedley (and her loathing of sex) by an ultimate act of humble acceptance: she will anoint his feet. But she finds she cannot do it; her revulsion toward sex and her hatred of people is so great that she succumbs instead to madness, living forever in her selective memory of that birthday party when violated people forgave each other and sat together at the same table.

In this way the birthday party functions as a kind of secular Last Supper, with Mrs. Sinnott as the saintly central figure, whose name (sin-not) and whose gentle behavior indicate her holiness. But in order to sit down at this table and not just photograph it from all angles as a spectator, Mrs. Eckdorf thinks she must participate in the ritual of cleansing that the "mandatum" of Maundy Thursday requires. Revealingly, the task she sets for herself is expressed not simply as *washing* the feet of the despised Mr. Smedley but as *anointing* them, a word that recalls not only Christ's washing his disciples' feet at the Last Supper but also Mary Magdalene's washing and anointing Christ's feet at an earlier supper. By her choice of words Mrs. Eckdorf betrays her deep feeling of sexual guilt; associating herself with Mary Magdalene, a prostitute, she takes on the lechery of the men and women in her life. Thus her frigidity is made to seem occasioned not by her loathing of the flesh of others but by revulsion against her sinful participation in their desires: if her father abandoned her, he must have known how wicked she was.

Unable to reckon with this buried guilt, unable to perform the act of penance she prescribes for herself, Mrs. Eckdorf must either renounce belief in her literalized metaphors and in the intrinsic truthfulness of her photos or else escape to an existence where metaphors and images constitute the only reality. From world traveler, successful photojournalist, and sophisticated visitor to Dublin Mrs. Eckdorf constricts herself to lunatic in an asylum, dwelling forever in mental images of a single afternoon, demonstrating by her choice that, for her at least, it is not the knowing of the truth but the forgetting of it that sets her "free."

Mrs. Sinnott, in her perpetual silence, presents an important contrast to Mrs. Eckdorf. Deaf and dumb since birth, unwilling to use sign language or read lips, preferring the slower process of writing, Mrs. Sinnott has amassed hundreds of red exercise books full of conversations. But they, unlike Mrs. Eckdorf's photo books, have not been shaped by narrative, true or spurious: as people come to see her, they record what they have to say on the next empty lines, and she responds on the next, and so on. Her books record "slices of life"; they do not present plots or arguments. Mrs. Sinnott's preference for the silence and tranquillity of writing (rather than the speed and vigor of lipreading or sign language) contrasts too with Mrs. Eckdorf's own violence of character (Mrs. Eckdorf loses control and screams in the streets; she physically attacks men, impaling the hand of one of her husbands with a fork, knocking Morrissey out with a paperweight). And unlike Mrs. Eckdorf, who panders to false emotions (beautiful photos of the poor for the coffee tables of the rich), Mrs. Sinnott elicits from her visitors the expression of deep feelings about themselves and their lives (Mr. Gregan, though he does not listen to his wife and feels his wife does not listen to him, is able to confide in Mrs. Sinnott not only because she seems genuinely interested but also because "it was easier not having actually to speak the words" [43]). And unlike Mrs. Eckdorf, incapable of human relationships, Mrs. Sinnott, though deaf, "had an ear for everything in your mind" (27). Unlike Mrs. Eckdorf, she allows people their privacy, as well as welcoming their intimacy; her daughter speculates that she did not read lips because she may have "preferred not to know everything that was going on about her" – her tranquillity and silence are thus "almost a blessing" (51).

So utterly unlike Mrs. Eckdorf, Mrs. Sinnott nonetheless has an analogous fate, though a more honest one. On the night of her ninety-second birthday, after her last supper, she has a dream full of pain and frustration and vivid visual images, a dream that in fact records her process of death. It ends with the tormenting image of an orphan's face (orphans had been her special concern): "The face went on suffering before her, until someone came and gently closed her eyes" (240). The orphan is herself, is Mrs. Eckdorf, is all who suffer. With her death the images in her mind also die; the exercise books containing a record of her compassion will be destroyed, and eventually her memory will fade, even among those whom she loved and who loved her (246). With death, darkness and silence engulf her completely, just as madness engulfs Mrs. Eckdorf in her asylum of "nonexistence." The truth of words is apparently as transient for the knower as is the truth of images.

There is a third woman mentioned several times in the novel who shares traits with both Mrs. Eckdorf and Mrs. Sinnott and whose mode of being owes much to images and words: Saint Attracta,[17] about whom Father Hennessey is writing a book. One of the red exercise books records that "Father Hennessey had spent an hour with [Mrs. Sinnott], showing her what he had written concerning the legend of St Attracta. . . . It was said that this hot-tempered saint had received the veil from St Patrick and had divided the waters of Lough Gara and had harnessed deer with her hair. *We must skim the truth from pretty myth*, Father Hennessey had written for her benefit alone.[18] *There is plenty of truth in St Attracta*" (35). Yet as he works on his book Father Hennessey is "assailed with doubts as to whether or not she had ever even existed" (126). As with photographs, the nature of the truth in legends is problematic: "The truth about any saint, he reflected, was particularly difficult to establish: saints went to people's hearts, they became decorated with legend, as statues of Our Lady were decorated with glass jewelry in Italian churches. There was no harm in that, except that the decoration too often obscured the reality, and even then one couldn't condemn because it was a form of worship" (126). Here Father Hennessey wrestles with the question of whether or not to demythologize religion: the jewelry may be false, but it lifts the heart to God; the legends may be false, but they aid worship. Yet beyond this issue lurks the question of why *this* "decoration"? Father Hennessey does not speculate on

"Why jewelry rather than Amazonian armor?" but does wonder, *"How can we reconcile the wild figure of Lough Gara with the humble nun? Why is there a tendency to turn our women into furies?"* (126). When he raises this question, Father Hennessey does not yet know Mrs. Eckdorf, and he never makes a specific connection between her and Saint Attracta (except to pray that "she would cease to distort the truth with dramatic adornment, as the truth about St Attracta and St Damien and St Cosma had been adorned" (238). But a parallel between them is clear: Mrs. Eckdorf too is hot-tempered, a wild figure, ranting in the streets of Dublin; she too is a virgin and ends her life enclosed, not in the veil of religion but in the veil of madness; she too works "wonders," not with loughs and deer but with photographs. Mrs. Sinnott also resembles Attracta, but the other side of her character: Mrs. Sinnott, too, runs a "hospice," and her works of mercy among the poor and orphaned, her gentleness and her silence, accord with the view of Attracta as "a humble nun" (Mrs. Eckdorf, seeing wonders of forgiveness in Mrs. Sinnott's household, even calls her a saint). Both women are in some ways like Attracta, yet no one would call Mrs. Eckdorf a saint and Father Hennessey will not allow Mrs. Sinnott to be considered one. Where do drama and decoration end and truth begin? Is it merely distance in time and pious elaboration of legend that make Attracta a saint, while Mrs. Eckdorf is simply a mad woman and Mrs. Sinnott simply a kind one?

These questions are implied throughout the narrative and explicitly worry Father Hennessey: "Did it matter if St Attracta had taken the veil from St Patrick or had lived a century later?" (129). And oddly enough, he goes on to speculate about these issues in a manner identical with Mrs. Eckdorf's: "Father Hennessey shivered, thinking of the people of O'Neill's Hotel: if the mysteries of the saints didn't matter there was the implication in his mind that the mysteries of the ordinary living did, and should instead be solved" (129). But unlike Mrs. Eckdorf, he can find no narrative solution to "living mysteries" and is "more at ease with dead saints than with the ordinary living" (128), with the narratives of legend rather than the narratives of life.

Mrs. Eckdorf from her intense personal need to find coherence among the details of life has searched for narratives to explain, to order, to redeem experience. Father Hennessey similarly has consoled himself with other kinds of narratives, legends of the saints, that also explain, order, and redeem experience. Faced with the shocking example of someone who took too literal an approach to this ordering of chaos, this solving of mysteries, Father Hennessey prescribes a cautionary penance for himself, going weekly to visit Mrs. Eckdorf in her asylum, talking with her about the only part of her life she remembers, her experience at O'Neill's Hotel. Like Mrs. Eckdorf, Father Hennessey sees his penance in terms of an image from Scripture, not anointing the feet of sinners but carrying his cross (264). Unlike her, however, he has not literalized the metaphor; unlike her, he is not insane; and unlike her, he does not dwell in unalloyed happiness.

By concluding the novel with the sentence "For her at least there was a happy ending" (265) Trevor points up the complicated issue of narrative in this novel. The novel itself is a narrative and has an ending that both shows something and asserts something. It shows a madwoman in an asylum dwelling in remembered images on which she has imposed her own interpretive narrative, all else in her life being forgotten, and it asserts that this situation constitutes a "happy ending." Happy for whom? Mrs. Eckdorf is said by people in the asylum to be "the happiest woman they had ever admitted" (263); Father Hennessey observes that this current state of happiness contrasts markedly with her previous distress; and Mrs. Eckdorf herself considers that she has died and gone to heaven (heaven being the warmth of family love she perceived at O'Neill's Hotel). But does this constitute a happy ending for the novel itself? The lives of those associated with O'Neill's Hotel have, in the narrative of the novel, been shown to be ordinary and not particularly happy. Father Hennessey drags out his life dutifully visiting Mrs. Eckdorf in her asylum once a week, in penance for his preferring the narratives of distant saints to the mysteries of present sufferers. Mrs. Sinnott's death is probably the best indication of the extent to which "happy ending" does not apply to the novel itself: unlike Mrs. Eckdorf, she really is dead, but there is no suggestion of a heaven for her, only the extinction of darkness and silence. And even her death itself, though apparently presenting an image of peacefulness to outside observers (245), was in fact a dreadful experience of pain and anguish, as her final dream records (239f). The "at least" in Trevor's final sentence underscores what the novel's narrative shows: that there is only the one happy ending within this story, the happiness of a woman who has fled the "truth" of all her memories and buried herself in selected ones, narrowing the focus of her awareness to such an extent that to everyone else she is insane.

This novel is a book about books and their relation to the truth: Mrs. Sinnott's red exercise books, recording conversations as they come, in no special order, the ordinary chaos of life; Mrs. Eckdorf's picture books, selected and arranged to tell a story, carefully controlled; the Scriptural story of foot washing, which Mrs. Eckdorf tries to apply literally. In its own process of selection, arrangement, and careful control the novel raises the inevitable question of whether what is called truth is merely the imposition of order on chaos, the fabrication of story to explain experience. Is Mrs. Eckdorf the freest one in this novel, or the most captive? What is the reader to make of the irony of her happiness? How coherent can metaphors be? Can one *live* a metaphor or inhabit a narrative explanation? Trevor never answers these questions, but he raises them again and again in his work.

Incremental References

Trevor's fiction does not usually include conventional symbols, but certain repeated items begin to take on additional weight and meaning as they recur thoughout his work; this is especially true of trees, gardens, orchards, fields, and islands. In its immediate context such a thing as an avenue of trees, for example, is just an avenue of trees. But as the story proceeds, those trees begin to stand for more than themselves, and in the context of all Trevor's work they acquire all the density of a symbol with none of the clumsiness.

In *Fools of Fortune* Marianne teaches her daughter, Imelda, about the moral structure of the world, as she sees it, by commenting on a tree where a man was hanged: "Just an ordinary tree, Imelda. You could pass it by and not know a thing."[19] Since this is the very tree on the Quinton's land where the informer Doyle was executed by the IRA, for whose death the Black and Tans burned the Quinton's house and murdered most of the family and servants, a series of events that ultimately leads to Imelda's illegitimate birth and her father's exile, this is hardly "just an ordinary tree." For Imelda it in fact becomes the tree of the knowledge of good and evil, because it serves as a focus for Marianne's answer to Imelda's earlier questions about her father, an answer that includes not only the Kilneagh fire, Willie's mother's suicide, Marianne and Willie's not being married, Marianne's parents' plan to put Imelda up for adoption, and Marianne's own insistence on keeping the child and living in the ruins of Kilneagh but also references to the famine, the Easter Rising, and various Irish martyrs and battles (163f). Marianne concludes her instruction by saying, "What I mean, Imelda, is that's how things happen. The most important things of all happen by chance" (164). The chain of events Marianne has just traced is made up of links that are and are not a matter of chance, just as the tree is and is not an ordinary tree. The point of her lesson – that "you can pass by anything and not know" (163) – is that *everything* has meaning, has antecedents and repercussions, has connections, even when those meanings and connections are not discerned by a given individual. Marianne's lesson to Imelda is Trevor's lesson throughout his work, throughout his elaborate system of correspondences.

Thus Doyle's tree is at once part of a larger pattern and "just an ordinary tree." Other ordinary trees in *Fools of Fortune* begin, retrospectively, to take on additional meaning from this axis of violence. Willie's great-grandfather, his "most extraordinary" ancestor who seriously depleted the estate for famine relief, "had planted two lines of beech trees on either side of the avenue to celebrate the victory at Waterloo" (12), an avenue through which Michael Collins drove when visiting the Quintons (who supported his forces fighting the British), an avenue that provided Willie's father with his most peaceful, most silent walk (14). Hence this avenue of trees, ancient and beautiful in its own right, is a sign of the paradox that characterizes the life both of the Quintons and of Ireland itself: to support both British victory and British defeat, to belong somehow to two worlds, to celebrate both peace and war, to foster both tranquillity and violence.

The mulberry orchard in *Fools of Fortune* is as complex in its associations as is the Quintons' avenue of trees. Planted in the nineteenth century by Anna Woodcombe, the first English bride at Kilneagh, in memory of her orchard at home, the Kilneagh orchard thus serves to link England and Ireland, as did the marriage between Anna and William Quinton, Willie's great-grandparents. Anna's heroic efforts at famine relief and her consequent death make her a saint of sorts; it is, in fact, in response to her later "apparition like the Virgin Mary" that William gives away "the greater part of his estate to those who had suffered loss and deprivation" (12). Accordingly, her orchard is associated with extraordinary conjugal and brotherly love, but with loss as well. Later another of the English "brides," Marianne, searching for Willie to tell him of her pregnancy and not knowing why he is mysteriously absent from Kilneagh, dreams that their reunion takes place in the original orchard at Woodcombe Park, its "heaven" contrasting with the ruin of Kilneagh (137); once again the orchard is associated in personal and social realms with both love and loss. The novel ends in the orchard at Kilneagh, Willie and Marianne an elderly couple deciding that the fruit must be harvested soon. This bumper crop, urged on by the summer's drought, is a little like their own lives, subject to a 50-year drought of separation but finally yielding the fruit of reunion and peace. As in earlier references to the orchard, however, the love ratified by this ending is complicated by the abiding presence of ruin and loss. Their years of devotion constitute a marriage of sorts, but a marriage devoid of official recognition (Marianne's family disowns her) and devoid of sexual fulfillment as well. Their only night of sexual union, just before Willie's killing Rudkin, has produced one child, who is driven mad by the violence of which Willie has been both victim and, later, perpetrator, a madness that paradoxically is also a blessing ("tranquillity is there, no matter how death came" [192]). The Quinton line, with its sacrificial loves, comes to an end with Imelda. These three will live together on the ruined estate, survivors of the violence just as the mulberry orchard has survived, united by love but themselves fruitless.

This paradoxical association of fruitful orchards with sexless relationships is also found in "Bodily Secrets," a short story published just after *Fools of Fortune*. Here a recent widow and a man whose homosexuality is a painful secret decide to marry, an arrangement of mutual kindness and support in which each will gain something needed (for Norah an escape from the role her adult children now assign her as "a remnant of the dead"[20] and for Basil Agnew something "to do with himself" [163] now that the toy factory, owned by Norah's deceased husband and managed by him for 17 years, is to be closed). Despite a slight difference in age and class, they like each other and enjoy dancing together; their social life at the club will go on without disruption. The separate bedrooms and his occasional weekends in Dublin remain their secret. The toy factory that, in different ways, had been a focus for their earlier lives is to be demolished; in its place they will plant an orchard: " 'Our wedding present to one another,' he explained [to their surprised friends]. 'Norah's trees and I shall tend them' " (170). Thus the orchard replaces the sexuality they cannot share; their mutual interest in nurturing the orchard is part of the "vague, unstated reassurance" (172) that serves as the basis of their marriage, offsetting the loss of physical beauty this aging woman finds hard to bear and the loss of self-respect this gentle man experiences because his homosexuality is furtive and drunken.

Gardens in Trevor's fiction, like trees and orchards, also take on complex associations with love, fruitfulness, fulfilled sexuality, and their opposites of sterility and loss. In *Other People's Worlds* it is reassuring to Julia that her fiancé, Francis, works in her garden, but this accommodation to the household needs and routines is as false as everything else about him, as her more discerning mother realizes: "The way he'd held the hosta leaf towards her had reminded her of another, or a continued, theatrical interpretation, as if greater significance should be attached to the gesture than the gesture itself implied. From being casually borne, the leaf had abruptly become precious, proffered on the palms of both his hands, a talisman or a dagger. Had he been a royal personage as he passed among the circular rose-beds, or a disaffected duke lost in melancholy and plotting?" (18). Francis, the actor, will not be any more authentic as a husband than he is as a gardener, as Julia finds out to her great grief on their unconsummated honeymoon. Conversely, in *The Love Department* it is only when James Bolsover gives up the job he hates and moves to the derelict garden he has inherited that there is the possibility of renewed love with his estranged wife, Eve. That garden offers them, if not paradise regained (or even the lawn restored, on which they celebrated their wedding many years before), at least the opportunity for trying again. As they reclaim this new garden they may also reclaim their lives together. "The Wedding in the Garden," with yet another variation on these themes of love and loss, plays on the ironies of sexual faithfulness as a form of hatred and revenge, set in a garden.

In "The News from Ireland" Trevor develops one of his more complex series of incremental references to gardens and to trees. The Irish estate from which the English governess writes her news was once prosperous, fell into decay under old Hugh Pulvertaft (descended from Elizabethan planters), then was restored by his English heirs: "along had come the Pulvertafts of Ipswich, taking on more staff, clearing the brambles from the garden in their endeavour to make the place what it had been in the past" (9f). The works project these Pulvertafts devise during the famine to provide employment and ultimately relief constitutes frivolous pleasure for the big house and insulting absurdity for the workers: a circular road to nowhere, its route devised by whim. One of the daughters hopes the road will "go round Bright Purple Hill" (14) and another that "copper beech trees mark the route" (15), to which their father enthusiastically agrees. This road, which he intends as "a memorial to this awful time" (15), will, however, serve just the opposite function: "What could be nicer [he speculates] than a picnic of lunch by the lake, then a drive through the silver birches, another pause by the abbey, continuing by the river for a mile, and home by Bright Purple Hill?" (14). The family eats while others starve. They celebrate their weddings with champagne (39). They give their scraps to the birds (37).

The estate is a garden of plenty and of beauty. So it has been in the past and so the Pulvertafts imagine it in the future. This past includes an abbey built by monks who selected the site for the perfect beauty of its landscape, monks who "cultivated a garden and induced bees to make honey for them" (28) and whose ruined buildings add to the contemporary charm of the scene. But the past that affects this estate goes back farther than to these monks. By including the governess's reference to the Legend of the True Cross, Trevor invokes a story that extends all the way to the Garden of Eden and to the beginning of human time, a story that accounts for the origin of the evil of which this curent famine is only one manifestation.

In this context, then, the purple beeches and the silver birches that decorate the Pulvertafts' estate are fraught with serious associations: they are more than pleasant elements of landscape design; by belonging to the same family as the Tree of the Knowledge of Good and Evil and the Tree of the Cross, they speak of sin and salvation and point to issues of moral responsibility. The half-mad butler, Fogarty, sees the moral discrepancy between the Pulvertafts' method of famine relief and the real aid that might have been provided. As he says to the governess, "A blind eye was turned, miss, you know that. The hunger was a plague: what use a few spoonfuls of soup, and a road that leads nowhere and only insults the pride of the men who built it? The hunger might have been halted, miss, you know that. The people were allowed to die" (42).

Fogarty's solution is paradoxical – salvation achieved by ruin: "If the estate had continued in its honest decline, if these Pulvertafts had not arrived, the people outside the walls would have travelled here from miles around. They would have eaten the wild raspberries and the apples from the trees, the peaches that still thrived on the brick-lined walls, the grapes and plums and greengages, the blackberries and mulberries. They would have fished the lake and snared the rabbits on Bright Purple Hill" (42). The exclusive garden would have been open to all. But even though the people were not allowed "without hindrance through the gates of the estate" (43) – which would have been as financially ruinous to the Pulvertafts as was the Quinton redistribution of land in *Fools of Fortune* and the Rolleston cancellation of rents in *The Silence in the Garden* – there will be ruin nonetheless. Fogarty has a prophetic dream in which he sees a Pulvertaft son shot in the hall of the house by descendants of the people who had been hungry: "The road that had been laid in charity was overgrown through neglect, and the gardens were as they had been at the time of old Hugh Pulvertaft, their beauty strangled as they returned to wildness" (44).

Since wilderness seems inevitable, Fogarty's solution is no solution, at least in the sense of making "everything, somehow and in the end, to be all right," as Willie had hoped in *Fools of Fortune* (31). But that may not be the point anyway. As these trees, these gardens, figure again and again in Trevor's fiction, they collectively suggest that, in the postlapsarian world that is his subject, every tree is related to every other tree and all of them to the original Tree of the Knowledge of Good and Evil. Although, as Marianne says in *Fools of Fortune*, "you can pass by anything and not know" (163), Trevor's fiction constantly points out the connections.

The Silence in the Garden combines a number of these important recurring references. The estate garden becomes desolate, and its fields are lost on an island that represents Ireland in miniature. Carriglas ("green rock") is an island (an "Emerald Isle") off the coast of County Cork, home of the Rollestons since the time of Cromwell, when they dispossessed another family, sending them to "the stony wilderness of Mayo" (41). The violence that marked the Rollestons' arrival continues (despite the beneficent Famine Rollestons), culminating in the cruelty of Villana and her brothers toward redheaded Corny Dowley, replaying in their children's games the persecution of Irish peasants by ascendant Anglo-Irish over the centuries. When this violence leads finally to murder, Villana realizing her culpability, breaks off her engagement, and condemns herself to a sterile, childless life. Her own childhood cruelty *"has turned around and damned a household"* (186); her own children cannot play in that same garden (187). As the family dies off, the garden will be silent and the estate of Carriglas will return to its clay (204).[21]

Trevor's incremental references are not straightforward symbols, with set meanings. They become clusters of associations, complicated and often made up of contradictory elements. Here too this association of the Rolleston garden with violence and evil does not assert that the settlers are evil and that restoring lands to their original owners provides a solution. (As Fogarty's litany of "visitors" in "The News from Ireland" indicates, there are no "original owners" [9].)[22] Indeed, at one point in *The Silence in the Garden* the Rollestons' estate involves four lost fields, like the four lost fields of Yeats's *Cathleen ni Houlihan* that stand for the four provinces of Ireland; the Rollestons have themselves been dispossessed of their estate, their "world," by their own generosity during the famine: "The four fields in question were now in the hands of a woman who was only distantly connected with the family which, three generations ago, the Rollestons had excused the payment of rent. Though it was not an issue . . . the woman in question came of fishing stock and could call on no inherited farming expertise. Deterioration of the land had set in over the years and was now continuing at a swifter pace than hitherto, the ill-drained acres . . . a tangle of brambles" (95f). Thus whoever the current holders of the land may be, on this island or its prototype they have neither special claim nor special expertise to validate their occupancy. The lawyer who has married Villana dreams of reclaiming the four lost fields, of restoring Carriglas to its former flourishing state: "He saw himself walking with his wife

through gardens in which there were gardeners again, by ripening
corn and healthy meadows" (96). But this golden world is an Eden
lost forever. The Rollestons will not allow lawsuits to recover the
land; nor will they continue their own hold on it by producing children to inherit it.

All these orchards, gardens, and fertile fields are places haunted
by their histories, places that ultimately come to seem both threatened and dangerous, like the garden at the Georgian country house
in Northern Ireland that in "Beyond the Pale" Dekko, Strafe, Cynthia, and Milly visit on holiday every year. Despite its sheltered figs
and long rhododendron drive, "quite majestic in its rather elegant
way," it has, nonetheless, "a garden running to the very edge of a
cliff" (691). An estate in decline may, as Fogarty suggests, become a
natural paradise, and cultivated gardens in any case have their fallow
periods. But as Trevor's incremental references grow, it gradually
becomes clear that the actual cliff over which a person can fall at the
edge of an island garden is the cliff of moral choice. The trees, the
gardens, and the fields persist in their own way through time, but
people affect that processs by their actions: as Fogarty explains to
the governess, who is in the process of trading moral awareness for
blind comfort, "The past would have withered away, miss. Instead of
which it is the future that's withering now" (44). Suddenly a word
like *wither* ceases to be a dead metaphor casually attached to "past"
and "future," and links time with every tree, every garden in Trevor's
work.

Names and Naming

Susan Scrimshaw, Larry Bird, Robin Popplestone, Anthony Trollope,
Carl Castle – real names in real life are often arrestingly mellifluous,
or slightly comic, or perilously similar to other words, or fraught with
possible meaning, symbolic or prophetic. But familiarity and actual
personality soften all that. Trevor's characters too sport memorable
names, often odd, even improbable configurations of sound, the
kinds of names that need to be spelled over the telephone
("'Jungbauer,' with a 'J' "). This very oddity gives the tingle of
verisimilitude to his characterizations – yet one more instance of
Trevor's precise rendering of the ordinary details of ordinary life.

But in fiction there is no real personality or actual familiarity to temper a name's effect; its comic and semantic potentials remain for the author to exploit. And Trevor does most interestingly exploit them, often using names as tags or little jokes, always aware of funny sounds and odd combinations. In *Miss Gomez and the Brethren* Mrs. Idle runs a "pleasure house" (189). *Elizabeth Alone* has a Mrs. Digg and a Mrs. Delve (though not in the same garden); a courting couple, Edward Tonsell and Carol Pidsley, whose names suggest their inconsequence (he the unnecessary tonsil, she his piddling companion); and a Mr. Rinsal, "in the bathroom showers business" (42). The surname of one of the major characters in the novel, Sylvie Clapper, hints at the venereal problems that have occasioned the hysterectomy for which she is hospitalized. In *Other People's Worlds* the charwoman, Mrs. Spanners, though intending to be helpful, is often a spanner in the works, as her employer suggests by commenting on both the oddity of the name and its suitability.[23] Sometimes names are obvious tags for characters who warrant only brief mention, such as the commodius Mrs. Commodium in *The Silence in the Garden*, who "squashed her neighbour into a corner of a pew" (139) during a tragicomic wedding. Sometimes they are authorial jokes that simply could not be passed by, such as the creation in The *Children of Dynmouth* of "a heavily-built girl called Grace Rumblebow" (30) who, with her orgies of doughnuts and beer, must have made up in rumble what she lacked in grace, or "Moult's Hardware and Pet Supplies" (9), with its beady-eyed birds no doubt molting in their cages. Sometimes characters make their own jokes, as when the unnamed narrator in *A Standard of Behaviour* asks his new girl-friend, Virginia, "Does your name still apply?" (45). Sometimes tag names attach to characters who are mentioned several times throughout a narrative, such as the voluble Miss Poraway in *The Children of Dynmouth*, or Swingler (the swindler), Nox (the noxious spoiler), and Mrs. Strap (the bossy charwoman) in *The Old Boys*.

Occasionally even an important character has what amounts to a tag name. Atlas Flynn, the brawny Irish demolition worker in *Miss Gomez and the Brethren*, is a titan whom neither London buildings nor Mrs. Tuke can resist. Though using a tag might suggest a substitute for character development, Trevor has in fact fleshed him out beautifully, sweat and all. In *Mrs. Eckdorf in O'Neill's Hotel* one of the major characters, as noted earlier in this chapter, is named Mrs.

Sinnott, an elderly woman whose deafness prevents her hearing evil, whose silence keeps her from speaking it, and whose retirement keeps her from seeing it. She does, of course, inevitably encounter evil, but she herself is like one who sins not, her saintlike character indicated by her name.

Not all tag names are immediately apparent in Trevor's work; some require recognition of perhaps obscure allusions, or knowledge of French or German, or a good grasp of the lives of the saints and the Bible. For example, the woman who runs a sexually liberated hippie ashram in *Other People's Worlds* is named Mrs. Tabor-Ellis, suggesting her own combination of that mountain on which, according to tradition, Jesus was transfigured (Mt. Tabor) and England's apostle of sexual freedom (Havelock Ellis). Mrs. Eckdorf's name may indicate that she is a liar by its combination of the sounds of "echt" (genuine, true, real, sincere) and "dorf" (as a card term, meaning "discard"); thus she is one who lies, who discards what is true, as indeed she actually does in various ways throughout *Mrs. Eckdorf in O'Neill's Hotel*.

Some of Trevor's tag names are used ironically. Verity was born of a marriage "riddled with . . . falsity" in "On the Zattere."[24] Prudence was born of Mrs. Tuke's imprudence with a lodger in *Miss Gomez and the Brethren*. *The Love Department*'s Lady Dolores Bourhardie, fat and 50, is not the smouldering Latin beauty Swinburne, Harold Pinter, and many a strip-joint marquee would associate with her first name.[25] In "The News from Ireland" George Arthur is christened for the two chief heroes of England, both powerful in battle (Saint George, dragon slayer, declared Protector of the Kingdom of England by Pope Benedict XIV in the Middle Ages, and King Arthur, whose court provided the legendary material of the founding of Britain). This George Arthur, however, will not follow a British military career, with its uncomfortable beds and bad water, but is persuaded to continue bravely in his father's footsteps as master of a grand estate in Ireland, where his own family is comfortable despite the famine outside.[26]

The association of certain names with particular saints is sometimes important in Trevor's work. There is a certain irony in Agnes being a prostitute in *Mrs. Eckdorf in O'Neill's Hotel*, since the virgin martyr Agnes is patroness of chastity; according to Butler's *Lives of the Saints* (which Trevor often describes his characters reading), the legend "alleges that she was unharmed in a brothel whither she was sent to break down her constancy to Christ, and put to death (by stabbing?) at a tender age."[27] Despite irony, the name is appropriate too, since in the novel Agnes emerges sufficiently unharmed from her trade to reform and go to work in a convent (197). There is also a touch of both irony and suitability in the fact that Alban Roche in *Miss Gomez and the Brethren* is named for an English saint, "the protomartyr of Britain," whose feast is celebrated "throughout England and Wales"[28] but not in Ireland, Roche's country of origin. Yet he, canny Irishman, triumphs over his English adversaries in London, England's own patron apparently on his side.

The connection between some of Trevor's characters and their patron saints can be problematic, or possibly so obscure as to be of no special consequence. Yet a reader is wise, when encountering an unusual name in Trevor's work, to check Butler's *Lives of the Saints* for whatever light it might shed. Villana in *The Silence in the Garden* is a case in point. In such later works as this names are less frequently comic but often have serious resonances. The Blessed Villana de' Botti was a fourteenth-century Florentine matron whose early piety had been abandoned for a life of "pleasure and dissipation" when she married, then was resumed again even more intensely after she saw her own gorgeously dressed form reflected in a mirror as a demon; thereafter she lived a life of prayer and great personal austerity, though continuing to fulfill "all her duties as a wife and as mistress of the house."[29] Her heroic penance and charity, as well as various marvels, made her honored as a saint from the day of her death. (In fact, her body is today still on view in Santa Maria Novella, where leaflets are available describing her life and cult.)[30] The Villana of *The Silence in the Garden* is no medieval saint, but her life does have an odd parallel. Her innocent childhood was interrupted by a period of wicked pleasure as she and her brothers and cousin persistently tormented another child, hunting him with a gun as if he were an animal. Then, as a young adult, Villana suddenly understands her own wickedness, realizes the evil she has done when she sees it mirrored in an act of violence that is intended to destroy her and her brothers but that in fact kills an innocent person instead. This realization, like a conversion experience, turns her to a life of penance, as she suddenly and unaccountably breaks off her engagement to the man she loves (her equally guilty cousin) and lives celibate; eventually she marries a man she does not love, with the stipulation that their life will be childless. Thus Villana, in the twentieth century, follows a path of self-denial, just as her medieval namesake did, in her own particular mode.

There are no indications in *The Silence in the Garden* that a holy Villana lived centuries before, to serve as model or inspiration for a contemporary one. But in *Fools of Fortune* the patron saint's relationship to her namesake is stressed as an important part of the novel. Marianne names her daughter Imelda, a significant choice for a Protestant in a Protestant household, living in the ruins of a big house surrounded by Catholics in County Cork in the early 1930s. Like Villana, Imelda is another fourteenth-century Italian "beata,"[31] from Bologna: "she is stated to have received her first holy communion miraculously, at the age of eleven, and to have died immediately after."[32] Blessed Imelda is prominent in Roman Catholic popular piety but not in the Church of Ireland, which in liturgy and devotions emphasizes its difference from the church of Rome. As the only Protestant student in the small local school run by nuns, Imelda experiences both kindness and, from one student, cruelty for her religious difference: "She didn't mind being different herself, not having a First Communion dress, nor rosary beads, not being able to walk in the Corpus Christi procession" (157), but she is fascinated by her Catholic patron saint, on whose day she was born and for whom, according to Catholic tradition, she was named. Complimented on her birthday by Mr. Lanigan – "And isn't Imelda a most beautiful name?" – she muses on details of the story, culminating in the experience of miraculous communion and simultaneous death (162); later, lingering in the reveries that will eventually claim her totally, she associates Imelda's story with the idyllic peace of a favorite poem ("The Lake Isle of Innisfree"): " '*I hear it in the deep heart's core,*' Imelda said aloud, lying down among the daisies on the river bank. She wondered what it had been like for the Blessed Imelda to experience the Sacred Host hovering above her while she knelt in prayer. She'd once asked Sister Rowan, who'd said that no ordinary mortal could know a thing like that. But it interested Imelda and she was curious" (169).

This Imelda is, however, no ordinary mortal herself. Curious not only about the experiences of Blessed Imelda but about those of her absent father as well, she begins to daydream about him, his childhood (as recounted thirdhand by Marianne), and about his act of vengeance. As she discovers details of the violent acts (both the Black and Tan murders at Kilneagh and Willie's eventual reprisal), they figure more and more prominently in her reveries. At first she focuses on her father's heroism, fueled by her mother's stories "of Ireland's fighting men, of the Earls of Tyrone and Tyrconnell who centuries ago had fled into exile, as the survivors of Ireland's lost battles had always fled." The nuns at the convent also speak of her father as a hero, never to be forgotten, like "somebody from a legend, Finn Mac Cool or the warrior Cuchulainn" (158). But the bloody details begin to predominate – "Was it Cuchulainn who had sent the headless bodies galloping to his enemy's camp in chariots?" (158) – until finally they swamp her completely. So vivid is her imagination that she identifies totally with her father's violent experience; she begins with fantasy and ends by reliving both the Kilneagh deaths and Willie's act of revenge: "She closed her eyes and in the room above the vegetable shop [where Willie stabbed Rudkin, nearly severing his head] blood spurted in a torrent, splashing on to the wallpaper that was torn and hung loosely down. The blood was sticky, running over the backs of her hands and splashing on to her hair. It soaked through her clothes, warm when it reached her skin" (174). Here Imelda has become Willie, experiencing the murder in much more specific detail than the newspaper reported or anyone could have told her – except Willie, whom she has never seen or spoken to. This violent fantasy merges with what she knows of the Kilneagh murders: "The screaming of the children began, and the torment of the flames on their flesh. The dogs were laid out dead in the yard, and the body of the man in the teddy-bear dressing-gown lay smouldering on the stairs. The blood kept running on her hands, and was tacky in her hair" (174f). Such excruciating reliving of two horrible events (events in which her idealized father is not entirely innocent, because though he is first victim, he is later agent), such intolerable pain drives Imelda whimpering into a corner, into perpetual silence, into madness.

She has learned how to get there from her patron saint and in the process becomes a kind of saint herself. Blessed Imelda had so wanted communion (so the story goes) that she was miraculously visited by the host, and in that communion she died, not as punishment but as reward, and was taken immediately to Heaven to be united forever with the one desired. This Imelda too has desired something ardently: to be with her father, not only dreaming about his life but also imagining meeting him herself, his returning especially to her. These dreams reach a climax in her complete union with him in his most searing experiences, and they constitute a kind of death for her. She passes through that climax into another world, a heaven where there is no violence, no ugliness, no ruin, where Willie's childhood home is rebuilt. Though there is a touch of cynicism in Willie's earlier reflection that his daughter is insane and that "in Ireland it happens sometimes that the insane are taken to be saints of a kind" (184), when he finally returns 10 years later and is living with her, he is grateful for her "quiet world," her shroud of happiness. He and Marianne "are aware that there is a miracle in this end, as remarkable as the Host which hung above the head of the child in Bologna" (192). By so emphasizing at the end of the novel this Imelda's connection with Blessed Imelda, Trevor shows that names not only can "tag" a person in some superficial way but also can serve as indexes of identity, as sources of personal power.

A negative example of this same phenomenon is found in Francis's use of names in *Other People's Worlds*. As a psychopath Francis has no real feeling or understanding of what other people experience and no real sense of his own identity either. He is an actor, both professionally and at the deepest level of his personality, always on show: "How he appeared to other people when he entered their different worlds was a constant concern" (39). His name is simply part of his stage makeup: "He hadn't changed his name for the Massmith sisters or for the doctor and his wife, but for the Kilvert-Dunnes it had seemed more suitable to be Adrian Staye, and for other couples to be Edward Osborne. He didn't know why he enjoyed having a different name for a while" (40). His name, like his "self," is entirely flexible because it is meaningless. His easy, arbitrary changing of his name is a sign that there is no stable identity within. That names *do* matter is indicated elsewhere in the novel, at a trivial level, by dogs' names: "Baloney" may seem strange to Mrs. Anstey, but it is nonetheless a name that is consistently used and recognized, acknowledged by the dog, its owner, and everyone else (26); that such naming, however fanciful, is important Julia indicates by her own inability to name the dog Francis has had sent to her: to

name it would be to give it a permanent place in her life, to accord it
an identity connected with herself.

The importance of names and naming is suggested more seriously in *The Silence in the Garden*. In the long history of the
Rolleston family in Ireland, since the time of the seventeenth-century
plantations, there is one generation in the nineteenth century
referred to as "the Famine Rollestons" because they "were widely
renowned for their compassion" (127). This epithet memorializes
their goodness, preserving forever their identity distinct from the
earlier Rollestons who arrived after Oliver Cromwell, *"with slaughter in their wake"* (188). Although by providing work and waiving
rents and tithes the Famine Rollestons ruined the family fortunes for
their own future generations, they have acquired in exchange a tag
name that both describes and honors them throughout subsequent
history.

Naming is indeed one of the ways history endorses events. The
Famine Rollestons are approved by the epithet given them. But the
twentieth-century family is denied approval when the bridge con-
necting their island to the mainland is named for Corny Dowley, the
slain IRA soldier whom Villana and her brothers hunted as a child.
They are shocked by the choice: "The Rollestons were the island
family; they had been humane at the time of the potato blight; they
had given generously, seeking no reward. Words on the bridge might
have remembered that, through a memorial to one of them" (74).
But Corny Dowley too came from that island, and it is his exploits as
national hero that the community chooses to commemorate. The
naming is a political statement (by the community, not by the novel),
permanently acknowledging Dowley's identity, encouraging his
"cult."

The power inherent in a name and in the act of naming, an
almost biblical use of name as efficacious power, is found in *Miss
Gomez and the Brethren*, where the titular character's name is of
utmost importance to herself and to the subject of the novel. As a difficult child in a Jamaican orphanage, she responds to the question of
what she would like to be by stating "that she'd be called Miss
Gomez when she left and that in her whole life she wouldn't permit
herself to be called anything else" (12). This equation of "being" and
"word," self and name, is not the careless non sequitur of a disturbed child but a firm metaphysical principle for Miss Gomez (and

an operative principle for the novel itself). She succeeds in making it govern her entire world: never once does the narrating voice disclose any other name; in the opening pages, before she has formally declared herself "Miss Gomez," she is referred to only as "the child" and addressed by orphanage personnel simply as "my dear." She does not permit herself in the whole course of the novel to be called anything else, either by the novelist or by a fellow character: what she would like to be, what she becomes, what she is, is "Miss Gomez."

The absence of a first name, a Christian name, is significant, because what she lacks is personal identity. She is part of a group, but she has no sense of herself as an individual in that group: "She loved the sound of Gomez, she said, because it had been her parents' name. Miss Arbuthnot hadn't said anything, believing at the time that Gomez had probably been a name they'd given her at the orphanage, knowing no other, as often was the case. But as Matron had just reminded her, this wasn't so: the child was right about her name" (12). This comment too is significant: the child is "right about her name," not simply that it is Gomez (rather than Sanchez or Gouveia) but that her assertion of identity through a name, a word, is the most accurate form of her existence. She goes forth as a word, and she has power as a word. But, of course, she is a person (in her fictive world), and she is a character (in her novel).

By employing a formal title, using a group name rather than an individual one, she herself makes explicit her sense of limitation, her fragmentary state. And Trevor, emphasizing this peculiarity of name and self, indicates the extent to which Miss Gomez is an "event," a "Gomez phenomenon," not a person, for herself and for all the people she encounters. As an event, as the instrument of a mission, she is oddly, paradoxically efficacious, blundering through her "good works" but seeming nonetheless to hold at bay that human cruelty which permeates Trevor's novels. As member of the Church of the Brethren she believes her prayers (and theirs) have alleviated the suffering she observes all around her in London, and there is no indication in the novel that she is wrong in her belief, even when she loses her faith (after all, Alban Roche does *not* murder Prudence Tuke, and Miss Gomez directly prevents Mr. Batt from committing suicide [225]).

Miss Gomez has no individual name and thus no personal identity, and neither do members of her church. Not only is the term *brethren* vague, despite its positive suggestions of fraternity and holiness, but the brethren themselves turn out to be non-existent, a sham religious group, a fantasy flock with an absent shepherd. The *name* of a church, the Church of the Way, has stood in for an actual congregation, yet, though hollow, that name has been effective. This name, this word, has fleshed itself in Miss Gomez, and she in turn, though a damaged person, has swept through London as a mighty power, making all sorts of comic errors, yet ultimately seeming to have offset disaster.

Whether mere tags or more profound designators of identity and power, characters' names in Trevor's work serve as yet another set of signposts in his cosmography, in the web of connections that makes Mrs. Idle an allegorically and immorally suitable madam for a house of pleasure and Blessed Imelda an appropriate patroness (across time and space) for the Imelda of Kilneagh.

Place-names do not usually have the same force as personal ones in Trevor's fiction. When names of geographic places or places of business are noteworthy, it is usually for their comic effect. Trevor is particularly adept at catching the amusing combinations and clichés in a typical streetfront: pathetically fallacious restaurants ("The Gay Tureen") and pseudoethnic pubs ("The Cruskeen Bawn Lounge"); alliterative establishments ("The Rhumba Rendezvous") and cultural contradictions ("Mecca Dancing"); genteel euphemisms ("Sundown Home"); playful misspellings ("Phyl's Phries"); cute admissions ("Camp Runamuck"); and Trollopian ironies ("the offices of Warboys, Smith and Toogood, Solicitors and Commissioners for Oaths"). Sometimes an ordinary enough name is made slightly comic by being inflated with an extra word: Great Western Royal Hotel and Church of the Holy Assumption are mocked by their superfluous "Royal" and "Holy" (just as "jumbo" added to "vin rosé" devalues it, or, for that matter, "British" modifying "sherry").

There are, however, a few place-names of real significance in Trevor's fiction. The Sansepolcro in which Willie of *Fools of Fortune* spends the last years of his exile is not merely a town in Italy but an indicator of the kind of life he is leading: he is in a sepulcher, dead to the normal life he would have led as husband, father, and landowner at Kilneagh (his "sepulcher" matches Imelda's "shroud," both father and daughter in a sense buried in their respective exile and madness).[33] The name Kilneagh "might possibly mean the place of the church, perhaps even a foundation of St Fiach"[34] – that is, the home of a renowned Irish hermit who spent his life in exile in France[35] (just as Willie has been a renowned Irish hero living a hermit's life abroad).

The name Carriglas in *The Silence in the Garden* is also significant. The first extended conversation Sarah has with the Rollestons, in whose house she is both cousin and governess, concerns *"places and their naming."*[36] In her diary, which makes up a large portion of the novel, she writes, *"Carriglas meant green rock, which was what the island in certain lights resembled when seen from the mainland. A deceptive image, Colonel Rolleston pointed out, for in fact the island was fertile"* (15). This fertile green island is Ireland in miniature, a little Emerald Isle in which the whole history of Ireland is played out, from ancient standing stones to holy well, with four lost fields, a decaying estate, a silent garden.

This geography of human relationships, these names that mark the moral and personal terrain, the mass of literary and rhetorical figures by which Trevor's elaborate system of correspondences is achieved – all contribute finally to the creation of a sense of linked good and linked evil so present that it envelops everything else in the narrative. In its complexity it could be considered the real subject of all Trevor's work.

Chapter Seven

Bildungsromane and Politics

Genre too is made to serve Trevor's system of correspondences. Trevor alters the classic *Bildungsroman* to make it also a political novel, showing how the protagonist's process of maturation in both *Fools of Fortune* and *Nights at the Alexandra* is affected by political events that shift his quest away from the traditional goal of social integration and toward discovery of and reconciliation with his deepest self. Thus the genre devoted to adolescent development, the *Bildungsroman*, is given an interesting new twist: the narrator or central character, whatever his odyssey, is really in search of himself; what he learns throughout his lifetime is really something concerning himself; his reconciliation at the end is not with the society that has failed him but with himself. By saying something important about the society and polity in which, or perhaps against which, the individual develops, such novels of development are also in effect political novels.

A number of recent Irish novels are written in this mode. William Trevor, John Banville, and Brian Moore have all written important novels where the central character's final state involves separation from his group and where the process of education and maturation involves return to something deep within himself: the protagonist is shown to be a wise child whose journey through life entails unavoidable progress out – into "the world" – and then deliberate return to his own original, isolated self. The particular kind of education and initiation found in Banville's *Birchwood* (1973) and its companion novel *Mefisto* (1986), Trevor's *Fools of Fortune* (1983) and *Nights at the Alexandra* (1987), and Moore's *The Mangan Inheritance* (1979) in various ways results in a discovery and affirmation of self that, in context, constitutes a political statement.

While it is true that almost all fiction deals with development of some kind (modifications of the central character's attitudes and values through the process of experience), such development does not necessarily have to do with maturation, education, apprenticeship, initiation in "life." (Banville's narrator in *The Book of Evidence* does not "mature"; neither do any of Trevor's old boys or Moore's Judith Hearne, despite profound changes in all their lives.) The classic *Bildungsroman*, however, according to standard definition, "recounts the youth and young adulthood of a sensitive protagonist who is attempting to learn the nature of the world, discover its meaning and pattern, and acquire a philosophy of life and 'the art of living.' "[1] Another description of the genre in its typical form asserts that the *Bildungsroman* shows "the formation of a character up to the moment when he ceases to be self-centered and becomes society-centered, thus beginning to shape his true self."[2] Such novels, especially in their English-language versions, tend to follow a formula: the young man leaves his home, leaves his parents and beloved, goes out into a new, alien world, and through this process of rejection and exile begins to discover what he must do, what he values, and who he is, typically in order that he may return to his society and assume a mature role in it.[3] Replete with rejections though the novel may be (e.g., Stephen Dedalus leaves family, faith, and nation), the protagonist asserts his adulthood by moving toward a new society (for Stephen, Europe and its vitality; for Paul Morrell, in *Sons and Lovers*, the city and its promising lights). Many recent Irish novels, however, describe a social and political situation that the child's newfound wisdom teaches him to avoid: alienation, not integration, is the mark of his hard-won maturity.

In Trevor's *Fools of Fortune* the shadow of the old *Bildungsroman* formula is clearly apparent and significantly altered. The young man does not leave his world; it leaves him. The "art of living" that he learns is the art of flight. The self and home he eventually regains, and chooses, are a ruin. Willie Quinton's early childhood is spent in the idyllic world of Kilneagh, a garden of innocence which he is loath to leave for formal education; he dreads being sent away to school, which is in effect to follow in his father's footsteps. In answer to arguments for his going – "Kilneagh isn't the world, you know"[4] – he counters, "But I'll live in Kilneagh when I'm grown up. I'll always be here." Although he prefers to stay with his mother, his sisters, and the defrocked priest (who teaches him Latin, history, and about the evils of violence), worldly "education" comes to him in the form of political terrorism: the killing of his family and the destruction of his beloved house by Black and Tans during the Anglo-Irish War. In one night of fire and bloodshed everything Willie most values is destroyed. Despite attempts to lead a normal life, go to school in a city, live with and care for his surviving (but emotionally destroyed) mother, he finds at the time of her suicide that he must kill the soldier who killed his family. And so he retaliates with a violence that equals the violence perpetrated ("*The head was partially hacked from the neck, the body stabbed in seventeen places*" reads the emotionless newspaper account of Willie's deed [172]). As a consequence of this murder Willie lives in exile, on the run, abandoning the unmarried cousin he loves and their baby. Only in old age are Willie and Marianne reunited, when life is virtually over and all that is left is memory of childhood and the task of caring for a daughter who, through madness (precipitated by the earlier violence), is fixed in a state of perpetual childhood in the orchard-garden where Willie originated.

Thus the plot of *Fools of Fortune* twists the conventional *Bildungsroman* away from travel as a way of finding self and values, to travel as exile, its goal being to preserve a self and values that have been endangered. Home has been ripped away, destroyed; in effect "home" has left the boy (rather than vice versa): thus he goes out into the world not in search of some gain but in flight from loss. In a an ironic twist to the *Bildungsroman* formula Trevor's protagonist does not return as an adult to his native country ready to take his place in society but instead gains his place of honor in that country by the very act that exiles him from it: his compatriots consider him a hero for his deed of reprisal, but as an outlaw he is forced to live abroad, in strange places like Sansepolcro. (The name of the town is significant, because Willie must live like one who is dead: the sepulcher may be a holy one, sainted, because he *is* a hero, but it is a grave nonetheless.)

Only when life is over, his deed forgotten, can Willie, in his seventies, reach out to what he might have had and been by returning to the place of his childhood. It is significant that he did not arrange for his cousin Marianne and their child, Imelda, to join him abroad; instead, they live together, finally, 50 years later, in the ruins of the burned house, with the scars of that early violence around them and with the paradox of the holy sepulcher (losing one's life in order to have it) literally personified in Imelda. She is a holy fool, a saint, able perhaps to cure others but herself dwelling in a kind of death: "Her happiness is like a shroud miraculously about her," the narrative states, and although Willie feels grateful to be able to spend his old age in his "daughter's quiet world, in which there is no ugliness" (192), that peace which he so valued as a child is available to him now only through her madness. The garden estate where as a child he thought he would always live and which as a young adult he desired to rebuild with Marianne (until his act of reprisal sent him into exile), has been restored in Imelda's fantasies; for her "in the scarlet drawing-room wood blazes in the fireplace. . . . [L]ights dimly gleam, and carved on the marble of the mantlepiece the clustered leaves are as delicate as the flicker of the flames" (192). These are Willie's cherished childhood observations alive in Imelda who has never seen that drawing room or heard Willie's description (her information is all thirdhand, through Marianne). This is essentially a false world now, a memory at best, an illusion, and yet Willie finds "there is a miracle in this end" (192). The self he asserts at the end of his life is one rooted in his earliest loves and memories, impervious to subsequent experience, his own isolated illusory dream of peace rather than society's actual violence.

In *Birchwood* Gabriel Godkin too has been reared on a grand country estate, but less idyllically than Willie, and he too has been thrust by violence out into "the world," a world of mirrors, in which he searches for what he thinks is his missing sister, only to discover a twin brother who incarnates the malignancy Gabriel fears to find in his home, in the outer world, and in himself. By traveling with the circus, by passing through a series of adventures – at once private and public, fantasy and history – he emerges finally at the place where he began, having learned that he does not have to be like his counterparts in society, that he is not his father, that he can live differently, that he can be himself, and that his initial impulses – not the models set for him by his family or by history – were the right ones.

In both these novels, Trevor's and Banville's, the boy finds his father to be remote and different from himself in some way, and the boy's discovery of self involves his realization that he does not have to be like his father. Although Willie "was fonder of [his father] than of anyone else" (43), his act of reprisal differentiates him from the "lazy-looking man in tweeds . . . very much the Irish seigneur" who "disliked noise or voices raised" (14); his gentle passivity did not prevent Mr. Quinton from supporting Michael Collins morally and financially, but that support did not extend to allowing Collins to drill troops on his land: like Father Kilgarriff, Willie's father deplored and avoided violence. Willie, by making violence and its permanent consequences the pivotal point of his life, has followed a different path.

In the final chapter of *Birchwood* Gabriel, who wryly speculates on himself as a "celestial messenger of hope,"[5] wants to make an announcement. Despite life-long taciturnity, his sense of discomfort with words, his repeated insistence that he does not "speak the language of this wild country" (170), despite all his various rejections of speech, he finally feels impelled to utter something about himself. This is Gabriel's important annunciation, by which he engenders himself: *"Look, I am not my father, I am something different"* (170). From this realization comes an important resolve: "I shall stay here [at Birchwood], alone, and live a life different from any the house has ever known. Yes" (170). Though not at home in the world outside or with the people who inhabit it, he now is reconciled to himself; he has made a vast pilgrimage through that world and has returned, and not to doomed repetition of his family's ways, not to duplication of his father's character – all of that belongs to death, and he says he has had enough of death. Like Willie, he is an old man now, with not much life left, but at last he embraces the strangeness he felt in himself as a child: it is not himself who will be integrated with society but rather society (represented by that house and its history) that will adjust itself to him – as he affirms with an emphatic "Yes" his right to live a life different from any the house has ever known. The ending of the novel is basically positive in tone: Gabriel, despite his age and oddity, really does have a message of hope.

Mefisto is *Birchwood* turned inside out. The number of parallels between the two novels is extraordinary: the central character is a young boy (with the same first name, Gabriel), and there is a lost estate, a great house and garden in decay, a significant explosion, a difficult father, violence against young women, and, most important, a double. But here the double is not a lost twin but a haunting figure, a bad angel ironically named Felix – happiness – whose malevolence and manipulation lead this Gabriel through an education in cynicism and "disillusionment." The horrible burning of Gabriel's body (which occurs midway in the novel) is a physical emblem for this disillusionment, leaving him – in a most telling allusion – a Lazarus who has to remake himself.[6] At the end of the novel, having refused to accompany Felix any farther (though he knows that haunting demon will return), Gabriel speculates about what he wants to be: "Naked. Flayed. A howling babe, waving furious fists. I don't know" (234). He has indeed been made naked and flayed by his burns. And now, like the Gabriel in *Birchwood*, he resolves to lead a different kind of life, a better one; the route to this new life involves return to origins, to childhood: "I have gone back to the very start, to the simplest things" (234), he says of his work in mathematics, but the remark applies as well to his resolve for a new mode of life. Whether this new mode will be successful or actually better is not an issue either *Birchwood* or *Mefisto* explores (though a case could be made that the signs are positive in *Birchwood* and negative in *Mefisto*). In both novels, however, the boy-become-old-man returns to his starting point, asserting himself and rejecting the society through which he has traveled.

What broadens these three accounts of a boy's individual development in Ireland beyond the merely personal and makes the novels also seem political are the many explicit references to national issues (such as the potato famine and the wars for independence) that figure significantly in the plot. Additionally, other, more subtle suggestions of political import are woven tightly into the fabric of the novel. Throughout *Fools of Fortune*, for example, Trevor frequently counterpoints love and war. To cite only one of many instances, Willie as narrator reminisces about three "love stories" (as he calls them) that fascinated him as a child (24-27), then immediately shifts to thoughts about Michael Collins, De Valera, an incident in 1797, Daniel O'Connell's pacific spirit, and World War I (28-32): that both subjects are profoundly related in Willie's mind is indicated not only by their juxtaposition but also by the fact that he uses the same sentiment – "I wanted everything, somehow and in the end, to be all right" (31; cf. 21) – to refer both to "this unsettling love" (31) and to "war and revolution" (21). Trevor never explicitly points out the connection between love and war in *Fools of Fortune*, but by saturating his narrative with references to various battles, raids, rebellions, retaliations, and formal wars throughout Irish history and by shaping his plot around some of these acts of violence, he makes the story of Kilneagh more than a chronicle of Willie and Marianne's frustrated love: this is not merely the story of a family; it is a story about Ireland itself, people and polity.[7]

Birchwood too is about more than just a family and an estate. At the personal level it is full of references to things Gabriel does not understand, mysteries of adult life from which he as a boy felt excluded: many of them have to do with sex, many with his family, and many with language. These three areas of mystery are significantly related: his personal experience of sex is understood in the larger context of his parents' experience of sex, and that complicated incestuous tangle in turn becomes a metaphor for the political and social entanglement of Irish and Anglo-Irish in Ireland. When in the first few pages of the novel the narrator (the old man Gabriel) uses the surprise of his first boyish exploration of a vagina to illustrate the difference between the way things are and the way he expected them to be, and then suddenly remarks, "That was how it was, coming home, always the unexpected" (5), the reader realizes that this is not a non sequitur but that "sex" and "home" are related in Gabriel's mind. When in these same opening pages he refers to a language he does not understand, it is clear that more is meant than Irish – there is an important link between Irish as an actual language and the metaphoric languages of "sex" and "family," which he also does not understand. By the time the reader gets to the aged Gabriel's final reference to language in the last few pages of the novel, these connections between public and private are unmistakable. The whole paragraph announcing Gabriel's new life illustrates this point by its sweep through time, space, weather, silence, history, and death, ending in an assertion of new life:

> The weather held for weeks, limpid and bright, wind all day, sun and rain and a luminous lilac glow above the trees, then the evenings, night and stars. At first the silence troubled me, until I realised that it was not really silence. A band of old women came one day and took away the bodies of the dead men down in the field. I watched from my window, fascinated. I wanted to go and help them, to say, *Look, I am not my father, I am something different*, but they would have run away from me, horrified. The poppies languished. I worked on the house, cleared out the attic, boarded up the windows, smashed during the siege, tended the flowerbeds, I do not know why. The summerhouse was invaded by pigeons, starlings, a hive of bees. I let them stay there. They were alive, and I had enough of death. Perhaps I

shall leave here. Where would I go? Is that why they all fought so hard for Birchwood, because there was nowhere else for them to be? Outside is destruction and decay. I do not speak the language of this wild country. I shall stay here, alone, and live a life different from any the house has ever known. Yes. (170)

In the previous paragraph Gabriel had lamented, "All that blood! That slaughter! And for what?" indicating that conflict among groups is futile, whether those groups be in society as a whole or within his immediate family. Indeed he does not speak the language of that wild country, where there is famine, rape, and murder; nor does he understand the language of his family, where there is exploitation, cruelty, and incest. Suddenly Birchwood seems an emblem for all Ireland and the incestuous household a type of the Irish themselves, Anglo and Norman and Celt, dwelling and breeding uneasily together, squabbling over the land. There is nowhere else for this people to go; the only hope is in living a life different from any their country has ever known. Gabriel's individual experience, his awareness of the crimes and cruelties of his father, and his resolve not to repeat them imply political as well as personal meaning.

The fathers in these novels, though quite different from each other, represent in their various ways the flaws that mar their societies, the defects and errors that the sons must avoid. Willie's father, in *Fools of Fortune*, is a good man but ineffectual; Gabriel Godkin's father, in *Birchwood*, is wicked and ineffectual; Gabriel Swan's father, in *Mefisto*, is boring and ineffectual. In all these cases the inability of the father to protect and foster his family (which is society in miniature) makes integration with society at large impossible for the son. The world over which these men preside is flawed, and although no specific suggestion is made of what the fathers might have done to mend that world, their very accommodation to its ways makes their sons exiles and solitaries.

Women in these novels suggest the possibility of escape from solitariness, but a possibility that is ultimately frustrated. In *Fools of Fortune* Willie's courageous mother is driven to her death; his courageous cousin, Marianne, shares his living death; and their daughter, Imelda, dwells in perpetual childhood, the only refuge from an impossible present in an impossible society. In *Birchwood* various women are destroyed by sexual mistreatment, and the ideal woman, that sister-twin Gabriel seeks, turns out to be nonexistent.

The darkest statement of all is found in *Mefisto*, where Gabriel's "education" in cynicism begins with Felix showing him that Sophie is not the pure and girlish spirit Gabriel thinks she is, that what he thinks is "wisdom" (Sophia) is false. Thus Gabriel is thrown back on the purity of mathematics and on the solitariness of his own mind, and goes back to "the beginning" (of which his childhood integrity is an emblem) in order to begin his life again. Whatever wisdom he is to have is within, not "out there." Whether he will indeed find a new and better way to live is not at all clear, however, and the overall impression of this novel is of a dark future in a basically cruel and destructive society.

Banville and Trevor are not original in shifting the conclusion of their hero's quest away from social integration and toward discovery of and reconciliation with the self. In fact, this latter element is present in varying degrees in most English-language *Bildungsromane* of the twentieth century. But unlike many of those novels, Trevor's and Banville's fiction sets the hero's development against a backdrop of significant political turmoil and significant resultant social change. Gabriel's odyssey from Birchwood takes him out into the actual world of the potato famine and the Molly Maguires. The other Gabriel's foray is into the next century's blight of drugs and unemployment. Willie's experience is set in the violent period of the Black and Tans. To appreciate what a different light such specific political and social facts cast on the account of a young man's development, it is only necessary to consider that other classic Irish *Bildungsroman*, *A Portrait of the Artist as a Young Man*. Stephen Dedalus left family, church, and nation because his soul's quest for artistic identity demanded it. Yet despite political references in the novel, there is no suggestion that had Parnell survived and continued to lead, that event would have made any difference in Stephen's world or to Stephen's life as an artist. Nor does *Portrait* show us the consequences of Stephen's quest, only the soaring hopefulness of its beginning. In whatever way a given reader might choose to use *Portrait* for political purposes, the novel itself cannot be considered anything but what its title asserts: a very individual portrait of a very special kind of person, presented in a very limited time frame. But both Trevor and Banville take their young men into old age and indict society by showing how those young men have been driven back into themselves because their fathers' world is ruinous: "All that blood! That slaughter! And for what?"[8] Family, country, beloved – all these have failed; the young man finds he has only himself. And as an old man recounting his story, he remains essentially solitary: Willie, focused on solitary Imelda, chooses not to rebuild his ruined house, and Gabriel, living alone, chooses not to learn the language of that wild country.

Two other novels provide useful contrast to these, showing how even different modulations of the *Bildungsroman* form can also function as political statement. Though slight, Trevor's *Nights at the Alexandra* (1987) brings together many elements from his other novels and stories (schooldays, movie houses, wartime, celibacy, provincial Ireland, lifelong devotion, gardens of happiness, and the phenomenon of storytelling itself); like *A Standard of Behaviour*, *The Love Department*, *Fools of Fortune*, and the later *The Silence in the Garden*, *Nights at the Alexandra* is in the *Bildungsroman* tradition, varying that form (as do the latter two novels) by focusing on youthful development from the perspective of old age. The story line is simple enough: announcing in three brief sentences his age (58) and his provincial, childless, unmarried state, the narrator, Harry, provides an account of his youthful meeting with a foreign couple who have come to live in Ireland during World War II; the influence Frau Messinger has on his adolescent emotional and cultural development; his early fantasy of becoming a servant in her house, keeping "the flower-beds tidy and the grass cut on the lawns"[9]; and his dedication to her memory as custodian of the Messingers' now-abandoned estate and as proprietor of the monument Herr Messinger built and named for her, the Alexandra cinema. Harry's family ("a Protestant family of the servant class which had come up in the world" [11] by acquiring a timber yard) consider that he has foolishly wasted his life running a now-defunct movie house; they pity him because he is "solitary and withdrawn," has not "taken [his] place," and is "left in the end with nothing" (80). Yet for the narrator "memory is enough" (80). The elegiac note sounding throughout this novella is particularly marked at the end by various references to loneliness and the narrator's own designation of himself as "the ghost of an interlude" (80). Even so, the narrative is propelled by more than nostalgia.

Nights at the Alexandra is as full of violence as are *Fools of Fortune* and *The Silence in the Garden*, but its events are not so sensational. Quiet violation of spirit is Trevor's particular forte, as in the celebrated short story "The Ballroom of Romance" and the recent "Kathleen's Field" (*Family Sins and Other Stories* [1990]). Here too a young woman is sacrificed to family needs: Harry's sister Annie resents not having been sent away to grammar school like her brothers, bound instead to dull employment in the small-town family business when she would rather be in Dublin (13). As a minor character in a short novel Annie does not get much attention, but at each appearance her discontent is indicated. At the end of the novel, however, her married state is flaunted as a triumph over her celibate brother: "For all my good fortune in being sent away to school, and my escape from the timberyard, she would outdo me in the end. She was outdoing me already, her manner implied, standing close to young Phelan" (74). Though apparently agreeing with this assessment, the narrator does not avert to Annie's marriage as a model of happiness. It is clear from her bondage to her family, the limitations of her experience, and the small number of eligible suitors in her provincial town that she has simply accommodated herself to the patterns of her group and not followed whatever dreams she might have had of other options. She has been subject to and has cooperated with that most prevalent form of quiet violence: conformity to social expectations. (The most dreadful example in the novel of such conformity is the seasoned marriage of her own parents, her father a thick, unhearing, opinionated man – head of the house – and her mother, hands red and rough from washing – the selfless woman – both parents distorted by a "trapped existence" (50).

The role of the Messingers in Harry's life is to show him the possiblity of a truly happy marriage. Ironically, they are both associated with modes of physical and emotional violence much more obvious than the forces of conformity in Harry's world: Frau Messinger and her mother were poor and beholden when Alexandra was a child, and moved ignominiously from relative to relative; Herr Messinger is in flight from Nazi Germany because he eschews the violence of that regime (even though some of his sons serve Hitler). Their marriage is actually occasioned by another form of violence, the assault of an illness – probably tuberculosis – that requires Alexandra to refuse the young man she loves, leaving her free later to marry the much older Herr Messinger. Although compromise has played its role in this marriage, it is compromise in which the two principals (unlike

Annie) triumph over circumstances. As Herr Messinger explains to Harry while his wife lies dying, "An old man marries for the time that is left, Harry. Both of us seemed not to have much time" (66). Frau Messinger's own assurance, "Harry, I have the happiest marriage in the world! Please, when you think of me, remember that" (9), confirms their triumph over the violent forces of social pressure, physical illness, and even war. Although the narrator states he has no answer to his family's accusation that he has wasted his life, his concluding memory of the Messinger marriage with its assurance that "there is happiness in spite of death and war" (80) seems to vindicate his choice.

But as always with Trevor's work, the "simple" endings are not so simple as they at first appear. Harry has not given in to pressures to conform (he does not return the tie pin Frau Messinger gave him for Christmas, disregarding his mother's hysterical insistence; he does not, like Annie, work in the family business and routinely marry). But neither has he shaped the world to fit his own dreams, as did Frau and Herr Messinger despite dreadful obstacles. However much he admires the spectacle of their happy marriage, their assertion of devotion, gratitude, and happiness in the face of war and death, he himself remains celibate.

Spectacle is his choice. First, the manifestation of the Messingers' own life as seen directly as well as heard in the stories Frau Messinger recounts. Second, the cinema, with its "sophisticated dreams," "heroes," and "sagas of great families" (74) – wonders so strong that they forestall Harry's brothers' sniggers, so potent as to silence even his father, soften "the tetchiness of the Reverend Wauchope," lift Mrs. Wauchope's sour disposition, and dissolve "the complicated shame" of Mr. Conron (74). This cinema, built at Frau Messinger's request because she too loved and approved the luxury and romance of the place, is a refuge from limitation and conformity, a miracle of escape – temporary for the townfolk and permanent for the narrator, who devotes his life to running it. But the spectacle that most occupies Harry is the movie he plays in his mind, the visual and auditory memories of Frau and Herr Messinger, who have been messengers from another world, providing him with an opportunity to escape his parents' world and supplying him with a vicarious one within himself.

Harry's vindication is and is not satisfying as a conclusion to the novel. In adolescence the "bigger world" offered him war (which was what the Messingers sought to escape by coming to neutral Ireland); the "little world" of his provincial town and family offered him narrowness and boredom (which the Messingers have avoided by cherishing their own stories and building their own cinema, being in but not part of the town). Neither choice of war or boredom is attractive, and so Harry opts for spectacle, imagination, vicarious pleasures, memory. Like Mrs. Eckdorf's faith in images, Septimus Tuam's ability to generate fantasies in others, and Mrs. Tuke's devotion to romantic novels, Harry's immersion in cinema and memory is problematic: is illusion worthwhile enough, authentic enough to base a life on? When the choices are war or boredom, perhaps the answer is yes.

Political elements in *Nights at the Alexandra* are muted but important. Frau Messinger is an Englishwoman; her husband is German. During World War II neither country would have afforded them congenial residence. What their own lives exhibit is the fact that, like Gabriel Godkin, people need not be like their "fathers"; they can repudiate both the silliness and the tragedy of war, as Frau Messinger explains to Harry:

> She would have been arrested and sent to an internment camp in Germany, as Herr Messinger would have been in England. Every indignity that could be devised would have been visited on them. And the one remaining free would have been reviled for marrying the other.
>
> "I am ashamed of my country when I think of that, Harry. As my husband is of his. That the innocent should be ill-treated, even allowed to die, in the glorious name of war: what kind of world have we made for ourselves?" (23)

Against the "we" of nations with its insane world of internment camps, Frau and Herr Messinger have made another world for themselves, reclaiming a derelict garden at their sanctuary-estate in Ireland (Frau Messinger boasts to Harry, "I knew nothing about a garden when first we came to Cloverhill. . . . He rescued it for me, you know" [63], and Trevor follows with a detailed paragraph about weeds and flowers). At 15 Harry learns from the Messingers that it is possible to repudiate both the "we" of nations and the "we" of his immediate society and make a world for himself, by himself, in which the spectacle of happiness first seen in adolescence can be preserved throughout a lifetime. Like Imelda, Harry in puberty chooses images of happiness, and, like Willie, Harry as an old man endorses that choice.

Trevor's fellow Irish-expatriate author Brian Moore in *The Mangan Inheritance* presents a somewhat different set of illusions: the Irish immigrant's descendant's notion that he can find his true self by returning to an idealized place of origin, not his own personal point of origin but that of his forefathers. This novel is, of course, not strictly a *Bildungsroman*, since its central character is 36 at the time of the main action, but its quest is similar. The protagonist leaves his country, his family, and what is left to him of his beloved and goes out into the world seeking his real identity, his real "face" and "true vocation."[10] Perhaps such a task taken up in middle age is a late twentieth-century equivalent of the adolescent crisis that has traditionally been the subject of the *Bildungsroman* (though it also has similarities to the kind of journey Dante followed, finding himself lost in a dark wood at 35). In any case Mangan tells his father that since his wife left him "something strange has happened to me. It's as if I – the person I was – your son – the person I used to be – it's as if there's nobody there any more" (43). Marriage and career to date have constituted a wasted life (61); he must begin again. Jamie Mangan's search for himself starts with two strokes of good fortune: (a) his discovery of an old daguerreotype, probably of the poet James Clarence Mangan, in which "the face in the photograph was his own" (48), a face he toasts as "my resurrection . . . my life!" (55), and (b) his inheriting his wife's riches after she dies in an accident before their divorce is final, money that allows him to go to Ireland, that green island, to seek his links with poetic genius. The main and longest part of the novel is taken up with this experience, flanked significantly with two short sections in America (United States and Canada) involving loss of his two most important loves, the first in which his wife dies and the last in which his father dies. Part 1 ends, "I will go to Ireland" (92); part 3 begins, "Mangan left Ireland" (331). What he discovers in the interval is not genius, however, but something important about the difference between art and life as well as his own problematic place as "his father's only son, continuance in a line which stretched back to Ireland and their grandfather's claim to be descended from the poet Mangan himself" (16).

The plot in this central section functions as "a bit of a detective story" (110), as one character describes Jamie's presence in a village outside Bantry in the dead of winter. Jamie and the reader are led through a series of mysterious hints to the shocking story that climaxes both part 2 and Jamie's own search. Romanticizing his origins, Jamie Mangan is not put off by the fact that some of his cousins seem to be "dirty, semiliterate gypsies" (124) living in a tacky caravan rather than in the abandoned old house nostalgia might prefer. With the dirt, drink, and easy sex, he finds himself feeling more at home than he ever had in New York or Montreal, his conjugal and paternal cities (138). He glamorizes the decadence of his distant look-alike relative and condemns his own tame life: "Perhaps that was why Jamie Mangan had never written great poetry [so he speculates about himself]. . . . He had not sought the life of his ancestor, a life of poetry induced by stimulants, by a deliberate derangement of the senses, by wandering the streets like a mendicant, sitting all evening in stinking taverns, everything in excess, even the poetry itself" (139). The phrase "*poète maudit*" recurs frequently in Jamie's descriptions of James Clarence Mangan, always with admiration, but as he succeeds in solving the mystery that lures him while he traces back his connections, when he actually encounters a living "damnéd poet," he finds the reality revolting.

Michael Mangan lives in hiding, as if dead, in the remote West, thinking of himself as an unappreciated genius, comparing himself with Yeats in his tower, glorying in his being "a *maudit*" (288). But after hearing his story, Jamie considers Michael merely a "foul, fawning child molester" (307) and an indifferent derivative poet. The striking facial resemblance that exists among James Clarence Mangan and certain of his descendants, such as Michael and Jamie, including loss of the same tooth,[11] is now rendered meaningless to Jamie. Rather than being an earnest of genius, this resemblance is, if anything, a mark of unglamorous evil. Like Synge's Pegeen Mike 70 years earlier, Jamie suddenly realizes the vast difference between words and deeds, between poetry and life. He rejects his former romanticizing of James Clarence Mangan by now calling him a "second-rate, rhyming jingler" (312) and discards the picture that before had seemed to promise resurrection and life. When Michael smashes the daguerreotype, Jamie sees "the face that was his face shattered beyond any possible repair" (313). Jamie has gone a long way out into the world of his past to discover it is not an Eden, that he cannot find himself there.

Michael's mad wife has proved wise in the question she earlier asked Jamie – " 'Why do so many Americans come here to look at graves?' she said. 'Do they not have graves enough in their own place?' " – and in her prediction that "if you keep looking over your shoulder, sir, you'll find things you don't want to find" (198). In his doubles – with the same face, the same calling – Jamie has discovered an ugly side of his history, an ugly side of his possible self, that he rejects. Coming to Ireland, he has found violence and nastiness: incest, child molestation, postpartum madness, postmolestation madness, castration, dereliction. Learning that mistreatment is not wiped out by immortal poetry, he leaves in anger and disgust. Whatever identity he wants for himself, it is not to be found in his "romantic" forebears.

Earlier Jamie Mangan had referred to himself as his father's only son; and in conversation with Michael he states "I'm the last of the line" (296). But returning home to his dying father's bedside, he learns something else important about himself: he is not now the only son. The dying old man leaves a pregnant young wife, whom Jamie promises to aid with money inherited from his own estranged and childless wife. Thus relationships from the old world continue in the new, but with an important difference: the taste for young women is there, and the tangle of connections, but the relationships are not actually incestuous, and the son who will carry on the line will not be subject to the Gothic distortions of rural Ireland.

As for the protagonist, Jamie Mangan himself, his "old face" in the daguerreotype has been destroyed. What, now, of his future? And how free is he, really, to shape his fate? His easy money from his movie-star wife has not been earned but "given." He in turn may give money to others (as he has to Kathleen, the young cousin he desired sexually in Ireland, and will give to Margreth, his father's young wife), but in using it for himself he has simply learned that another of his inheritances was a dead end (the decadent poet's bad life and second-rate poetry).

Everything given him from the past, from outside himself, has disappointed him. His glorious Irish heritage is sham. Not only are his poet ancestors morally execrable and poetically mediocre; they are quite unheroic: the only ancestor killed in 1916 died not in the fight for independence but in an ordinary pub brawl (290). Poetry, politics, Eros, his Irish past, and his Irish present all fail Mangan: his line of descent entails romantic illusion about all those graves he has come to see, hoping to find the people who made him what he is today (133). He mistakenly thought he needed to explore that Irish past because there are no graves in America (199), but by the end of the novel he knows there are: his father will be buried in America. As for the future, it belongs to his father's other son. Jamie Mangan's inheritance is nothing at all. Whatever self he has must be made by himself, and he may well have missed that opportunity.

Moore's novel is sensational in some of its details and extreme in its conclusion. With more subtlety Trevor shows similar failed heritages in many of his later narratives, his also often involving failed or absent father's (or forefathers). In *The Silence in the Garden* the Rolleston children's father is absent owing to his military career (and so cannot curb their hunting Cornelius Dowley) and Tom's father is absent owing to a terrorist bomb (and so cannot legitimize his existence). Several stories in *Family Sins* contain fathers who are useless or even damaging to their children. Deborah's father, in "Coffee with Oliver," is a foul parasite; her only hope of a future lies in her rejecting him completely. In "Children of the Headmaster" Jonathan's father knows nothing of the students he supervises or of his own son and consequently offers them no real support or guidance: Jonathan "had even wanted to protect his father because he didn't know enough, because he blustered and was oppressive, and went about things stupidly."[12] The story ends with Jonathan running away from his father's office, "through the empty corridors of the school. . . . [A]long the sea-front, looking for his sisters" (206). Like some of Banville's boys, Jonathan may spend his life looking, without success, but at least he knows he does not want to be like his father. The protagonist of "In Love with Ariadne" finds his father less stupid than the headmaster but no more effectively helpful (" 'You'll get over her,' his father had said in the holidays, guessing only that there had been some girl");[13] this young man's search for the sister, the beloved, proves unsuccessful, only "a useless longing to change the circumstances there had been" (97). Years later he finds himself a split character: "A lone figure stares out into the blurred night, hat-

ing the good sense that draws him away from loitering gloomily outside a convent" (98). That lone figure is his fragmentary real self that
wanted to rescue Ariadne, to persuade her that love was possible
(97); the good sense drawing him away is a personification of that
part of him which accepted his father's advice, values, and world.
Thus whatever life he has is blurred and dark, ruined by his inability
to reject his father and endorse his own goals himself.

"August Saturday" provides a telling glimpse of some of the
issues involved in Trevor's various narratives where fathers have
failed their children.[14] The central event involves an August Saturday
when Grania has sexual intercourse with a stranger from England,
thus providing her husband, Desmond, with the only child they have
("I am going to do this because I want a child," she remembers herself thinking).[15] When that stranger returns 16 years later to live on
the estate he has just inherited from the relatives he had been visiting before, Grania is faced with the prospect of his presence in their
social group and his eventual realization that he must be Judith's
father. Her initial discomfort and confusion clears as she realizes that
she has no regrets.[16] But this bald summary of events is not what the
story glimpses. As is so often the case in Trevor's work, names and
places convey the story's import.

The stranger himself has no name in the narrative. Although on
his initial visit he was introduced and then, on return 16 years later,
his earlier visit is recalled by virtually all the set at the tennis club, no
one ever calls him by name, and Grania is mistaken thinking his surname the same as the family from whom he inherits the estate. He is
simply an Englishman: that is abundantly clear in the narrative (209)
and to the Irish people in the small town outside Dublin where
Grania and her tennis friends have spent their lives. This Englishman
may not warrant a name, but he is quite effective as a lover, able to
achieve in one night what Grania's husband could not accomplish in
24 years. Contrasting with this nameless stranger, Grania's husband,
Desmond, bears the name of a distinguished Old Irish family famous
for fighting English usurpation of their lands. Despite the fact that
here in this corner of modern Ireland Desmond is "the pick of the
tennis club" and has "worn better than any of" the other men (219),
this named "hero" does not possess "his land," has not sown his
seed to produce the daughter he thinks is his. He has been cuck-
olded by an Englishman. With various telling details Trevor highlights

the English-Irish opposition between the two men: Desmond is red-headed (209),[17] and he and his friends are all Catholic; the stranger, on the other hand, is part of a family that used to belong to the tennis club but feels there is "a different kind of lot these days" (211). Grania – whose name is used often throughout the story – is, like her mythical namesake, a woman desired by two men, husband and lover. Unlike mythical Grania, she does not desert her husband; in fact, she loves Desmond and has no desire to run away with the stranger. Nonetheless, by giving her the name of the famous faithless bride of a famous Irish king, Trevor underscores her identification with Ireland and points up the political resonance of the sexual success of her lover, so clearly identified with England. Thus "August Saturday" presents the most extreme form of parental failure: the father who is no father at all. And it places that failure in the context of national differences: the invader-settler Englishman successful where the local-hero Irishman is not. Trevor's point here is not to champion England or insult Ireland but rather to show the hazards and falsities of any "national heritage."

Since the focus is on Grania's adultery, not on her child Judith's search for herself, this story is, of course, not like a *Bildungsroman*. But by its subject – the failed father, the illusory heritage – it shows the persistence of an important theme in Trevor's fiction. The fathers and forefathers of that green rock which is Carriglas, that orchard garden of Kilneagh, that rural tennis club of "August Saturday," fathers Catholic and Protestant, have failed their children, providing no congenial society with which they can integrate themselves, leaving only a wilderness where there might have been a garden.

Chapter Eight

Children, Celibates, and Holy Fools

The question inevitably arises as to whether Trevor's view in his fictional world is optimistic because of his frequent comic elements or is pessimistic because of his focus on what seems an endlessly multiplying series of evil events – or, to use Trevor's metaphor, whether the garden can be redeemed. To what extent does Trevor's work provide resolution for the intricate evil it explores originating in the Garden of Eden and permeating the many gardens found in his short stories and novels? The answer to this question is found in certain kinds of characters that appear in Trevor's fiction from the very beginning, three types of persons – some comic, some tragic – who in various ways both manifest evil and transcend it: children, celibates, and holy fools.

Some characters belong simultaneously to all three categories. In *The Love Department* the adult Edward Blakeston-Smith is really just a child whose task in life, as posed by himself and everyone else in this novel, is to grow up. Although his mission has taken him to the Love Department, where he works for Lady Dolores Bourhardie defending love in marriage, he himself is not married and never will be; his chosen vocation in life is to remain celibate, as a brother of Saint Gregory's. Thus as a monk he partakes of a traditional "holy folly," to lose his life in order to gain it.[1] So successful is he in this vocation that he even reaches that ultimate state of sainthood, at least in the popular mind, becoming the patron saint of married love. In this early novel Trevor presents a character who becomes a comic paradigm of qualities to be found in many of his other major characters.

The chief difference over the years is this: in the earlier novels these characters are amusing, cartoonlike grotesques; in later novels they often become serious and at times even tragic. Yet the basic set of traits remains. Tom, for example, in *The Silence in the Garden*, is presented in detail as an actual child; then that childhood is shown to affect his adult life so profoundly as to color all his later years. He is not childish, as is Edward Blakeston-Smith, but he continues as the scarred child he was even into his maturity. He too chooses celibacy, not because he cannot appreciate adult sexuality, not from Edward's imaginative incapacity for participating in it, but because he will not allow himself marriage. Though Tom himself does not enter a monastery, he is associated with religious and ascetic life: his vocation manqué is a much more serious one than Edward's flight from messy adult sexuality to regular meals, charitable companions, and pleasant checker games in the garden, where nothing very real is at stake. Edward seeks out a womb for his infancy, takes refuge in a prelapsarian world. Tom, a much more serious character, lives out the pain of being born in sin and living on in guilt and shame. Both, however, bear their childhood alive within them, choose celibacy, and associate themselves with "the holy."

From 1966 to 1988, between these two extremes of Edward and Tom, Trevor created a variety of other characters who combine or emphasize the traits of child, celibate, or holy fool to a lesser or greater degree. Celibates are particularly plentiful in Trevor's work. (Has any other author written so frequently of unmarried, unattached, or sexually inactive people, their inactivity being an important part of the narrative?) Miss Gomez and Mrs. Eckdorf, though one was a prostitute for a time and one was nominally married, are both effectively "celibate," untouched by, uninterested in sex, unallied with anyone. The short stories abound with bachelor and spinster bores, cowards, deviants, and victims: Raymond Bamber ("Raymond Bamber and Mrs Fitch"), Mr. Mileson ("A Meeting in Middle Age"), Miss Fanshawe ("Going Home"), Mr. Dukelow ("A Choice of Butchers"), Francis ("Death in Jerusalem"), Mulvihill ("Mulvihill's Memorial"), Justin Condon ("Music"), Helena ("Her Mother's Daughter"). Sometimes celibacy is the result of impotence ("Cocktails at Doney's"); sometimes it is the result of an earlier sexual experience ("The Printmaker"). Most of Trevor's celibates are virgins; some are unmarried but sexually active ("The Forty-seventh Saturday"). And some noncelibates, though technically married, have unconsummated relationships ("The Bedroom Eyes of Mrs Vansittart"). Trevor contrives many permutations on these issues of spinsterhood, bachelorhood, asexually or homosexually motivated avoidance of marriage, unconsummated or discontinued marriages. Often such characters in the short stories are simply wounded people – usually wounded from some childhood experience (e.g., the narrator of "The Death of Peggy Morrissey"). Occasionally a story will show questions of celibacy and marriage, sexual deprivation or deviancy in a larger social context, with political overtones ("The Distant Past," "Beyond the Pale," "Attracta," "The News from Ireland," and the novels *Fools of Fortune* and *The Silence in the Garden*).

Several pieces in *Family Sins and Other Stories* show sexual deprivation as a price extracted by families and by "the land." The murder/suicide horror in "Events at Drimaghleen" (regardless of which version of events is true) shows the fatal effects of a mother's attempts to prevent her son's marriage, which she does both for her own sake and for the sake of their farm. "A Husband's Return" shows a woman yielding to family pressures, condemned to live the rest of her life without her husband, lacking the courage either to welcome him back to the family farm or to run away to join him. And "Kathleen's Field" shows a girl sacrificed for her family's needs, her life as a servant exchanged for a fertile field (like Mary in *The Killeen*, having "the cravings of her own body . . . driven underground by the urgent hungers of the land").[2] Though all these stories show an adult child damaged by a parent who must put individual needs aside for the sake of the family farm, there is no indication that the enforced celibacy is "redeemed" in any way, by holy folly or anything else.

Among the sexually inactive are idealists, such as Charlotte ("The Printmaker"), who enshrines a brief adolescent romance as the ultimate erotic moment of her life; quasi-incestuous brothers and sisters, such as Edward and Emily Tripp ("The Original Sins of Edward Tripp"), who live together in an embrace of mutual cruelty; and passive creatures, such as Francis ("Death in Jerusalem"), so bound to mother and motherland that he cannot experience anything else. Not all Trevor's celibates are willingly so; there are the many women whose spinsterhood results from limited opportunity (Bridie, in "The Ballroom of Romance," were she eventually to marry, would have to make serious compromises, compromises Attracta was unwilling to make and Sarah, in *The Silence in the Garden*, unable to make).

Among the many varieties of celibates is a special group, whose unmarried or sexually inactive state results from mental imbalance or oddity of some kind: the "holy fools," the "saints." In *Mrs. Eckdorf in O'Neill's Hotel* the titular character becomes devoted to a woman she considers a saint (Mrs. Sinnott), and as a result of this intense devotion and her own peculiarities, enters a "heaven" of madness, giving all she has of life for this one idealized vision of goodness. Miss Gomez, though not so extreme in madness, also gives her entire life to a vision of order and goodness without which she could not bear to live. The two chief examples of such holy folly, however, are Imelda in *Fools of Fortune* and Tom in *The Silence in the Garden*. At one extreme Imelda (like Mrs. Eckdorf) is truly insane, living within her own idealized vision of goodness, impervious to the actual evil around her: she *sees* the destroyed house restored, the garden reclaimed, even though it is not (192). So untroubled is her spirit that she seems haloed and perpetually youthful ("Her smooth blonde hair has a burnished look where the sunlight catches it; in her middle age she is both elegant and beautiful"), but with a youthfulness that is essentially false ("her face meticulously made up" [191]). The local people consider her a saint; they bring the afflicted to her for cures. This action – along with Willie's earlier observation that "in Ireland it happens sometimes that the insane are taken to be saints of a kind" (184) – sets Imelda's private vision in a larger, public context. Thus virgin Imelda, like various saints in Alban Butler's *Lives of the Saints*, has given all for her holy state, an asceticism, a martyrdom that has placed "happiness . . . like a shroud miraculously about her" (192). Like her beauty, this happiness is ambiguous (a "shroud"). Yet in her own way she, like the official saints, is dead to this world, but alive to a heaven of imagined goodness.

At the other end of the spectrum is Tom, mentally quite normal yet in his own way also a holy fool. From childhood he has been associated with a revered tradition of saintly asceticism: hoping to offset the taint of his bastardy, the local priest, the nuns, and his mother have set him the task of tending the holy well, touching the holy clay, at the "ruined abbey on the island, where the saint had had his bed long before the abbey had been built to commemorate him" (35). Tom indeed "benefited from the holiness of the well"

(112) in that he too, like its saintly hermit, chooses a solitary, celibate life. Unlike Imelda, proclaimed a saint in her extreme removal, Tom lives an ordinary life, his celibacy a quiet form of expiation. Yet in this he too does his part, not only to atone for what he and the community consider to be his personal contamination (no one wants to touch him, because he is a bastard) but also to continue the Rolleston children's self-punishment: to live celibately, to avoid producing other children. Tom belongs, unacknowledged, to that long tradition of monks and hermits, the other holy fools, whose remains lie *"at the heart of the island"* (17).

The most frequent allusion to a specific holy fool in Trevor's fiction is to the early Irish saint Attracta, who supplies a name for one of his most important titular characters and who also appears as a significant concern in *Mrs. Eckdorf in O'Neill's Hotel*. What is particularly interesting about Attracta is that she, or someone with the same name, is also an important Irish mythological character, prominent in Yeats's play *The Herne's Egg*. That Trevor had this myth in mind, as well as the saint's legend, is indicated by the parallels between events in "Attracta" and *The Herne's Egg* (in both cases a woman is raped by seven men so that she will conform to their view of the way she should live her life). Yeats's Attracta is a priestess, betrothed to the Great Herne and guardian of his eggs. Congal, King of Connaught, thinks her merely mad, "thrown into despair / By the winter of [her] virginity."[3] Thus the wisdom of this world, represented by the men of power, considers her foolish and denies what she sees to be the only reality. Undeterred by the fact that "people say that she is holy" (50), Congal and his fellow heroes determine to cure her by raping her, "and do her a great good by that action" (49), that she may "live as every woman should" (50). But she transcends their wisdom, making the rape a union with the Great Herne ("I lay beside him, his pure bride" [58]), while they, having stolen and consumed the eggs she guards, must all die. The myth shows that the divine cannot be put to personal uses (the consecrated eggs cannot be stolen and consumed with impunity). Attempts to make the divine ordinary (the rape of Attracta) lead to death. Thus the shadow of Yeats's Attracta on Trevor's character Attracta[4] raises her life from mere accidental spinsterhood to an exalted celibacy and gives her schoolteacher's role the function of a priestess. Thus associated with Christian saint and mythological priestess – both

Irish – Attracta too, with Tom, belongs to that tradition of holy fools whose stories lie *"at the heart of the island."*

Celibacy and holy folly, however, are not the usual state of most people, and consequently characters like Edward, Mrs. Eckdorf, Miss Gomez, Imelda, Attracta, and Tom may seem quite alien. Some early reviewers tended to dismiss Trevor's novels and stories as unrealistic accounts of abnormal personalities in bizarre events. Yet what is interesting in Trevor's work is the way characters who at first glance seem like oddities or monsters are shown in fact to be part of an ordinary human community. This realization he achieves most strikingly in his studies of children. Children, of course, are celibate (at least temporarily), youthful, and foolish (though not caught in the abnormal agelessness of Edward and Imelda) but at the same time represent a stage of life every reader has experienced. Although children also partake of evil and sometimes even seem like monsters, Trevor's studies of them demonstrate a principle that runs through all his thought: what is monstrous is not necessarily egregious; what ravages society is not outside but within, not an intruder but an ordinary member. Timothy Gedge in *The Children of Dynmouth* is just such a "monster"; he is, however, not alone, as the plural noun in Trevor's title suggests.

Mrs. Blakey's observations are fairly typical of the way adults view Timothy. Puzzled, she watches through the window as 15-year-old Timothy talks with her charges, Kate and Stephen, both 12:

> The boy looked strange, loose-limbed and broad-shouldered, with his very fair hair. The children seemed quite tiny beside him, Stephen even frail. He kept grinning at them as though they were all three the very best of friends, but clearly that wasn't quite so. He was so very familiar on the streets of the town, with that zipped yellow jacket and his jeans, yet he looked like something from another world in the garden. He didn't belong in gardens, any more than he belonged in the company of two small children. His presence puzzled her beyond measure.[5]

Familiar yet alien – that is the abiding sense adults have when they encounter Timothy. Here Mrs. Blakey's puzzlement can be explained by the simple fact that the three children belong to different social classes and different age-groups and have no real reason to visit each other; as guardian of the two younger ones while Kate's mother and

Stephen's father (old friends newly married) are away on honeymoon, Mrs. Blakey is bound to be vigilant. But the language Trevor has used to express the nature of her concern is highly charged. The opposition of "another world" to "garden" and the use of the impersonal "something" suggests a more extreme contrast than the situation actually warrants. Although Mrs. Blakey cannot hear Timothy's next remark – "A person has temptations" (121) – her visual perceptions accord well with the word *temptation* and with Kate's later certainty that Timothy is possessed by the devil. Here, without quite understanding what is wrong, puzzled "beyond measure," Mrs. Blakey has the sense that an idyllic world, their garden, has been invaded by a powerful, loose-limbed creature whose "light" hair and clothing are somehow strange, whose ingratiating manner is false and somehow sinister. These images, of course, suggest the serpent in the Garden of Eden, the wily Lucifer, angel of light, tempting the first couple to sin, a couple who were then innocent as children. Now another child-couple is also, it would seem, being threatened by temptation. But what exactly is the nature of that temptation? And what is the point of the word *quite* in Mrs. Blakey's noting that these three children are not quite the very best of friends? Answers to these questions reveal a concept central to this novel and to the structure of Trevor's moral universe generally.

But first Timothy's relationship to Kate and Stephen requires a closer look. Like Mrs. Blakey, they have a puzzled response to Timothy, and, like her response, theirs seems especially charged. It is perfectly understandable that the two younger, well-bred children would be embarrassed by Timothy's coarse talk about sex ("He described the scene he'd witnessed in his mother's bedroom" [99]) and offended by his subsequent references to their parents on honeymoon ("Your dad'll enjoy that, Stephen. Your dad'll be all jacked up" [99]). Unused to this kind of talk, they are further unsettled by the apparent lack of logic and good taste as Timothy talks about going to funerals, tells them a few flabby jokes, describes his act for the Spot the Talent competition at the Easter fete (a comic impersonation of the famous bride murderer, George Joseph Smith), and then asks to have Stephen's dead mother's wedding dress, after having described surreptitiously watching Stephen's father put it away in a trunk (100f).

That Stephen and Kate, upset by this bizarre series of remarks, suddenly run away from Timothy makes sense. But what seems odd is the intensity of Stephen's anger and his mode of expressing it when later Timothy persists in asking for the dress and talking about what other people are going to contribute to his act: " 'It's all lies what you're saying.' Stephen's face was flushed" (120). What the "it" refers to is not entirely clear, but the implication is that nobody could approve this "comic" act, contribute to it, or think it would be a success. Later passages in the novel, however, add the fact that Stephen knows nothing about a wedding dress and denies the truth of the scene Timothy described. As Timothy persists day after day in asking for the dress, blandly ignoring Stephen's anger and distress, it becomes important for Stephen to discover if there really is such a dress packed away by his father in an old green trunk. Its existence would prove something – but what?

Timothy had told Kate and Stephen a series of shocking stories about other people: Miss Lavant's illicit love of Dr. Greenslade; Commander Abigail's secret homosexuality; Publican Plant's many adulteries; Mr. and Mrs. Dass's violent rejection by their son; and, after days of innuendo, his most outrageous story, that he witnessed Stephen's father push Stephen's mother off the cliff so that he could marry Kate's mother (127-29). The children's attempts to dismiss Timothy as mad become less effective as various assertions begin to seem probable and some are apparently corroborated ("the sight of Commander Abigail on the green-painted seat made all the difference," "the fantasies of Timothy Gedge . . . were turning out not to be fantasies at all" (132f), the children think. For Stephen the truth of the murder story seems to hinge, illogically, on whether or not there actually is a wedding dress. After days of brooding he finally goes to the attic: "When he opened the faded green trunk the wedding-dress was there, at the bottom, beneath clothes that were familiar to him" (151). His giving the dress to Timothy signals Stephen's capitulation to what he takes to be the truth of the story.

But why does the presence of the dress prove the murder? And why give the dress away; why not cherish it all the more? Convinced of Timothy's veracity on one point (there really is a dress), Stephen is willing to believe him totally, because to Stephen that story fits what he feels: so suddenly bereft of his mother, he cannot really welcome his father's new wife; mourning for his lost home, he cannot really rejoice in moving to Kate's. His attempts to be brave and reasonable (assuring his father "I'm sure it'll be all right" [36]) do not work at the level of emotion: the horrible story matches the horror he feels, seems to account for what he feels, gives him an excuse to feel what he feels. And in giving away the dress he participates also in the murder, rejecting his mother and her marriage, just as his father apparently did. Viciously turning against Kate (149f), with whom he has for years had a relationship similar to the comfortable one with his mother (34), he also acts out his father's alleged violence against his mother, as well perhaps as his own anger against her for deserting him by death. Timothy's story becomes the occasion for Stephen to express complex and conflicting feelings hitherto kept in check by his schooling ("You must be brave, old chap" [38]). Timothy's story tempts Stephen to face the "truth" of his own hidden feelings, to taste fruit of his own branch of the tree of the knowledge of good and evil – evil he finds both outside and inside himself.

Stephen's giving Timothy Gedge the wedding dress to use in his comic murder act is paralleled by Mrs. Abigail's giving Timothy her husband's houndstooth suit for the same purpose: "Quite suddenly it seemed fitting that the suit of her husband should garb a man who had slaughtered his brides: there was in that, somewhere, a gleam of relevance" (156). Angry with her husband for his homosexuality and her consequent sexless marriage, she extracts her revenge by this donation: "He'd know what had happened to the suit, and it seemed right that he should: this small tribute to the truth that had been exposed seemed at least her due. She left the doors of the wardrobe open" (156). In both cases a "bride" has been slaughtered, a love lost, a terrible truth brought to light.

As the bearer of that light Timothy is literally a "Lucifer." But of what sort – darkened angel, Father of Lies, roaring lion going about the world seeking whom he may devour? When accused of lying, he protests that he only tells the truth. And indeed the narrating voice frequently corroborates the accuracy of some of Timothy's stories (Captain Abigail really is homosexual; Plant really is prodigiously adulterous, etc.). Yet not all his stories are true. Timothy clearly is one of those pathological types, with no strong feelings, no capacity for sympathy, and no real sense of the difference between fact and fiction. His stories are sometimes true because he is a full-time

Peeping Tom and knows how to use the information gained for his advantage, usually through blackmail disguised with his apparent ingenuousness. But when the information does not fit his purpose or his fantasy as well as it might, he simply invents (e.g., his silly insistence that Miss Lavant is Mrs. Abigail's sister, despite Commander and Mrs. Abigail's repeated denials [65]). But this novel is not a study of the pathology of liars or the methodology of the devil, however much Trevor draws on both traditions. The novel centers itself, rather, on the stories that are partly true, partly false, stories that for their acceptance require collaboration by their auditors.

The murder story is one of these. It completely upsets the two children, ruins their friendship, and casts a permanent shadow on the family formed by the new marriage – despite the fact that when Kate finally confides in an adult, she discovers that the account is false: Stephen's father was on a train when his mother fell, and so he could not have pushed her. And yet, the novel suggests, perhaps even so, there was a murder of sorts. After Kate's hysterical request that the rector, Mr. Featherstone, exorcise the devil from Timothy, the rector visits Timothy to try to straighten things out. When confronted with the information that Stephen's father was away when the accident occurred, Timothy still insists on murder: "She went down the cliff because he was on the job with the other woman. He was fixing to get rid of the first one in the divorce courts" (171). That this assertion may well be correct is indicated by Timothy's next sentence: "I was up at Sea House one night, looking in through the window – " Featherstone cuts him short ("I don't want to know what you were doing") but does not contradict him. Timothy has recounted a series of events that make the "accident" or the "suicide" seem like a murder: "I heard them having a barney, Mr Feather. A different time that is, if you get me. She's calling the girl's mum a prostitute. I heard her, sir: 'Why don't you throw me down?' she says. He told her not to be silly" (171). Mr. Fleming may not have physically pushed his wife over the cliff, but he certainly gave a psychological push by his adultery and decision to divorce. Or so would be the case if Timothy's account is correct.

Believing or disbelieving Timothy becomes an act of collaboration both on the part of his various auditors and on the part of the reader. Stephen was willing to participate in the more direct and physically violent version of the story because of his own emotional needs. Kate can only allow the story to be a diabolic lie, for reasons of her own. Mr. Featherstone, a kind and sensible cleric, though indignant at Timothy's distressing Kate and Stephen (but discounting the extreme explanation Kate advances: possession by the devil), does accept Timothy's synthetic account: "It was true [Featherstone thinks], it had the feel of truth: the woman hadn't just fallen over a cliff" (177). But his gentle humanity supplants clerical belief in the value of truth[6] with the question, "Yet what good came from knowing that a woman had killed herself?" (177).

Is Timothy Gedge's account of Mrs. Fleming's death correct? Although he is a terrific liar, much of what he tells is shown to be true. Rifling through his father's desk, Stephen comes on two sets of love letters – in one drawer a set from his mother, with a few to her from his father, and in another drawer a second set; both sets are "full of love and promises" (140). Letters from the latter group have no dates and contain such tantalizing sentences as *"It's hard to wait"* and *"Nothing makes sense without you."* Can Stephen – can the reader – legitimately conclude from this that the second love brought about the murder of the first? Or does Mr. Fleming's keeping his first wife's letters, and her wedding dress, argue innocence? Certainly the evidence on either side is inconclusive. What remains is the extent to which Mr. Featherstone, or any other resident of Dynmouth, or any reader of the book, finds Timothy's version of what happened to have "the feel of truth." And that involves a complex process of collaboration with the narrative.

Repeated references to windows and to seeing allow Trevor to manage the "feel of truth" in this novel and its requisite process of collaboration. In the passage where Mrs. Blakey sees the three children in the garden, she watches them through a window of their handsome Georgian house: all three are "distanced" by such observation, not only by the actual spatial distance but by the fact that she can see them but they cannot see her; she is inside, presumably safe, and private, while they are outside, more vulnerable, and more public. Yet even that "outside" is divided into regions: the garden is walled, set apart; Stephen and Kate belong there but Timothy does not (he has even left open the white iron gate set in the archway). Timothy is thus made to seem the most distant, and in this passage he appears as an intruder "from another world." That, however, is Mrs. Blakey's *view* of the situation.[7]

For Timothy windows have served as a way of spying on other people unobserved, from the outside looking in. Virtually every story he tells that is corroborated has involved his peeping through windows, or in a few cases through doorways. His position here too, it would seem, is that of an outsider. And when he is inside his own space at home, he reverses the situation, protects himself, keeps all the world away by closing his own curtains. (He is in fact the only character in the novel who does close curtains. The rest of Dynmouth's inhabitants, it would seem, fight, commit adultery, and transact secrets of all sorts without bothering to cover their windows.)

Is he, then, as a voyeur, an outsider? Do the windows separate, or do they connect? Certainly Mrs. Blakey's response to Timothy is representative of that of everyone else in the town: he does not belong. Virtually every person in the novel who has extended contact with him tells him to go away and never come back. (And he really is a dreadful person; the reader has no difficulty accepting that everyone rejects him. It is a wonder that the Abigails, the Dasses, and the Featherstones were so forbearing.) But showing Timothy to behave monstrously, showing that other characters in the novel see him as a moral monster and thus reject him, does not necessarily make Timothy an outsider. There is still that "quite" in Mrs. Blakey's observations.

If it is not "quite so" that Timothy is "the very best of friends" with Kate and Stephen, the very form of the denial implies *some* connection, some degree of friendship and therefore some community with these "normal" children. Then, when their normality is examined, further connections appear. Stephen, as has been seen, is immensely cruel to Kate after he has been told her mother was involved with his mother's death, and his line of reasoning about that death makes him a participant in the "fact" (if not the act) of murder. All Stephen's responses make "psychological sense": he is simply a young person who is suffering terribly; he does not seem like a monster. And yet his feelings and behavior are not so very different from Timothy's, though in context more "understandable." Kate too is paired with a supposed freak, a benign monster, Miss Trimm, though the one is an ordinary little girl and the other a senile spinster who thinks she has mothered another Jesus Christ (166); in listening to Kate's hysterical attempts to make sense of what Timothy has said by reporting that he is possessed by the devil, Mr. Feather-stone perceives a similar need in both these parishioners to over-simplify the moral structure of the world (and he can imagine Kate as an old woman being very much like Miss Trimm). Still, taken in context, Kate's monstrous insistence that a stake should be driven through Timothy's body and his bones burned to cinders (167) becomes an index of her suffering, not something that suggests she herself is a monster. Why is Timothy crazy or evil and Stephen not? Kate not? Perhaps the point is that Timothy is not so egregious as he seems: Mr. Featherstone tries to explain to Kate that good and evil are not separate qualities:

> He said there was a pattern of greys, half-tones and shadows. People moved in the greyness and made of themselves heroes or villains, but the truth was that heroes and villains were unreal. The high drama of casting out devils would establish Timothy Gedge as a monster, which would be nice for everyone because monsters were a species on their own. But Timothy Gedge couldn't be dismissed as easily as that. [Kate] had been right to say it was people like that who do terrible things, and if Timothy Gedge did do terrible things it would not be because he was different and exotic but because he was possessed of an urge to become so. Timothy Gedge was as ordinary as anyone else, but the ill fortune of circumstances or nature made ordinary people eccentric and lent them colour in the greyness. And the colour was protection because ill fortune weakened its victims and made them vulnerable. (168)

Kate is not persuaded or comforted by this argument. Nor perhaps is the reader. These few passages near the end of the novel come per-ilously close to seeming like "the moral of the story," but Mr. Feath-erstone is saved from seeming an authorial spokesman by his own uncertainties and his own sense of helplessness. Speaking later with his wife, he describes Timothy as a battered child, even though no one had actually battered him, a child whose very existence is a hor-ror: "What use were services that recalled the Crucifixion when there was Timothy Gedge wandering about the place, a far better reminder of waste and destruction? What on earth was the point of collecting money to save the tower of a church that wasn't even beautiful?" Mr. Featherstone feels like "a laughable figure, with his clerical collar, visiting the sick, tidying up" (179). His inability to do anything to

help Timothy calls into question his entire vocation, that very vocation which allows him to counsel Kate about moral complexity.

Everyone who lives in Dynmouth was once a child. And children
everywhere, as the narrating voice asserts early in the novel, are the
same: they all lead "double lives" (8f). That duplicity not only refers
to the fantasy worlds the narrating voice then describes but also
applies to the mix of good and evil, truth and lies, that the whole
action of the novel contains. In the process of growing up the adults
in Dynmouth may have given up the distinctive reveries of childhood, but they have perfected their skills of lying, especially to themselves. Mrs. Abigail does not leave the Captain, as she had determined to do in the first revelation of his homosexuality, but settles
back into a marriage she has always felt to be false;[8] Publican Plant,
who makes love first to a customer and then, later in the same
evening, with his wife, enjoys the contrasts, and "for their parts, the
women had appeared to be satisfied" (68), although had the adultery been open, implications are that the wife would have been
angry; Mr. and Mrs. Dass do not talk about their devil of a son, but
Mrs. Dass spends her invalid days reading novels like *To the Devil, a
Daughter*. Even the minister's wife mourns a child lost through miscarriage while at the same time being very impatient with her young
twins. All these lived lies require self-deception and collaboration in
glossing over unacceptable information. The adults of Dynmouth
may live with their house windows open, but inner feelings and
motivations are carefully curtained; lies and truth coexist. Their need
to see evil as "the other," the devil as not belonging in *their* garden,
the difficult boy as an alien, shields them from their own implication
in what they reject. All those glassed windows present barriers
against what is "outside" and at the same time by their transparency
imply that there is nothing "inside" to conceal. The novel, however,
demonstrates the falsity of that distinction.

The designated "outsider" in Dynmouth functions as a kind of
center: looking, watching, spying through windows, Timothy gets
"inside" the truth. Unwilling to face that truth, citizens of Dynmouth
perceive him as a monster and account for his monstrosity by various
proposed causes: his actually witnessing a murder (152, 165, 172), or
simply watching too much TV (175f); adolescence (159) or the mere
fact of being born (177f); parents, devils, or just bad luck (180). But
Trevor ends his novel with a cluster of fantasies that, more than any-

thing else, both account for Timothy's apparent monstrosity and indicate his place inside the community.

Timothy's final, consoling fantasy, reported to a deaf old man, is a "beautiful story," as he repeatedly calls it, about true love:

> It was beautiful, two people loving one another all these years and Dr Greenslade being too much of a gentleman to leave his wife and family, and Miss Lavant giving birth to a baby and the baby being handed to a Dynmouth woman. It was beautiful how they'd laid it down that the baby should be brought up in Dynmouth so that they could always see it about the place. . . . Fifteen years ago . . . , they'd brought their love affair to an end because the baby had been born. . . . It would always be a secret: even if the doctor's wife died and the doctor married Miss Lavant it would still be a secret about the child that had been born, because they'd never want it to be known out of respect for the dead. It would be a secret carefully kept. . . . It would just be there, like a touch of fog. (189)

In this story all Timothy's traumas are reversed: the father who deserted him and his mother is replaced by a loving and chivalrous man ("elegant . . . like Cary Grant almost"); his slut of a mother is replaced by a beautiful woman who cares about his welfare and gives him sweets (and his actual mother is dismissed as merely "a Dynmouth woman"); it is a story in which three constitutes a triad of perfection and not, as his sister regularly says when he tries to join her and their mother, "a crowd" (29); it is a fantasy designed to redeem all sorrows, a secret known only to a few that justifies his wretched state by making him the object of a transcendent love.

Thinking for a moment of two other, quite different pieces of literature, *King Lear* and *The Wild Duck*, helps illumine the turn Trevor has given his narrative through Timothy's fantasy of being the special, the beloved son. At the end of his novel Trevor in effect poses the same problem that so empowers Lear's death scene: of what value is happiness based on falsity? If Lear dies redeemed of sorrow because he thinks Cordelia lives, he dies deceived. (If Timothy lives thinking he is Dr. Greenslade's cherished son, an incarnation of true and selfless love, he lives a lie.) Shakespeare's scene leaves the realization conveyed by that final "look there, look there" (5.3.312) absolutely ambiguous, and that ambiguity, more than Lear's actual death, charges the scene: is it the vision of life or death that fixes Lear's own final moment of existence? Does Lear die crushed by the truth or redeemed by a lie? Trevor's novel, of course, does not have the grandeur of *Lear*: his novel ends showing Timothy in the full grip of his self-deception, believing his own story and Petula Clark's fatuous message, missing altogether the irony with which the words of her song contrast with the narrative they close ("everything was going to be all right" [188]). This irony seems to condemn happiness based on falsity, especially since there is no "tragic greatness" to elevate the deception.

Should Timothy, then, be brought to realize the falsity of his consoling story? This is, of course, the same problem explored in *The Wild Duck*, which demonstrates both the prevalence of "life lies" and the damage resulting from their exposure. That play does not answer its question outright any more than *Lear* or Trevor's novel does, but it does suggest that meddlers are execrable and self-deceivers are tragicomic, as Trevor's work too demonstrates time and again.

Timothy's ultimate personal fantasy is reinforced by two attendant "myths" from the "outside" world. Over the loudspeaker Petula Clark sings that "everything was going to be all right" (188), "How can you lose? . . . Things will be great" (189), supplying through the clichés and ephemera of popular culture a philosophy of life that Timothy has readily seized and that pointedly, and ironically, ends the novel. In addition, Trevor has placed his whole narrative against an older story, reenacted in the liturgy of Holy Week, a story of betrayal, misjudgment, brutal suffering, and death, followed by new life, resurrection, and redemption. But this story is quietly in the background, providing the time frame for the novel and the social occasion for the Easter fete (at which Timothy had proposed to reenact his own favorite story of betrayal and death, George Joseph Smith's bride murders). Except for Mr. Featherstone, who questions the usefulness of "services that recalled the Crucifixion" when there are people as battered as Timothy Gedge about the place (179), few explicit connections are made between the novel's narrative and the Christian story of redemption.[9] But the analogy is clear enough, though muted in its presentation. Timothy's fantasy of being the cherished child is a grotesque secular equivalent of a sacred story about a beloved suffering son who rises from the dead. ("How can you lose? . . . Things will be great.")

The novel is, however, no devotional tract. Everything is *not* all right. Mrs. Featherstone's realization that she ought to minister to Timothy, a real, existing child, rather than lament her miscarriage (187f), is balanced by Mr. Featherstone's informed conviction that no ministry will save Timothy (179). And while Timothy's fantasy of being a very special child in the town is comforting, it simply is not true: no one he tells believes it, and the final picture of him reciting the story is, significantly, to a deaf man. Like the windows in the novel, this deaf man suggests both connection and separation: he cannot hear what is being said, and yet he stands there, he attends, he responds in whatever way he can. Like Mrs. Featherstone, he wants to be attentive; like Mr. Featherstone, his attention is ineffectual. By such scenes Trevor begins to demonstrate that the town's image of Timothy is wrong: he is not an "outsider" but rather lives in their midst as a stumbling block, a paradox.[10]

But whatever larger significance is invoked by Trevor's reference to the Christian story of crucifixion and redemption is kept in the background. In the foreground characters and events present a mix of the mundane and the grotesque. Timothy simply is a sick kid, with a sick sense of humor and some crazy fantasies used to bolster his ego. His Dynmouth is a kind of Everytown, with a collection of characters all shown in one way or another to lead double lives and, like him, to be comforted by lies as well as by truths, grown-ups and children alike needing a redemption that can be supplied only by ministering to what lives, not by mourning what has miscarried.

That such ministrations will *not* make everything all right is the point of the ironic end of the novel; that such ministrations are required nonetheless is the point of the entire narrative. An impossible task constitutes the mandatum of Trevor's moral universe, the only way to reclaim the desolate garden of Dynmouth.

Jennifer Johnston's novel *Shadows on Our Skin* (1978) is in some elements of character and plot very similar to Trevor's *The Children of Dynmouth* but quite different in its mode of presentation. Comparison between the two novels, published within a year of each other, helps highlight important elements in Trevor's fiction. Johnston too has as central character a boy who is odd, apparently different from others in his society, a boy whose truth-telling precipitates damage and suffering, damage which cannot be undone and suffering for which there is no real remedy. But Johnston sets her novel not against myths (whether couched in popular songs or in Bible and liturgy) but firmly in an actual political context.

Joe is Timothy's age, and is as poor a student, finding classes boring, school a waste of time, taken up instead with his own fantasies. He lives in Derry, during the Troubles of the 1960s and 1970s, is Catholic, poor, and painfully alienated from his father, resentful of the camaraderie between his father and his older brother, Brendan. The novel begins with Joe's fantasy of his father's death and his own grim wish it would occur. But Joe, unlike Timothy, does not seem monstrous: as he ignores what is clearly a very dull geometry lesson and elaborates instead his father's epitaph, it is clear that his hatred of his father is real (and will later be shown to be justified), that his activity does not constitute escape from reality but confrontation with it, and that his mode of confrontation is constructive and balanced. He is in fact a budding young poet struggling with the right words, the right shape for his expression. Timothy too had wanted to be an artist, but his planned creation misfired (alienating rather than amusing his proposed audience) and his method of achieving fame was unrealistic (a famous comedian would be in the audience at the church fete, he assumed, spot his talent, and immediately put him on his television show). Joe, on the other hand, is shown during the course of one geometry class progressing from easy doggerel to better-crafted lines, crisp and appropriately sardonic. He is not a poet yet, but he may become one. That he floats through his world, taking refuge in his own verbal creations, makes perfect sense given his boring classes; his drunken "hero" Republican father; his tense, overworked mother; and the bombings, shootings, and night raids he experiences. When he meets a young woman, a teacher of English, who is as alienated from this world as he is, who values words and recognizes what he is going through, his adolescent friendship-crush is entirely convincing, as is his jealousy when his older brother makes a play for her. The moment of deadly truth-telling also seems normal: Kathleen had confided in Joe that she was engaged to a British soldier, stationed then in Germany; that she had come north from her home in the south of Ireland because she thought "it would be a good thing to do"; and that soon she would be leaving for England.[11] When Brendan tells Joe he is planning to give up the Provos, go back to England (where he had been working before returning to participate in his father's idealized "heroism") and perhaps marry Kathleen, Joe is so angry and jealous that he blurts out Kathleen's engagement as proof that she would never marry Brendan. This information, in that troubled world, is as shocking as Timothy's story of cliffside murder. But this story is true and has results not uncommon in Derry: Brendan flees (in trouble with "the boys" for telling Kathleen "everything" in his wooing her), and when Joe goes to visit Kathleen he finds her packing to leave, her hair cut off, her face and body badly beaten by Brendan's "friends" in reprisal for her consorting with a soldier.

This novel, like *The Children of Dynmouth*, also ends with a bit of popular verse: on the first page of an old book Kathleen gives Joe as a parting present is the childish inscription,

> Kathleen Doherty is my name,
> Ireland is my nation.
> Wicklow is my dwelling place,
> And heaven my destination. (198)

There is irony in these words too, as there was in Petula Clark's song, but it applies to a political situation and not to the protagonist's individual life. The gift book itself, *A Golden Treasury of Verse*, constitutes an endowment from a fairy godmother, an outward sign of Joe's vocation. Her giving it signals her forgiveness; his acceptance indicates his ability to be forgiven: "Carefully he put the book into his pocket and started off home to get his father a cup of tea" (198). Armed with this literary excalibur, Joe is no longer the boy he was when the novel began: he knows he has courage (because he smuggled his brother's gun out of the house during a raid); he can make adult decisions about politics (he disposed of the gun on his own authority, throwing it in the harbor) and about his personal life (he conducts his friendship with Kathleen even though he knows his mother would disapprove); he knows there are other ways to live, other ideas to hold besides what he is used to (Kathleen has embodied a variety of alternatives); and he knows that words and actions have consequences – consequences for which he may be responsible even when he is not guilty. He goes to make his father's tea not from childish obedience to family force but as a free young man who knows he carries a future with him.

By linking her story of individual growth with an actual political situation, showing the damage families can cause against the backdrop of actual violence in a real social group, Jennifer Johnston has emphasized how plausible are Joe's uses of the imagination. Her narrator invokes no myths, just history, and the residual myths clinging to certain characters, such as the father's myth of himself as great nationalist hero, are debunked. Her protagonist lives through horrific experiences but stays human and sympathetic and grows toward maturity. The political problem is not solved; the damaging results of truth-telling are irrevocable (Kathleen will always remember that beating, even if she is not physically scarred; Joe will always remember being the immediate cause of violence he did not intend). But even so, the novel contains no suggestion that the truth should not be told, and certainly no suggestion that it cannot be told. The novel ends with the hopeful indication that, despite evil, there is a future of real places to go to and real things to do, poems to be written and imaginations to shape them. It suggests as well that these poems, these imaginations, and the societies in which they exist are made up of diverse elements that can coexist profitably, for Joe is enchanted by both the English and the Irish languages. He savors an old Irish poem, "The Scholar and His Cat" (9), which he memorizes in Irish as part of his homework (the only schoolwork he enjoys and gets right), and he also treasures a book of verse in English, which is his native tongue, the language in which he writes his own verse, the language that makes him the particular kind of Irishman he is in twentieth-century Derry.

Newspaper accounts of the kind of real event that occurs in Johnston's novel tend to use the word *tragic*, while Trevor's kind of event is sometimes described with terms like *grotesque*, *bizarre*, and *Gothic*. Yet interestingly enough, these bizarre events place Trevor's narrative closer to the realm of the tragic than Johnston's. In tragedy what is human is always shown in some kind of distortion (typically, man as king, thus rendered larger than life). To recognize the man in the king may be one of the results of reading past literature; to provide a narrative in which the reader suddenly realizes the ordinariness of an apparent monster is the skillful function of Trevor's work. That there is no escape from evil, suffering, and death is the moral of both. But that comedy and hope always intrude someplace is their actual lesson. Speaking about *The Children of Dynmouth*, Trevor insists that Timothy "would have recovered": "I think he would have recovered from his appalling experiences because I believe that *at that age*, most people would recover. I don't think that people are as easily damaged as we make out. They are damaged in other ways, but a child can go through what Timothy or Willie went through and can be perfectly normal."[12] By linking his English Timothy with his Irish Willie, his tragicomic *Children of Dynmouth* with his serious, elegiac *Fools of Fortune*, Trevor indicates once again the bonds that exist between all his characters at all points of his fiction. Whether the subject matter is from fantasy or history, evils remain paradoxical: the Ireland that preoccupies Trevor's work is a microcosm of all space and time; its evils – suffered and perpetrated – come from within. Hope and deliverance are also within. Apparent monsters are not outside the community but part of it, just as the snake was part of Eden. At every point, goods and evils touch and mirror each other; loss may be gain; the same earth is both garden and wilderness.

From first to last these connections and paradoxes dominate Trevor's work. Two recent narratives from the early 1990s, *My House in Umbria* and "Lost Ground," continue to develop the view that good and evil are not unambiguously separate. In these stories too the garden is the primary metaphor, and children, celibates, and holy fools are significant agents.

The novella *My House in Umbria* presents an international group (American, English, Irish, Italian, German) affected by a terrorist bomb blast. While recuperating in the same Italian villa, this random collection of strangers becomes a family; recognizes that the lovely estate lacks only one thing, a garden; and plants the wilderness as a mark of gratitude to their fellow victim and hostess, Mrs. Delahunty. "A garden can't make up for anything," the old general remarks to her. "But at least it will mark our recovery in your house."[13] As usual in Trevor's fiction, neither the problem nor the solution is simple or straightforward. Since the narrator, Mrs. Delahunty, is a manipulative, self-deceived liar and drunk, her story with its idealization of the garden is suspect. Throughout the narrative her plethora of anecdotes suggests that "reality" is a mix of slanted "truths." Piling up scenarios – from her dreams, her fictional romances, her memories of her own past, movies, biblical stories, her amalgam of fantasy and information about the people around her, the fan mail from readers who recount their own lives and speculate about characters in her novels as if they were real people – she concocts a picture from "that higgledy-piggledy mass of jagged shapes," demonstrating clearly that "survival's a complicated business" (335). Like Mrs. Eckdorf, Mrs. Delahunty is both deluded and insightful. Her self-deception, her violent outbursts against men, her childhood sexual abuse, and her final drunken stupor (a form of asylum) make her life and character similar to Mrs. Eckdorf's. She too seeks something she considers to be a miracle – to plant a garden and thus redeem all sorrows: "There had been a terrible evil . . . but in this little corner of Italy there was, again, a miracle. No one could simply walk back into the world after the horror [the terrorist bomb blast] of Carrozza 219. Three survivors out of all the world's survivors had found a place in my house. One to another they were a source of strength. Again I referred to the garden" (355). Her notion that making a garden is like casting out the devil, her belief that "When evil was made good it was as though the evil had never existed" (361), seems in context both inspiring (because a man too old to work and a man who has lost an arm actually succeed in creating the garden) and fallacious (because her continued drunkenness and the melancholy fates of the other survivors suggest that merely making the garden is not redemptive enough).

Mrs. Delahunty is one of Trevor's holy fools manqué, like Miss Gomez, Mrs. Eckdorf, and Edward Blakeston-Smith. But another of the survivors is no such comic grotesque: the American child, Aimée, bereft in an instant of mother, father, and brother, slowly recovers, moving gradually over a period of weeks from shock and silence into the screams and terrors of remembering, then into the solace of a new family – her fellow survivors – and finally toward the hope of a new life with her uncle in America. Aimée, representative of life and hope, at first seems to have no connection with gardens: she is not involved in the planning or making of the garden at the Umbrian estate; the earth-moving equipment for its terracing arrives as she leaves, as if those events were somehow counterbalanced. Yet Aimée, the child, is at the heart of the garden metaphor in this novella. Not only has Mrs. Delahunty connected the real Aimée with the fictional girl in the garden of the novel she was beginning to write as the bomb went off (238, 297), the child and the actual garden suffer similar fates: nine years after its planting the garden lies neglected, returning to wilderness from lack of water, just as Aimée the characters comes closest to understanding the nature of evil and the paradoxes of good. Invoking a motif he has used often in the past (most notably in "Events at Drimaghleen" and "Kathleen's Field"), Trevor here presents his garden in the form of a farm, the land, and shows how political and familial violence feed each other, creating an endless cycle of suffering, which only the "holy fool" can stop.

The holy fool in this story is Milton Leeson, 15-year-old son of a Protestant farmer in County Armagh, who is visited in the orchard by a strange woman identifying herself as Saint Rosa and giving him a holy kiss with the injunction not to be afraid "when the time comes."[14] Outraging both his Orange-parading family and the local Catholic priest, Milton begins to preach against violence and reprisal, citing as an example of reconciliation the fact that Saint Rosa, a Catholic saint, mourns one of their own murdered neighbors, a Protestant member of the Ulster Defense Regiment. Assuming he is crazy, the family tries to keep Milton locked up. But when they are away at a 12 July march, Milton is shot in his room by "unidentified strangers" (who include his brother, Garfield, butcher's assistant in Belfast and boasting Protestant paramilitary).

Particularly interesting in this story is not only its similarity to earlier pieces (such as "Beyond the Pale" and "Attracta") but the way it connects land with issues of national identity, and then identifies the notion of national identity as an important ingredient in a prevalent form of evil, political violence. These connections are made through a series of puns in the title. By calling the story "Lost Ground" Trevor not only suggests the many elements in the plot that literally involve ground – earth, land that has been lost – but he also firmly connects the horrific events in this story with the reader's own world: "lost ground" is an idiom used by ordinary people in ordinary contexts, an innocent metaphor (like "beyond the pale") shown through fiction to be anything but innocent. The phrase also helps structure the plot of the story: because the oldest son, Garfield, would sell the farm and because the youngest son is mentally retarded, the only possible male heir is Milton; thus his death deprives the family not only of a son but of their very future on this land they have worked for nearly 200 years. Through this murder they literally lose ground. In addition, the phrase operates metaphorically in the story. Garfield's "hardman reputation had been threatened [by Milton's preaching], and then enhanced [by his too has relapsed into her earlier mental illness – both began in hope; neither now flourishes.

There is another garden spot in this novella, however, one Aimée has actually visited and embraced. On the only outing the group of survivors ever takes together, to Sienna, they stop at a Benedictine monastery set in a forest of trees: elated, Aimée finds it delightful, "really beautiful" (328f). The whole day has been an occasion of great joy for her, climaxing in this visit to "the abbey, Monte Oliveto Maggiore, as close to heaven on earth as you will ever find," Mrs. Delahunty comments (328). This "heaven on earth" continues the paradoxical view of good and evil that permeates Trevor's fiction: the Mount of Olives is the place where Jesus sweated blood, anticipating his crucifixion, the suffering and death that brought new life. As he did explicitly in "The News from Ireland," Trevor again draws on the ancient Christian tradition linking gardens, the tree of Eden and the tree of the cross. Only through paradox could such a place as the Mount of Olives be consoling, and this paradoxical place is the garden Aimée knows and loves, not the one Mrs. Delahunty thinks will annihilate suffering.

Although the novella ends with all the survivors damaged in one way or another – the general dead; Otmar, disappeared into oblivion; Mrs. Delahunty, sunk in alcoholism; Aimée, in an asylum – nonetheless the final effect is not unmitigatedly pessimistic. The child, Aimée, has truly been loved, as her name suggests; the survivors truly survived for a time and made some recovery; the Umbrian garden was actually created and, though parched, remains sufficiently intact for German tourists to "shake their heads in disapproval [of its neglect]" and for English tourists to "get the hose going and water the azalea urns" (375). Despite an endlessly multiplying series of evil events, the garden is not yet dead and might even be restored. Despite suffering and incomprehensible persistent horrors, hope intrudes. At the very least, the aged self-deceived narrator intends "making the most of the colours while they last and the fountain while it flows" (375).

"Lost Ground" takes a different approach to similar issues. Focusing on Northern Ireland and conflict between Catholics and Protestants, the story mercilessly lays bare the hatreds and self-deceptions on both sides as it develops its analogy between a single family and the body politic. Here too there is a holy fool, who of

murdering Milton]" (56); thus Garfield had metaphorically lost personal ground "in certain Belfast bars and clubs" that could be regained only by this fratricide. The Leesons have lost more than a son and more than a farm, however; they have lost their personal peace because they are all individually and secretly aware of their complicity in silence, as are their neighbors, and must continue to live consciously for the rest of their lives with lies about "the scalding agony of what had happened" (56). The final and greatest lost ground is peace itself: instead of making progress toward recognizing their brotherhood and learning to live together, this community has lost ground by fostering and condoning fratricide.

Thus by a series of puns Trevor points up problems inherent in the association of land with national identity. Those who possess the land (in this case hardworking Protestants with well-kept fields) lose it because of their insistence on identifying themselves with a particular national group and their abhorence of another national group. By giving his own twist to a familiar biblical paradox, Trevor shows that those who attempt to keep their land actually lose it. And he also shows that families attempting to save what they consider to be their honor and their place in society actually destroy themselves if they destroy one of their members. This story, like the rest of Trevor's work, is profoundly moral; the detached simplicity of the narrative has the resonance of a well-told parable: the Leesons' murder of Milton is only a specific instance of a larger, more prevalent fratricide. The story never states outright that all men are brothers, but the implication is clear. Garfield's shooting his own brother, Milton, is no worse than the paramilitary of one group shooting the paramililtary of another; both actions destroy and deny an essential brotherhood and thus continue a series of concatenated evils.

Trevor ends this story by highlighting the place of lies in the propagation of evil: "The family would not ever talk about the day, but through their pain they would tell themselves that Milton's death was the way things were, the way things had to be. That was their single consolation" (56). Living their lie (pretending not to know who killed Milton), the family generates yet another lie (this is "the way things had to be"). By facing the reader with such conscious lies (to which the response is easily made, "No, that is not the way things have to be"), Trevor raises again the problem that permeates his fiction: what lies, what truths, what goods, what evils are to be embraced? And can they indeed even be sorted out from each other? Milton found his answer in an orchard, a garden: it seems the only possible solution to political and familial violence – forgiveness and reconciliation – but does his madness discredit his answer?

Is his world of imagined goodness as false as Imelda's vision of a restored Kilneagh? Is pursuing the impossible mere folly? Can a wilderness become a garden?

The wilderness in *King Lear* and the wilderness-loft in *The Wild Duck* are places of confrontation with the truth about the nature of human life and are at the same time places where salutary lies offer redemption. The many damaged gardens in Trevor's work have a similar function, wildernesses where truth and lies shoulder each other in search of a possible good to be gained. Whether there really was a garden in the past – an Eden lost – is never clear to his characters, but (for both individuals and the group) the cycles of order and disorder, the waves of planters and marauders, have the testimony of history: gardens have indeed been set, gone to wilderness, then been reclaimed; avenues of trees established, four fields lost, mulberries harvested, pansies destroyed, rhododendrons acclaimed (*"famous . . . the length and breadth of Ireland, miss"*).[15] Trees have been both gallows and comforting presence. This wilderness-garden is Ireland. Trevor's fiction traces its paths, vast and intricately connected, like a "cobweb of human frailty,"[16] in which nonetheless (despite cruelty, violence, sterility, madness) some weddings do occur, from which children are born and, however imperfectly, flourish – making Trevor's characters and his readers wonder if that reclaimed garden belongs to the past or to the future. Speaking of his own writing and comparing its raw material to a felled tree, Trevor affirms that "out of the chaos . . . you have to create order. The whole thing really is the order."[17]

Notes and References

Chapter One

1. "Writers in Profile: William Trevor," Radio Telefís Éireann (filmed 6 August 1976 for broadcast on 18 October 1976), a 30-minute videotape available in the Irish Studies Collection of Boston College's Media Center, O'Neill Library. Unless otherwise indicated, quotations in this chapter are taken from this valuable interview.

2. This novel has since been repudiated by being dropped from lists of Trevor's published work; in a letter to me (21 March 1990) Trevor dismissed it in parentheses with the single word *worthless*.

3. *The Children of Dynmouth* (Harmondsworth, England: Penguin Books, 1979), 100.

4. Irish language patterns, "local color," details of characterization, and love of storytelling; Celtic motifs and structures; centuries of Irish history and the current Troubles – all these elements are present in Trevor's work, and all are discussed by him in various interviews throughout his career. But Trevor never feels the need to define what constitutes "an Irish author" or Irish literature. He avoids such oversimplifications and reductions in both his introduction to *The Distant Past* (the author's choice of his Irish short stories [1979]) and his edition of *The Oxford Book of Irish Short Stories* (1989). Like Oliver Goldsmith, Maria Edgeworth, Oscar Wilde, and Elizabeth Bowen, as well as Daniel Corkery, Seumas O'Kelly, Liam O'Flaherty, Frank O'Connor, Edna O'Brien, Desmond Hogan, and the others he includes in that Oxford volume, Trevor is Irish; he is an author: he is an Irish author. Perhaps the best indication of Trevor's stature as an Irish author is to be found in the opening sentence of the chapter "Irish Fiction 1965-1990" in the important *Field Day Anthology of Irish Writing* ([Derry: Field Day Publications, 1991], 3: 937), which leads off with his name in its brief list of Irish authors with international reputations, climaxing with "and, of course, Samuel Beckett."

5. "Lost Ground," *New Yorker,* 24 February 1992, 36-56.

Chapter Two

1. "The News from Ireland," in *The News from Ireland and Other Stories* (London: Bodley Head, 1986), 38f.

2. *A Writer's Ireland: Landscape in Literature* (New York: Viking Press, 1984), unpaginated [28].

3. F. J. E. Raby, *A History of Christian-Latin Poetry from the Beginnings to the Close of the Middle Ages*, 2d ed. (Oxford: Clarendon Press, 1953), 88.

4. "The Original Sins of Edward Tripp," in *The Stories of William Trevor* (Harmondsworth, England: Penguin Books, 1983), 72; first collected in *The Day We Got Drunk on Cake and Other Stories* (1967).

5. "Beyond the Pale," in *The Stories of William Trevor*, 696; first collected in *Beyond the Pale and Other Stories* (1981).

6. *Fools of Fortune* (Harmondsworth, England: Penguin Books, 1984), 31.

Chapter Three

1. "The Original Sins of Edward Tripp," in *The Stories of William Trevor*, 70f; first collected in *The Day We Got Drunk on Cake and Other Stories* (1967).

2. Despite the difference in sound between short and long *e*, Mrs. Mayben's name suggests the "may have been" of Edward's hopes as well as the "has been" implied by her refusal.

3. "The Original Sins of Edward Tripp" was not included in Trevor's selection of his Irish stories, *The Distant Past*, although "Miss Smith" was. It is interesting that Trevor thinks of the latter story as being "set in a town in Munster," even though no name, phrase, or detail suggests Ireland. The kinship of the two stories is clear, however, both showing children participating in games of destruction, games that destroy children.

4. *A Writer's Ireland: Landscape in Literature*, 136.

5. "The Distant Past," in *The Distant Past* (Dublin: Poolbeg Press, 1979), 67.

6. Archibald MacLeish. *J.B.* (Boston: Houghton Mifflin, 1958), 11.

7. *Elizabeth Alone* (London: Triad/Panther Books, 1977), 279. First published by Bodley Head (1973).

8. *Other People's Worlds* (Harmondsworth, England: Penguin Books, 1982), 142.

9. See Matthew 5: 38-42, especially "And if any man will sue thee at the law, and take away thy coat, let him have thy cloke also. . . . Give to him that asketh thee, and from him that would borrow of thee turn not thou away." See also Luke 6: 29.

10. Francis plays a minor role in a TV program about a nineteenth-century girl, Constance Kent, who was herself mistreated as a child and who later butchers her baby half-brother. Her story parallels Francis's and Joy's experiences of abuse passed from generation to generation. Francis feels closer to "the real Constance Kent" than to anyone else (86).

11. The theme of incomprehensible judgments at the bar of life – the desire for favor and the madness of expecting it – is supported throughout the novel by references to Mrs. Anstey's reading Dickens's *Bleak House*; the only lines actually quoted concern "*a little mad old woman in a squeezed bonnet, who is always in court, from its sitting to its rising, and always expecting some incomprehensible judgement to be given in her favour*" (182).

12. Yet another instance of Trevor's device of significant simultaneity. Virtually all the characters involved in this novel are described as watching or not watching the broadcast of this program, as are other people all over Britain that same night, people known to each other and people not known to each other, in different rooms but linked by a common interest in or indifference to this event (218f).

Chapter Four

1. In a 1990 interview with Gail Caldwell, Trevor remarked, "Leaving Ireland enabled me to see Ireland through the wrong end of the telescope. You've got to write about the parochial in the most universal way you know how" (*Boston Globe*, 30 May 1990, 44).

2. In an interview with Jacqueline Stahl Aronson in the *Irish Literary Supplement* (Spring 1986, 8) Trevor cited an early novel, *The Old Boys*, as one of his "most cheerful books" and agreed with the interviewer that it is "hard to write cheerful books these days."

3. *A Standard of Behaviour* (London: Sphere Books, 1967), 60. The biographical sketch printed in this paperback edition lists the initial publication date incorrectly as 1956 but on the copyright page provides the correct date, 1958.

4. *The Old Boys* (Harmondsworth, England: Penguin Books, 1984), 35.

5. Of course, other authors have also used this device (see, for a variety of examples, Virginia Woolf's *Mrs. Dalloway*, Ngaio Marsh's *Death of a Peer*, James Plunkett's *Farewell Companions*, and Iris Murdoch's *The Book and the Brotherhood*), but none has used it so persistently or quite so distinctively as Trevor.

6. In the editions cited here *A Standard of Behaviour* has 122 pages; *The Old Boys*, 189; and *The Boarding-House*, 254 (*The Boarding-House* has more lines of type per page than do the other two volumes).

7. *The Boarding-House* (Harmondsworth, England: Penguin Books, 1983), 83.

8. Such analogies are not absent from the narrator's mind, for on the second page of the story a one-sentence character is economically described as "a Dickensian ancient" (6).

9. *The Love Department* (Harmondsworth, England: Penguin Books, 1981), 37.

10. There are also passing references to West Indians.

11. The three seem at times a parody of the manipulative trinity in T. S. Eliot's *The Cocktail Party* (first produced at the Edinburgh Festival, 1949).

12. James O'Connell, *The Meaning of Irish Place Names* (Belfast: Blackstaff Press, 1979), 79.

13. In the short stories published during this early period of Trevor's work, the few brief references to the Irish also serve to indicate stereotype and prejudice: in "The Penthouse Apartment" the Irish are referred to as heavy drinkers; in "The Introspections of J. P. Powers" an embarrassing grammatical error is seen as "the way the Irish talk"; in "A School Story" there is an opening reference to trite jokes about "the Englishman, the Irishman and the Scotsman." Aside from the only story specifically Irish in setting and characterization, "The Original Sins of Edward Tripp," these are the only references to the Irish or Ireland in the entire collection, published as *The Day We Got Drunk on Cake and Other Stories* (1967). Other objects of prejudice in this first volume are Jews in "The Table" and bores, homosexuals, and Jews in "Raymond Bamber and Mrs Fitch."

14. James Joyce, *Dubliners* (New York: Viking Press, 1968), 223.

15. My readings disagree substantially with those of Gregory A. Schirmer, who finds *Miss Gomez and the Brethren* to be "certainly the bleakest of Trevor's novels," nadir in a "slough of despondency [which] he will never leave . . . completely behind him" (*William Trevor: A Study of His Fiction* [London: Routledge, 1990], 53f).

16. *Miss Gomez and the Brethren* (London: Triad/Panther Books, 1984), 81.

17. Miss Gomez's childhood in a Jamaican orphanage (7-14); Alban Roche's childhood in Ireland (72-78).

18. Prudence too has been hurt by her parents – her mother, who did not want her to be born, and her beloved father, who suddenly withdrew his attention when he discovered he was not her father – and she too is healed by this new love. But there is no sentimentality in this "cure": "she felt that if they could view this moment from a vantage point in time they'd see each other as each other's stepping-stones from their separate pasts. Yet she knew that they were fortunate in their love, even if it lasted only six weeks more" (217).

19. Schirmer (*William Trevor*) is incorrect in stating that "Miss Gomez's first sexual experience" occurred in the London brothel (52). See *Miss Gomez*, 14.

20. Mr. Tuke, whose life is in ruins since losing both Prudence and Rebel, has found a similar faith: "In the Witnesses' meeting-room Mr Tuke prayed for his wife, believing now that he had been induced to marry her for this purpose alone: that through his constant intervention and the intervention of others she should find salvation" (243).

21. Trevor's assertion that "her faith was defiant in adversity" (256) echoes "Gold is tried in the fire, and acceptable men in the furnace of adversity" (Apocrypha: Ecclesiasticus 2: 5).

Chapter Five

1. Toni Morrison, *Beloved* (New York: New American Library, 1987).

2. *The Silence in the Garden* (New York: Viking Press, 1988).

3. Mary Leland, *The Killeen* (London: Hamish Hamilton, 1985).

4. The appearance of the supposedly murdered child as a young adult at the end of *The Heart of Midlothian* and his function as ironic nemesis make an interesting parallel, however, to Corny Dowley's role in *The Silence in the Garden*.

5. Romans 9: 25 serves as the book's epigraph: "*I will call them my people, which were not my people; and her beloved, which was not beloved.*"

6. The Song of Solomon 2: 16.

7. "I am Beloved and she is mine" (210).

8. There is one exception to this generalization: Villana's cousin, Hugh, one of the hunters and the man she would have married, has had three children but only by virtue of stepping into another world (going to England, "not a place [Villana] would care to find herself in"; marrying an unnamed girl; and having unnamed children [55], this namelessness making them seem like phantoms to those in the "real world" of Carriglas).

9. The connection between terrorism and child murder, sterile relationships and child murder, is also indicated in *Other People's Worlds*, 56 and 137, and in "Beyond the Pale," 704f.

10. There is a strangely messianic ring to this passage, not only in the concept of one body with many branches and the related notion of an offering made on behalf of a people, of a wonderful child who is nonetheless despised and rejected, but in the very language as well: the words *branch*, *offered*, and *rejected* are not the usual diction Michael employs, and in rendering his thoughts with words used in familiar biblical passages the narrating voice suggests an association between these sons, Thomas and Michael, and another Son given over to suffering and death.

11. "Events at Drimaghleen," in *Family Sins and Other Stories* (New York: Viking Press, 1990), 13.

12. Trevor has stated that he shares "an obsession, or point of view" with two American novelists, William Faulkner and Carson McCullers, both noted for their rural Gothic fiction. See Caldwell interview, *Boston Globe*, 44.

13. Other stories in the same volume present similar situations; see "A Husband's Return" and "Kathleen's Field."

14. Gayatri Chakravorty Spivak, "The Politics of Interpretaton," in *In Other Worlds: Essays in Cultural Politics* (New York: Routledge, 1988), 129.

15. Gayatri Chakravorty Spivak, "Subaltern Studies: Deconstructing Historiography," in *In Other Worlds*, 197.

16. *Other People's Worlds*, 179.

Chapter Six

1. *The Distant Past*, 5.

2. The story actually seems more English than Irish, not only in its diction and phrasing but also in such details as the schoolroom's having "pictures of kings on the walls" (139).

3. "Attracta," in *The Distant Past*, 103.

4. Note, for example, the prayer repeated during Stations of the Cross ("Holy Mother, pierce me through, in my heart each wound renew, of my Saviour crucified") and the mystic experience of stigmata (for example, that of St. Francis of Assisi).

5. See, for example, Frank O'Connor, *The Lonely Voice* (London: Macmillan, 1963).

6. **pale**: "a stake of wood driven into the ground for fencing: any thing that encloses or fences in: a limit: the limit of what can be accepted as decent or tolerable *(fig.)* . . . **beyond the pale**: intolerable: unacceptable" (*Chambers 20th Century Dictionary*, New Edition [Edinburgh: W & R Chambers, 1983], 911).

7. "Beyond the Pale," 707.

8. Trevor uses red hair as a tag for "Irish" in several stories: Cornelius Dowley is described as a red-haired boy long before he is identified by name in *The Silence in the Garden*; S. J. Studdy (*The Boarding-House*), Atlas Flynn (*Miss Gomez and the Brethren*), and Desmond ("August Saturday" in *Family Sins*) are also redheads.

9. Trevor's choice of the Glens of Antrim is particularly apt for this story. Geographically they are relatively lush fingers of garden reaching into the bleak Antrim plateau. As a Catholic oasis in the midst of a Protestant county, and reminders as well of Ireland's ancient Catholic-Gaelic connection with Scotland, they thus reinforce the redheaded young man's right to be there. But they also suggest that long history of mutual colonization which sent Celts from the Antrim coast to settle Scotland (ultimately giving it its name) and later sent Protestants from Scotland back to settle Northern Ireland, thus ironically calling into question the whole issue of exclusive rights.

10. "Irland . . . is deuyded in ii partes, one is the Engly[sh] pale, & the other, the wyld Irysh" (*Oxford English Dictionary*, 2057).

11. John 13: 34.

12. John 13: 4-15.

13. Trevor uses the same allusion in "The News from Ireland" when Mrs. Pulvertaft, anxious about the starving workers outside her gates, dreams about a command to wash and dry the feet of Jesus but feels "unhappy because she does not know which of the men is Jesus" (in *The News from Ireland*, 34).

14. John 8: 32, quoted in *Mrs. Eckdorf in O'Neill's Hotel* (Harmondsworth, England: Penguin Books, 1982), 123.

15. Trevor often makes use of tag names and suggestive names: there may be a hint that Eckdorf indicates "liar" (i.e., someone who discards what is true) by the combination of "echt" (genuine, true, real, sincere) and "dorf" (as a card term, meaning "discard").

16. Using the city as grid for the action is reminiscent of *Ulysses*, even in some particular details, and is at times as comic: both involve quest for a parent, references to hospital confinement and birth, pub scenes, brothel scenes, significant juxtapositions (who is where when), failure to cross paths, and eventual climactic meeting, and both end with references to a woman's mind – Molly postorgasmically contented in a bed that for her is all the world; Ivy, insanely contented in an asylum that for her is all the world.

17. Attracta, or Araght, is a fifth- or sixth-century virgin whose feast day is 11 August. "Attracta is said to have founded a hospice for travellers on the shores of Lough Gara in Ireland and also to have performed a number of somewhat unlikely miracles," according to *The Saints: A Concise Biographical Dictionary*, ed. John Coulson (New York: Hawthorn Books, 1958), 58, 481.

18. Father Hennessey's conversations with Mrs. Sinnott were kept in separate books from all the rest, as is appropriate for the confidentiality of her relationship with   her relationship with her priest.

19. *Fools of Fortune*, 163.

20. "Bodily Secrets," in *The News from Ireland*, 170; first published in the *Irish Times* (1984).

21. Fogarty uses the same image in his prescription for the Pulvertaft estate ("The News from Ireland," 10).

22. This is a concept that Trevor subtly suggests many times in his work. In "Attracta," for example, he follows Mr. Purce's bigoted assertion of Protestant superiority and mistreatment at the hands of Catholic revolutionaries with a reference to the young Attracta's homework assignments, including "a chapter of her history book to read, about the Saxons coming to England" (*The Distant Past*, 115); thus Trevor indicates, without comment, that Ireland was not the only island to be invaded, colonized, and subjected to struggles involving domination, assimilation, revolution, and

counterrevolution. Trevor suggests as well, at least in the voices of several
characters, that the results in daily life of these ubiquitous struggles is actually of no great consequence: "green-painted pillar-boxes [rather than red]
and a language that nobody understood" (*The Distant Past*, 62; see also
Fools of Fortune, 48). (These old mailboxes, of course, can still occasionally
be found in Ireland, cast with the British royal emblem but now painted
green.)

23. *Other People's Worlds*, 27.

24. "On the Zattere," in *The News from Ireland*, 53.

25. See Algernon Charles Swinburne, "Dolores," in *Poetry of the Vic-
torian Period*, rev. ed., ed. George B. Woods and Jerome H. Buckley
(Chicago: Scott, Foresman, 1955), 682-86, and Harold Pinter, *The Home-
coming* (New York: Grove Press, 1967), 74.

26. "The News from Ireland," in *The News from Ireland*, 42.

27. See *A Dictonary of Saints,* comp. Donald Attwater, based on Alban
Butler's *Lives of the Saints* (New York: P. J. Kennedy & Sons, 1958), 6.

28. Ibid., 8.

29. *The Lives of the Saints, Originally Compiled by the Rev. Alban Butler*, ed. Herbert Thurston and Donald Attwater (London: Burns Oates &
Washbourne, 1933), 2: 385f.

30. Trevor "now lives half the year in Italy and Ticino, Switzerland,
where he does most of his writing. 'For me, it's essential, the distance,' he
says now. 'Leaving Ireland enabled me to see Ireland through the wrong
end of the telescope' " (Caldwell, *Boston Globe*, 44).

31. In the canonization process, being declared "blessed" is the step
just before formal declaration of sainthood; since the full procedure
involves a certain amount of ecclesiastical politics, remaining for centuries
at the "blessed" stage does not impugn the individual's sanctity or bar
devotion. Since there is no comfortable English noun for "blessed," Imelda
will here sometimes be referrerd to as a "saint."

32. A *Dictionary of Saints*, 128f.

33. For the prominent social importance and public ritualization of
death in the actual town, San Sepolcro, see James R. Banker, *Death in the
Community: Memorialization and Confraternities in an Italian Commune
in the Late Middle Ages* (Athens: University of Georgia Press, 1989).

34. *Fools of Fortune*, 10.

35. See *A Dictionary of Saints*, 95.

36. *The Silence in the Garden*, 15. It is also significant in this novel that
Villana does not want to know the names of Hugh's wife and children in
England, thus minimizing their existence (55).

Chapter Seven

1. C. Hugh Holman and William Harmon, *A Handbook to Literature*, 5th ed. (New York: Macmillan, 1986), 35.

2. Roy Pascal, *The German Novel* (Toronto: University of Toronto Press, 1956), 11.

3. See, for example, Jerome Buckley's account in *Season of Youth: The Bildungsroman from Dickens to Golding* (Cambridge: Harvard University Press, 1974).

4. *Fools of Fortune*, 31.

5. John Banville, *Birchwood* (New York: W. W. Norton, 1973), 153.

6. John Banville, *Mefisto* (London: Secker & Warburg, 1986), 130.

7. In a 1990 interview Trevor stated that "almost any story set in Ireland is bound to reflect the history of that distressful country," but his reasons are different from the "centuries of oppression" usually cited: "There are pressures of history in France or Italy, but they're different pressures, because Ireland is a rural country. It's so new; people forget this, especially the Irish. They forget that we've only been there as a state since the early 1920s, which is no time at all. We need a good 300 years to sort ourselves out – to actually be something. We have no traditions except a few literary traditions, which are somewhat vague." But whether old wrongs or new political structures account for it, "you can scarcely move in Ireland without being aware of history. I don't try to weave history in, it just creeps in – it's unavoidable" (Caldwell, *Boston Globe*, 44).

8. *Birchwood*, 170.

9. *Nights at the Alexandra* (New York: Harper & Row, 1987), 33.

10. Brian Moore, *The Mangan Inheritance* (New York: Farrar, Straus & Giroux, 1979), 61.

11. Jamie loses his in a pub brawl in Bantry exactly as Michael had in the same way in the same town.

12. "Children of the Headmaster," in *Family Sins and Other Stories*, 205f.

13. "In Love with Ariadne, " in *Family Sins and Other Stories*, 97.

14. Trevor has defined the short story as "the art of the glimpse" (Caldwell, *Boston Globe*, 44).

15. "August Saturday," in *Family Sins and Other Stories*, 226.

16. Grania herself may have no regrets – attaining the child she wanted and giving Desmond the pleasures of paternity in a world where having children is important (228) – but she has violated all the mores of her group (virginity at marriage, sexual fidelity afterward) and for the rest of her life carries a secret she is all too conscious of and cannot share.

17. Trevor often uses red hair to indicate a character is Irish.

Chapter Eight

1. See 1 Corinthians 1: 18-31 and 3: 18-20, especially "God hath chosen the foolish things of the world to confound the wise" and "If any man among you seemeth to be wise in this world, let him become a fool, that he may be wise. For the wisdom of this world is foolishness with God," and see Luke 17: 33, with its paradoxical "Whosoever shall seek to save his life shall lose it; and whosoever shall lose his life shall preserve it." See also Philippians 1: 21 and 3: 7-8, John 12: 24-25, and I Corinthians 15: 36.

2. Mary Leland, *The Killeen* (London: Hamish Hamilton, 1985), 136.

3. W. B. Yeats. *The Herne's Egg and Other Plays* (New York: Macmillan, 1938), 15.

4. Trevor's Attracta in imagination has become one with Penelope Vade, who was raped by seven terrorists in Belfast for her unwillingness to live an ordinary life of bigotry.

5. *The Children of Dynmouth*, 120f.

6. "And ye shall know the truth, and the truth shall make you free" (John 8: 32, cited in *Mrs. Eckdorf in O'Neill's Hotel*, 123).

7. Mr. Blakey too has seen Timothy through a window, at night in the storm, as a puzzling intruder in the garden, lighted up suddenly by a flash of lightning, a sinister presence that he does not mention to his wife.

8. "A message, unspoken, was there between them: he was to be a new man, there was to be a new relationship. But beneath the surface of resolution she knew he would regain his former self and enjoy again the shame of his surreptitious ways" (155).

9. Kate's theory of diabolic possession is less a formally religious issue and more a mishmash of elements from horror movies; her solution to the problem involves not only exorcism but the sort of treatment deemed appropriate for vampires.

10. See 1 Corinthians 1: 23 and Matthew 12: 39.

11. Jennifer Johnston. *Shadows on Our Skin* (New York: Doubleday, 1977), 122.

12. Aronson interview, *Irish Literary Supplement*, 7f.

13. *Two Lives: Reading Turgenev and My House in Umbria* (New York: Viking, 1991), 327.

14. "Lost Ground," 36-56.

15. *The Silence in the Garden*, 11.

16. "Two More Gallants," in *The News from Ireland*, 261.

17. Caldwell, *Boston Globe*, 44.

Selected Bibliography

PRIMARY WORKS

Novels

The Boarding-House. London: Bodley Head, 1965. Harmondsworth, England: Penguin Books, 1968, 1984 (paperback editions).

The Children of Dynmouth. London: Bodley Head, 1976. Harmondsworth, England: Penguin Books, 1979, 1982 (paperback editions).

Elizabeth Alone. London: Bodley Head, 1973. London: Triad/Panther Books, 1977 (paperback edition).

Fools of Fortune. London: Bodley Head, 1983. Harmondsworth, England: Penguin Books, 1984 (paperback edition).

The Love Department. London: Bodley Head, 1966. Harmondsworth, England: Penguin Books, 1970, 1981 (paperback editions).

Miss Gomez and the Brethren. London: Bodley Head, 1971. London: Triad/Panther Books, 1978 (paperback edition).

Mrs. Eckdorf in O'Neill's Hotel. London: Bodley Head, 1969. Harmondsworth, England: Penguin Books, 1973, 1982 (paperback editions).

Nights at the Alexandra. New York: Harper & Row, 1987.

The Old Boys. London: Bodley Head, 1964. Harmondsworth, England: Penguin Books, 1966, 1984 (paperback editions).

Other People's Worlds. London: Bodley Head, 1980. Harmondsworth, England: Penguin Books, 1982 (paperback edition).

The Silence in the Garden. London: Bodley Head, 1988. Harmondsworth, England: Penguin Books, 1989 (paperback edition).

A Standard of Behaviour. London: Hutchinson, 1958. London: Sphere Books, 1967, 1982 (paperback editions).

Two Lives: Reading Turgenev and My House in Umbria. London: Viking Press, 1991.

Short Story Collections

Angels at the Ritz and Other Stories. London: Bodley Head, 1975.

The Ballroom of Romance and Other Stories. London: Bodley Head, 1972.

Beyond the Pale and Other Stories. London: Bodley Head, 1981.

The Day We Got Drunk on Cake and Other Stories. London: Bodley Head, 1967.

The Distant Past and Other Stories. Swords, County Dublin: Poolbeg Press, 1979.

Family Sins and Other Stories. London: Bodley Head, 1990.

Lovers of Their Time and Other Stories. London: Bodley Head, 1978.

The News from Ireland and Other Stories. London: Bodley Head, 1986.

The Stories of William Trevor. Harmondsworth, England: Penguin Books, 1983 (paperback collection of *Angels at the Ritz and Other Stories, The Ballroom of Romance and Other Stories, Beyond the Pale and Other Stories, The Day We Got Drunk on Cake and Other Stories*, and *Lovers of Their Time and Other Stories*).

William Trevor: The Collected Stories. New York: Viking Press, 1992.

Plays

Autumn Sunshine. In *Best Radio Plays of 1982*. London: Methuen, 1983.

Beyond the Pale. In *Best Radio Plays of 1980*. London: Methuen, 1981.

The Girl. London: Samuel French, 1968.

Going Home. London: Samuel French, 1972.

Marriages. London: Samuel French, 1973.

A Night with Mrs. da Tanka. London: Samuel French, 1972.

The Old Boys. London: Davis-Poynter, 1971.

Scenes from an Album. Dublin: Co-Op Books, 1981.

Unpublished and Miscellaneous Materials

The Last Lunch of the Season. London: Covent Garden Press, 1973. Covent Garden Stories no. 6.

Old School Ties. London: Lemon Tree Press, 1976. Fragments of stories, memoirlike passages.

Ed. *The Oxford Book of Irish Short Stories*. Oxford: Oxford University Press, 1989.

"Writer in Profile: William Trevor." Thirty-minute television interview with Jack White; part of a Radio Telefís Éireann series on Irish writers; filmed 6 August 1976 for broadcast on 18 October 1976. Video print available in the Irish Collection of Boston College (Media Center, O'Neill Library).

A Writer's Ireland: Landscape in Literature. New York: Viking Press, 1984.

SECONDARY WORKS

Aronson, Jacqueline Stahl. "William Trevor: An Interview." *Irish Literary Supplement: A Review of Irish Books*, Spring 1986, 7-8. Useful discussion of various themes in Trevor's fiction from *The Old Boys* to *Fools of Fortune*, his mode of writing, his comic view.

Brady, Anne M., and Brian Cleeve. "Trevor, William." In *A Biographical Dictionary of Irish Writers*, 239. New York: St. Martin's Press, 1985. A brief entry in a volume of brief entries, interesting for its length relative to other authors of the Irish canon (about the same as Frank O'Connor's, a third of James Joyce's).

Caldwell, Gail. "A Gentleman of Substance." *Boston Globe*, 30 May 1990, 37, 44. An account of Trevor's reading at the Irish Literature Festival in New York; perceptive discussion of his work, including Trevor's own comments.

Firchow, Peter, ed. "William Trevor." In *The Writer's Place: Interviews on the Literary Situation in Contemporary Britain*, 304-12. Minneapolis: University of Minnesota Press, 1974. An interview that includes discussion of the economics of being a writer, various media, literary agents, the book-reviewing establishment, current promising young writers, best-sellers, Ireland.

Fitzgerald-Hoyt, Mary. "The Influence of Italy in the Writings of William Trevor and Julia O'Faolain." *Notes on Modern Irish Literature* 2 (1990): 61-67. Describes how both authors "use Italian settings to frame their characters' dramatic emotional choices, but with varying results."

Gitzen, Julian. "The Truth-Tellers of William Trevor." *Critique* 21 (1979): 59-72. Discusses "the theme of loneliness and hunger for love" that distinguishes characters in Trevor's melancholy comedy, particularly their capacity "for creating and sustaining illusions"; although all Trevor's fiction contains characters who tell the truth, his plot contains situations in which "the question of illusion is difficult to resolve." This perceptive essay concludes by observing that "William Trevor not only values and seeks psychological truth but recognizes the point at which it retreats into metaphysical mystery."

Halio, Jay L. "Trevor, William." In *Contemporary Novelists*, 4th ed., edited by D. L. Kirkpatrick, 816-18. New York: St Martin's Press, 1986. Similar to entry in *Dictionary of Literary Biography*; adds only *Fools of Fortune* to its brief discussion. Sees Trevor as "an heir along with Iris Murdoch to the Anglo-Irish tradition in fiction that has given us the superb novelist and short-story writer Elizabeth Bowen."

_____, and Paul Binding. "William Trevor." In *Dictionary of Literary Biography: British Novelists since 1960*, vol. 14, part 2, 723-30. Detroit: Gale Research, 1983. A sound general account of life and work to 1981.

Hogan, Robert. "Old Boys, Young Bucks, and New Women: The Contemporary Irish Short Story." In *The Irish Short Story: A Critical History*, edited by James F. Kilroy, 169-215. Boston: Twayne Publishers, 1984. Contains unsympathetic discussion of Trevor's short stories (182-86), seeing them as characterized by "an increasingly comprehensive moroseness": "Astonishingly, some critics have commented upon Trevor's humor; but what sounded to them as laughter strikes this commentator as a death rattle."

Lane, Denis, and Carol McCrory Lane, eds. "Trevor, William (1928-)." In *Modern Irish Literature*, 658-64. New York: Ungar, 1988. A volume in the series "A Library of Literary Criticism." Contains a selection of excerpts of reviews and commentaries published from 1964 to 1984.

Morrison, Kristin. "Trevor, William." In *Reference Guide to English Literature*, 2d ed., vol. 2, 1334-36. London: St. James Press, 1991. General critical introduction to Trevor's work.

_____. "William Trevor's 'System of Correspondences.' " *Massachusetts Review* 28 (1987): 489-96. Special Issue on Contemporary Ireland. Demonstrates through discussion of "The News from Ireland," *Fools of Fortune*, and "The Original Sins of Edward Tripp" that Trevor's fiction deliberately connects political acts, historical events, and moral states in such a way as to suggest that each is an analogue of the other, that public and private worlds mirror and affect each other. Argues that this "system of correspondences" constitutes the intellectual framework of all Trevor's fiction.

Morrissey, Thomas. "Trevor's *Fools of Fortune*: The Rape of Ireland." *Notes on Modern Irish Literature* 2 (1990): 58-60. "The psychological damage done to the characters of this novel, whether the result of a sexual violation or terrorist attack, is [like] . . . rape trauma syndrome."

Mortimer, Mark. "The Short Stories of William Trevor." *Etudes Irlandaises* 9, n.s. (December 1984): 161-73. Rather general discussion; notes humor but complains of Trevor's lack of "normal" people.

_____. "William Trevor in Dublin." *Etudes Irlandaises* 4, f.s. (1975): 77-85. Appreciative discussion of Trevor's "masterly control over words; his brief, telling portraits; his uncanny use of the banal and of cross purposes in presenting a richly humorous picture of life," especially in his "slices of Irish life."

O'Malley, William T., ed. In *Anglo-Irish Literature: A Bibliography of Dissertations, 1873-1989*, 191. New York: Greenwood Press, 1990. Lists three dissertations dealing with Trevor's work: 1980, Maryland; 1985, Saskatchewan; 1987, California-Santa Barbara.

Ralph-Bowman, Mark. "William Trevor." *Transatlantic Review* 53/54 (1976): 5-12. Interview, including discussion of Trevor's mode of writing, his "telling the truth" about his characters, his "pre-war Edwardian style," his use of cliché, the particular novelists he likes. One of the richer interviews.

Rhodes, Robert E. "William Trevor's Stories of the Troubles." In *Contemporary Irish Writing*, edited by James D. Brophy and Raymond Porter, 95-114. Boston: Iona College Press / Twayne Publishers, 1983. Perceptive, detailed discussion of five stories ("The Distant Past," "Saints" [later to be revised and expanded into *Fools of Fortune*], "Attracta," "Autumn Sunshine," and "Another Christmas") dealing with "the renewal of Ireland's ancient Troubles in Northern Ireland since the late 1960s and the impact of that violence on people in the North, the Republic of Ireland, and in England." An important essay.

Schiff, Stephen. "The Shadows of William Trevor." *New Yorker*, 28 December 1992 / 4 January 1993, 158-63. A general appreciation. Quotes Trevor's insisting "I am Irish absolutely to the last vein in my body."

Schirmer, Gregory A. *William Trevor: A Study of His Fiction*. New York: Routledge, 1990. A general discussion, organized chronologically, with chapters on "The Early Novels," "The Middle Novels," "The Late Novels," "The Short Stories," "The Irish Fiction." Argues that "the tension between [E. M.] Forster's 'Only Connect' and [T. S.] Eliot's 'I can connect/nothing with nothing' has provided the governing moral force of [Trevor's] work." Like several earlier reviewers and critics, considers Trevor to be caught in a "slough of despondency" that "he will never leave . . . completely behind him."

Stinson, John J. "Replicas, Foils, and Revelation in Some 'Irish' Short Stories of William Trevor." In *Canadian Journal of Irish Studies* 11, no. 2 (1985): 17-26. Appreciates "Trevor's masterly economy, lightness, and rich suggestiveness" in constructing stories in which "moments of real insight come about for the characters precisely as a result of their seeing some aspect of their own selves highlighted by the presence of opposed characteristics in people in some way similar to themselves." Discusses "An Evening with John Joe Dempsey," "The Paradise Lounge," and "Teresa's Wedding."

Tolomeo, Diane. "Modern Fiction." In *Recent Research on Anglo-Irish Writers. A Supplement to Anglo-Irish Literature: A Review of Research*, edited by Richard J. Finneran, 295. New York: Modern Language Association of America, 1983. Lists a few of Trevor's books and one critical essay about his work.

Weaver, Jack. "Trevor, William." In *Dictionary of Irish Literature*, edited by Robert Hogan, 664-65. Westport, Conn.: Greenwood Press, 1979. Brief entry, marred with a few careless errors (e.g., his "Agnes Eckdorf" conflates two of Trevor's characters into one; he supplies an incorrect date, picked up by other critics, for *Marriages*).

Index

The Author

Kristin Morrison is professor of English and a member of the Irish Studies Program of Boston College, where she teaches twentieth-century Irish fiction and drama. She is the author of *Canters and Chronicles: The Use of Narrative in the Plays of Samuel Beckett and Harold Pinter* (1983) and has published numerous articles on narrative technique and on drama in such journals as *Nineteenth-Century Fiction, Texas Studies in Literature and Language, Quarterly Journal of Speech, American Imago, Modern Drama,* and *Comparative Drama*. She has contributed essays on Samuel Beckett's work to such volumes as *Drama in the Twentieth Century* (1984), *Women in Beckett* (1990), and *Approaches to Teaching Beckett's "Waiting for Godot"* (1991). She is a member of the American Conference for Irish Studies and of the International Association for the Study of Anglo-Irish Literature.